Education Policies in Pakistan

Politics, Projections, and Practices

Education Policies in Pakistan

Politics, Projections, and Practices

SECOND EDITION

Shahid Siddiqui

OXFORD
UNIVERSITY PRESS

OXFORD
UNIVERSITY PRESS

Oxford University Press is a department of the University of Oxford. It furthers the University's objective of excellence in research, scholarship, and education by publishing worldwide. Oxford is a registered trade mark of Oxford University Press in the UK and in certain other countries

Published in Pakistan by
Oxford University Press
No. 38, Sector 15, Korangi Industrial Area,
PO Box 8214, Karachi-74900, Pakistan

First Edition published in 2016

This edition in Oxford Pakistan Paperbacks 2021

ISBN 978-0-19-070789-7

Typeset in Minion Pro
Printed on 68gsm Offset Paper

Printed by Mas Printers, Karachi

To the dream of quality education for all

Contents

List of Tables

List of Abbreviations and Acronyms

ACR	Annual Confidential Report
AD	Associate Degree
AIDS	Acquired Immune Deficiency Syndrome
AIOU	Allama Iqbal Open University
AV Aids	Audio Visual Aids
BA	Bachelor of Arts
BEd	Bachelor of Education
BS	Bachelor of Science
BSc	Bachelor of Science
BTech	Bachelor of Technology
CBE	Competency Based Education
CPD	Continuous Professional Development
CT	Certificate of Teaching
DPI	Director Public Instructions
ECCE	Early Childhood Care and Education
EFA	Education for All
FCC	Forman Christian College
GCI	Global Competitive Index
GDP	Gross Domestic Product
GER	Gross Enrollment Ratio
GNI	Gross National Income
GoP	Government of Pakistan
GPI	Gender Parity Index
GRE	Graduate Record Examination
HDI	Human Development Index
HEC	Higher Education Commission
HEIs	Higher Education Institutions
HIV	Human Immunodeficiency Virus
ICT	Information Communication Technology
IER	Institute of Education and Research
IPEMC	Inter-Provincial Education Ministers Conference

KP	Khyber Pakhtunkhwa
LAMEC	Literacy and Mass Education Commission
MDGs	Millennium Development Goals
MNA	Member National Assembly
MPA	Member Provincial Assembly
MPhil	Master of Philosophy
NAB	National Accountability Bureau
NCAAA	National Council for Academic Awards and Accreditation
NCC	National Curriculum Council
NCF	National Curriculum Framework
NECTE	National Accreditation Council of Teacher Education
NEP	National Education Policy
NEPF	National Education Policy Framework
NER	Net Enrollment Ratio
NETCOM	National Education and Training Commission
NFE	Non-Formal Education
NGO	Non-Governmental Organization
NTS	National Testing Service
ODL	Online and Distance Learning
OOSC	Out of School Children
PEC	Pakistan Engineering Council
PLL	Practical Lab Learning
PMDC	Pakistan Medical and Dental Council
PML-N	Pakistan Muslim League-Nawaz
PNA	Pakistan National Alliance
PPP	Pakistan Peoples Party
PSLM	Pakistan Social and Living Standards Measurement
PTC	Primary Teacher Certificate
PTI	Pakistan Tehreek-i-Insaf
SAP	Social Action Plan
SDG	Sustainable Development Goals
SNC	Single National Curriculum
TOEFL	Test of English as a Foreign Language
TRC	Teachers' Resource Centre
TVE	Technical and Vocational Education
TVET	Technical, Vocational Education and Training

UIS	UNESCO Institute of Statistics
UNDP	United Nations Development Programme
UNESCO	United Nations Educational, Scientific and Cultural Organization
UNICEF	United Nations International Children's Emergency Fund
UPE	Universal Primary Education
USA	United States of America

List of Appendices

Preface

Policies play an important role in the progress and development of a country. A policy document usually deals with three important tasks: identification of areas of improvement, decisions about the targets to be achieved, and strategies regarding the implementation of promised targets. Preparation of a policy depends heavily on reliable data and consultations with relevant stakeholders. Education is considered an important factor in the socio-economic development of a country. The role of education has become increasingly significant in contemporary times; the focus has shifted to a 'knowledge economy', and 'human capital' has become the most desired kind. In this scenario, an education policy emerges as a significant document that is potentially interlinked with the social and economic development of a country.

Pakistan, since its independence in 1947, has faced challenges of access and quality due to insufficient educational institutions and lack of qualified teachers (Kardar, 1998; Rahman, 2004; Aly, 2007; Siddiqui, 2010, 2012; Pakistan Education Task Force, 2011). Over the years, many important education policies were released in an attempt to tackle the education problem. These policies came at different times, during different regimes, and with diverse policy documents. They varied in their size, intentions, and seriousness.

THE IMPACT

Despite detailed policies, educational outcomes remained unsatisfactory. According to the Global Competitive Index (GCI, 2019) Pakistan's score on health and primary education is 114, which is dismal compared to Bangladesh (92), China (39), India (109), Malaysia (65), and Sri Lanka (42). It is important to note that the higher the number, the lower the performance, which means Pakistan lags behind the rest of the countries mentioned in the list.

Studying policies in terms of their preparation processes and implementation phases is becoming popular in the contemporary academic environment. Such studies are helpful as they identify areas for improvement, facilitate the modifications in the existing policy contents along with its implementation process, and help prepare a new policy with realistic targets and attainable implementation strategies. There is growing realization about the significance of the role the implementation process plays in the success of education policies. Research such as Huberman and Miles (1984), Fullan (1986), McLaughlin (1987), and Schorr and Schorr (1989) explored processes, steps, and factors involved in the process of implementation. Most of this research is situated in the North American experience and attempts to discuss the implementation of reforms related to school development.

POLICY IMPLEMENTATION

In Pakistan, there have been sporadic attempts to study the implementation of policies on education. Some of these studies included Bray, 1983; Bengali, 1991; Ahsan, 2003; Warwick, et al., 1991, 1992; Saigol, 2003; Rahman, 2004; Ali, 2006; Khan, 1997; Barber, 2010; Andrabi, et al., 2010; and Siddiqui, 2011. Most of these attempts were at the report or paper level and had a narrow and limited focus. There is no book with a critical and comprehensive analysis of education policies in Pakistan and written exclusively from an indigenous perspective.

Being associated with the educational system of Pakistan for more than three decades, I always felt a genuine need for a comprehensive study of the education policies in Pakistan and decided to work along these lines. The first task was to gather all the relevant policy documents. I was surprised to note that the policies were not available online, with the exception of two. After visiting libraries and departments and tapping a number of resources, I finally managed to collect the documents required for an in-depth study.

RATIONALE OF THE BOOK

This book is an attempt to study the education policies in Pakistan in a critical and holistic manner. It captures the important aspects of education policies in terms of their preparation processes, socio-political contexts, thematic targets, and implementation strategies. Offering a comprehensive critique of the policies in a logical manner, each chapter focuses on a specific theme, highlights its role in a broader educational context, tracks the remedies offered by different policies, and identifies the gaps between promises and practices. Each theme is studied across all the education policies from the Pakistan Education Conference held in 1947 to the most recent education policy launched in the first quarter of 2021. Each chapter contains an analysis and discussion section that offers a critique of the initiatives in the selected domain of education. Chapter 14 focuses on the implementation of policies and underlying challenges, and offers some viable recommendations.

Being the first comprehensive critique of educational policy documents, this book is useful to academics, students, researchers, curriculum planners, and policymakers in the fields of education, policy studies, gender studies, teacher education, and politics. It should also be useful to members of civil society as it deals with crucial issues related to the processes of policy planning and implementation. The book does not take prior knowledge of the readers for granted and thus tries to present the content in a simple and coherent manner, making it equally palatable for technical and non-technical readers.

ORGANIZATION OF THE BOOK

The 'Preface' provides the background and rationale of the book. It offers an elaborate sequential organization of the book and highlights the central theme of each chapter. The preface also delineates the implications of the book for the different strata of the society.

Chapter 1, 'Education Policies: Rationale and Process', deals with the rationale behind having an education policy. It also examines the process of policy preparation and the various phases involved, i.e. identification of areas for improvement, decisions about setting targets, and measures to be taken for implementation.

Chapter 2, 'The Sociopolitical Context of Education Policies', underlines the fact that policies are greatly influenced, in terms of their preparation and implementation, by the milieu in which they are situated. Some important social, political, and economic trends and developments are briefly described as a historical backdrop to facilitate the readers in understanding and analysing policies in a meaningful way.

Chapter 3, 'Education Policies: Vision and Ideology', studies the vision across education policies from 1947 to 2009. The chapter highlights the significant role that a vision plays in a policy and demonstrates how most of our policies were personality-driven, as the ruler of the time imposed their vision without going through a participatory, consultative process. The chapter also discusses the role of donors and the associated influence that comes with foreign consultants impacting a policy vision. It also studies the inconsistency among policies in terms of vision and goals.

Chapter 4, 'Literacy', examines the recommendations made by various education policies and the measures taken by different governments to realize the targets of their policies. The chapter discusses the skewed approach of policies in favour of a quantitative expansion of literacy. It draws attention to the qualitative aspects of literacy by making a useful distinction between functional and critical literacy.

Chapter 5, 'Universal Primary Education', unpacks the term Universal Primary Education (UPE) and traces the promises and deadlines given by each policy for UPE. The proclaimed deadlines for achieving the targets were never realized and each subsequent policy kept on extending them.

Chapter 6, 'Higher Education', critically analyses the role of higher education in the development of a country. It identifies the pendulum movement between primary education and higher education, focusing on the quantitative growth and challenges of qualitative improvement of higher education.

Chapter 7, 'Female Education', delineates the challenge of female education. It examines the quantitative and qualitative gaps between male and female education with special reference to the measures proposed by education policies. The chapter also discusses the issue of the relatively lower participation of educated women in the national workforce.

Chapter 8, 'Language Issues', examines how language is not just an effective tool of communication but also an important identity marker at the individual and societal level. The chapter discusses the proposals of various education policies regarding the national language, official language, and regional languages. The chapter unveils the contradictory policies towards languages and their impact at the national and regional levels.

Chapter 9, 'Technical and Vocational Education', highlights the role of technical and vocational education in the development of a country. It examines the measures proposed in various education policies for technical and vocational education and their outcomes.

Chapter 10, 'Special Education', examines the theme of special education which becomes more challenging in a South Asian context where, due to socio-cultural reasons, children's disabilities are hidden by their parents. Furthermore, only a few facilities are available for children who have disabilities. The chapter studies the theme of special education in education policies from 1947 to 2009.

Chapter 11, 'Religious Education and *Madrasahs*', traces the ideological component in education policies and focuses on the 1979 policy (GoP, 1979) that was launched during General Zia ul-Haq's regime (1978–88). The thrust of the policy was to Islamize the whole educational system of the country in terms of its objectives, curricula, textbooks, pedagogy, and assessment practices.

Chapter 12, 'Curricula and Textbooks', focuses on the curriculum orientations in different policies and analyses the tension between indigenous content and imported ideas. The chapter also discusses the initiatives announced in different policies regarding the content, publishing, and provision of textbooks to students.

Chapter 13, 'Teachers and Teacher Education', underlines the central position of teacher education in the improvement of the educational system of a country. The chapter critically analyses the measures proposed by each education policy from 1947 to 2009 and the outcomes of those measures for school improvement.

Chapter 14, 'Implementation: Challenges and Recommendations', analyses critically the implementation challenges present at the state, organization, and individual levels. The chapter also offers realistic recommendations based on a thorough analysis of the policy planning and implementation processes in Pakistan.

Chapter 15, 'Post-2009 Education Initiatives', critically analyses the educational initiatives during the post-2009 period up to the first quarter of 2021. These documents were initiated by three different governments, i.e., the Pakistan Peoples Party (PPP), Pakistan Muslim League-Nawaz (PML-N), and Pakistan Tehreek-i-Insaf (PTI).

Chapter 16, 'Where Do We Stand Today?', examines the recent status of educational areas including public expenditure for education, literacy at different levels, female education, early childhood care, higher education, out of school children, dropout from schools, the quality of education, curriculum initiatives, and medium of instruction issues.

Acknowledgements

I would like to express my gratitude to all those who helped me in completing this project over the past three years. Without their support this book would not have been possible. I would like to thank Javaria Siddique whose consistent support and meticulous organization of research documents facilitated the writing process. I feel indebted to Aamir Riaz, Uzma Dawood, Umer Anjum, Sofia Hussain, Zia ur Rehman, and Rabia Khan for their help in reading the manuscript and providing useful feedback. I am thankful to various libraries and departments for their generous help in procuring some necessary and rare documents.

Chapter 1

Education Policies: Rationale and Process

The process of planning is important in order to conceive a policy and implement it. There is ample literature available about the processes of policy planning and implementation. Different steps of a policy may include the areas that need to be improved. Such identification is possible in the presence of reliable data and a comprehensive consultation process. This stage is vital as the lack of consultation with the stakeholders or relying on data which is not authentic could blur the vision at the very outset. The second important stage is deciding on the measures to deal with the identified areas of improvement and setting goals. The potential problem faced by policymakers during this stage is that they usually come up with very ambitious targets which are unrealistic. The goals and targets thus need to be set keeping in view the financial, human, and physical resources available at the time and their consistent supply during the period of implementation. Another important consideration for setting goals is their ownership by different stakeholders and their compatibility with indigenous culture and values.

Implementation, which is the final stage, is crucial as policies, especially in developing countries, fail because of poor execution. An effective implementation process requires thorough planning and a detailed action plan, assigning the responsibility of different tasks to specific organizations and individuals. There should not be any ambiguity or duplication of tasks in terms of responsibility. Likewise there is a need for strong coordination between the departments, organizations, and agencies doing similar work. In the absence of such coordination, efforts remain fragmented and no holistic outcome can be expected.

During the implementation phase a continuous monitoring system needs to be in place through which progress can be tracked effectively. There needs to be a proper evaluation mechanism as well to assess a policy in terms of its objectives, implementation, and impact and the evaluation report should be shared with the stakeholders.

SOCIOPOLITICAL ASPECTS OF POLICY

We briefly looked at the stages of policy from planning to implementation but in real life things are not that simple. Policy planning has to take care of some important considerations. These considerations and pressures exist both at internal and external levels. Such considerations and pressures play their part in weaving the fabric of the policy text. External considerations may include the social, political, economic, and technological trends at the global level. Besides global pressures, certain developed countries have a special relationship with some developing countries and are in a strong position to influence education policies. For example, USA and Saudi Arabia, because of their special relationship with Pakistan, are in a position to influence its education policies and have done so in the past. Internal considerations may be historical, political, ethnic, religious, ideological, and resource-driven.

EDUCATION POLICIES IN PAKISTAN: THE PROCESS

In Pakistan, a number of policy documents were prepared and presented during different times. Some of them were comprehensive documents that dealt with educational issues in detail and offered elaborate recommendations, e.g. the 1959 report of Commission on National Education was spread over 370 pages and the 1992 Education policy comprised of 232 pages. On the contrary some policies were sketchy in nature, e.g. The New Education Policy presented in 1970 had only 26 pages. Table 1 contains some major education policy documents.

Table 1: Education Policies in Pakistan

Year	Policy Document	Total Pages
1947	Pakistan Educational Conference	91
1959	The Commission on National Education	370
1969	Proposals for a New Educational Policy	89
1970	The New Education Policy	26
1972	The Education Policy 1972–1980	110
1979	National Education Policy and Implementation Programme	45
1992	National Education Policy 1992	232
1998	National Education Policy 1998–2010	134
2009	National Education Policy 2009	71

Besides the policy documents mentioned in Table 1, there are a couple of reports which are not dealt with here. For instance the report of the Second Education Conference held in 1951; this report was abandoned before implementation. The other document is the 1966 report on students' unrest, which was narrow in its scope and was not a reflection of stated measures by the government, unlike other policies mentioned in Table 1.

PAKISTAN EDUCATIONAL CONFERENCE, 1947

It is important to note that for a number of years there was no state organization or department dedicated to planning. The Pakistan Planning Commission was not instituted until 1955. Much before this, however, the first policy document came out in the form of a report based on the findings of the Pakistan Educational Conference in 1947. The conference was held from 27 November 1947 to 1 December 1947, three months after Pakistan had achieved independence, with a view to assist the education division of the Ministry of the Interior in determining the future educational policy and programme of Pakistan. The conference was a high level gathering that attracted top office bearers of the government and other important individuals. There were forty-eight participants at the conference excluding the nine officers of the education division (Ministry of Interior). The minister for interior, Mr Fazal-ur-Rahman, read out a written message by Quaid-i-Azam, Muhammad Ali Jinnah (Appendix-A). Mr Rahman also made aspeech (Appendix-B) touching upon the important aspects of education.

SUBCOMMITTEES OF THE CONFERENCE

The chairman of the conference instituted the following subcommittees to consider and report on the relevant items on the agenda.

1. Scientific Research and Technical Education Committee
2. Adult Education Committee
3. University Education Committee
4. Primary and Secondary Education Committee
5. Women's Education Committee
6. Committee for Scheduled Caste and Backward Classes Education
7. Cultural Relations Committee

All committees were given terms of reference for effective operations. A proposal by Mr Rice, then principal of Forman Christian College (FCC), was attached with the conference report as an appendix. The proposal was about overhauling university-level education. All the reports of the committee were shared with the participants on 29th, 30th November and 1 December 1947.

Though the conference tried to do its best in the given period of time, the consultative process was limited and the main decisions could not be implemented. The external consideration was the legacy of the English language that was linked with the major domains of power, e.g. the army, the bureaucracy, and the judiciary. World War II (1939–1945) had just ended and there was an obsession with the notion of morality. This could be seen in the 1947 conference report where one of the focal points was the teaching of morals. Historical considerations incorporated the role of religions as the Pakistan Movement had pleaded its case as a separate nation on the basis of a different religion, culture, and language. All these considerations were reflected in the report of the 1947 educational conference that recommended Urdu as the lingua franca, and Islam as the way of life.

COMMISSION ON NATIONAL EDUCATION, 1959

The following important policy document was produced as a result of the work of the Commission on National Education. Since the Commission was headed by S. M. Sharif in 1959, the report was also popularly known as the Sharif Commission report. The Commission on National Education was appointed by a resolution adopted by the Government of Pakistan on 30 December 1958. Pakistan was under the military regime headed by Field Marshal Ayub Khan who had taken over in 1958 and declared himself the President of Pakistan. The commission started its work with a formal inauguration when Field Marshal Mohammad Ayub Khan addressed the commission on 5 January 1959.

The commission sent out a questionnaire about various aspects and levels of education and had it published in the press. The commission also met educationists and visited various institutions (GoP, 1959: 1). There were, however, no exact figures given about the total number of questionnaires sent out and the number of respondents. Dr I. H. Qureshi was also a member of the subcommittee on University Education in the 1947 conference. Between February to April, the commission met educationists and leading public figures in East and West Pakistan and in the Karachi Federal Area to discuss the needs and problems of our educational system. The commission generally held these discussions in educational institutions in order to meet their staff and inspect their facilities. From May till August, the commission deliberated and prepared its report.

External pressures came with the contribution of donor agencies. The Commission Report (GoP, 1959: 9) acknowledged this in the following words:

> The work of the Commission has been greatly helped by the generosity of the Ford Foundation in making consulting services available to it and in giving valuable material assistance. This aid is most warmly acknowledged, as is the continued and sympathetic cooperation of the resident representative of the Foundation.
>
> We gratefully record also our thanks to UNESCO for its assistance in securing information on overseas practices and for the services the members of the Secretariat have rendered to the Commission.

This excerpt from the report reflects the foreign economic and technical input in the preparation of the Commission Report which is considered the most comprehensive document in education and greatly influenced the educational scenario of Pakistan. It is, however, interesting to note that two out of the four experts engaged in the preparation of Pakistan Education policy were foreigners, i.e. Dr Herman B. Wells, President of Indiana University, Bloomington, USA, and Dr John C. Warner, President Carnegie Institute of Technology, Pittsburgh, USA. The two other Pakistani experts, Dr I. H. Qureshi and Dr Abdus Salam, were also engaged in teaching in foreign universities—Dr Qureshi at Columbia University, New York and Dr Salam at Imperial College, London.

It is important to note that there was a consultant from Indiana University who was involved in the policy planning process and that the very next year an Institute of Education and Research was set up in the University of the Punjab with the cooperation of the University of Indiana. A similar institute was set up in the University of Dhaka in East Pakistan. In these institutes foreign faculty members, usually from the University of Indiana, were engaged in teaching and research. Selected students of these institutes were given scholarships for university programmes in the USA.

PROPOSALS FOR A NEW EDUCATIONAL POLICY, 1969

In 1969, a detailed document spread over eighty-nine pages with the title 'Proposals for A New Educational Policy' was released. The document was based on a research study which was intended to review existing education policies, identify the areas of improvement, and put forward a set of recommendations for the formation of an education policy. The document can itself be considered as a policy document. As a result of the review of the earlier education policies, the 1969 policy (GoP, 1969: 1) recommended that '... if education is to be an effective instrument of national development and consolidation, nothing short of a radical departure from the existing policies would be required.' The policy concluded that English education (a legacy of the British empire in India) and *madrasah* education (traditional religious education in the subcontinent) cannot meet the educational challenges independently. The policy proposal (GoP, 1969: 2) concluded that education policies in the past had failed 'to promote a national consensus, play a proper role in national development, reduce unemployment among educated youth, and enhance the educational standard in the country.'

NEW EDUCATION POLICY, 1970

The 1970 Education Policy was a relatively slim document comprising only twenty-six pages. This policy came in the context of tremendous ethnic and political pressure at the internal level as President Field Marshal Ayub Khan had been forced to resign and Yahya Khan was in the presidential seat. The universities were abuzz with protests. The province of East Pakistan was simmering with protest. The policy document looked like a formality to appease the concerns of students and teachers on campus, at least at a rhetorical level.

The New Education Policy, 1970 used text from a presidential press conference held on 26 March 1969 in its introduction. The President announced that his government attached a high priority to the problems of education and would make every possible effort to meet the educational needs of students. According to the policy (GoP, 1970: i):

> ... an intensive review of the entire educational system was undertaken by a number of study groups, both at the Centre and in the Provinces.

In the light of the review, a few proposals were made which were distributed for feedback and as a result 15,000 pages of comments from different sections of society were received. In the light of this feedback the document was reviewed in a series of meetings with representatives of professional groups and organizations. The revised proposals were further reviewed by the cabinet committee. The cabinet committee report was discussed by the cabinet on 13 and 26 March 1970. The policy was finally adopted by the cabinet on 26 March 1970 (GoP, 1970: i).

The major internal consideration for the 1970 Education Policy was the unrest of students and feelings of animosity in East Pakistan where people believed that they were denied their legitimate political, economic, and cultural rights. The interesting part of this policy was that the military government of General Yahya Khan knew that, with general elections to be held in the coming months, it would not be there for the implementation of this policy.

NATIONAL EDUCATION POLICY, 1972

The New Education Policy 1972 was presented by the government of the Pakistan Peoples Party, headed by Zulfikar Ali Bhutto. There is no mention of the process that led to the formation of the policy. Two important events happened between 1970 and 1972. First was the war between India and Pakistan in 1971 and the second was the separation of East Pakistan (now Bangladesh) that same year. The internal considerations, after the shock of losing East Pakistan, were national cohesion and the role of ideology as a uniting force, addressing the challenge of literacy and underlining the role of students and teachers in national development.

NATIONAL EDUCATIONAL POLICY AND IMPLEMENTATION PROGRAMME, 1979

General Zia ul-Haq, who assumed power in 1977, convened a meeting of educationists, scholars, lawyers, teachers, and students to give recommendations for the 'reconstruction' of education in the country. Some of the salient features of these recommendations were announced in October 1978 by the Minister for Education. This led to a public debate in seminars and discussion groups. According to the foreword of the policy (GoP, 1979: iii) the suggestions, made collectively or individually, were keenly studied in the Ministry of Education and incorporated in the implementation programme. The draft work plan was presented to the cabinet in December 1978 where, after detailed discussions, a standing committee was constituted for further examination of the document. The implementation work plan was studied by the cabinet committee in consultation with governors, provincial education advisers, secretaries, vice chancellors, representatives of the Pakistan Medical, Engineering, Bar and Agricultural councils and educationists.

The 1979 policy came at a very crucial time, when General Zia ul-Haq was in power and USA and Saudi Arabia were exerting 'friendly' pressure. An important global event was the revolution in Iran, which emboldened religious elements within Pakistan. The strongest indigenous consideration was aligning the educational stance with the *Nizam-e-Mustafa Movement,* which had been instrumental in bringing Zia ul-Haq in to power. The foreword of the policy explained that a National Education conference was convened where representatives of educationists, scholars, lawyers, teachers, and students expressed their views. The important features of the proposal were presented by the education minister. These points were circulated for debate before the final policy was announced. The policy laid emphasis on Islam, the ideology of Pakistan, and the Urdu language. It claimed a shift to the indigenous models of education.

Understandably, foreign pressures and considerations came with foreign funding. The policy (GoP, 1979: 11) acknowledged the economic role of international donors:

> A number of international agencies like UNDP, UNICEF, and UNESCO will be interested to support this innovative activity through supply of free books, teaching aids, kits, and other contingent items.

Similarly, on another occasion (GoP, 1979: 107), the role of foreign donor agencies was mentioned in the following words:

> International agencies such as UNDP, UNESCO, and UNICEF have shown keen interest in providing grants for experimentation with innovative programmes included in the National Education Policy.

The external considerations and pressures were not just confined to Western powers as there were some Islamic countries that also provided funding and had their say in the education policy. For instance there was extra importance given to the Arabic language in the policy by announcing the setting up of thirty Arabic language centres. As for the expenses, the policy (GoP, 1979: 48) claimed:

> Arab countries have promised to provide books and reading material for these Centres. Books so obtained will be made available in these Centres.
>
> (xiii) The Arab countries have promised to provide teachers and to arrange their training. These facilities will be utilized properly.

The foreign considerations in education policies thus came along with the material benefits.

EDUCATION POLICY, 1992

A number of steps were involved in the preparation of the 1992 policy. According to the policy (GoP, 1992: 2), a series of educational conferences were held in the provinces to gather input from various sections of society. A national conference was also convened and a number of proposals were sent in response to a letter from the Ministry of Education. The minister for education discussed the proposals with the education committees of the Senate and National Assembly. Later the draft policy was discussed in an interprovincial ministers' meeting. The policy was finally presented on 15 September, 1992.

The 1992 Education Policy (GoP, 1992: III) acknowledged international developments and trends as an important consideration for the preparation of the policy:

> Convulsive changes are taking place in the world. The turnover of knowledge in all fields is unprecedented. The economic future of developing nations lies in their abilities and capacities to transform knowledge into new technologies. The world is moving towards a period of intense competition. All this calls for the preparation of a highly competitive society in Pakistan, a society which could stand up to the challenges of the future.

The policy, at the outset, explained the process of planning by mentioning that in April 1991, under the direction of the federal education minister, a national conference was convened where a cross section of society comprising scholars, writers, newspaper editors, scientists, teachers, and lawyers discussed education-related proposals. A large number of these proposals based on educational parameters were received from intellectuals and educationists in response to a letter written to them by the Education Minister.

EDUCATION POLICY, 1998

The 1998 Education policy (1998: 2) alluded to important considerations for the preparation of the policy:

> In view of the rapid developments taking place all over the world and the enormous changes in the socio-economic fabric of our own society, it was deemed essential to express the aspirations and

> intentions of the government in the crucial area of education with renewed vigour and fresh outlook.

According to the policy (GoP, 1998: i) the process began with the Prime Minster instructing the Education ministry to prepare a new education policy. The ministry consulted scholars, administrators, opinion leaders, and representatives of non-governmental organizations to design an initial draft. These deliberations helped the ministry to draw up the major features of the policy which were reviewed by the cabinet. The cabinet suggested extending the range of consultations. The Ministry placed advertisements through the print and electronic media within the country to invite ideas and concrete proposals on national educational issues. The cabinet appointed a subcommittee to scrutinize the proposals and the ministry to finalize the policy. Six committees of experts from the ministry of education were constituted to look at the 4,025 proposals received from all over the country.

According to the foreword of the policy (GoP, 1998: i) the cabinet committee studied the proposals in consultation with educationists. The first draft was presented to the cabinet on 19 February 1998. The Prime Minister, Nawaz Sharif, announced salient features of the policy on 21 February in a national convention on education. More feedback was invited on the draft policy by 15 March 1998. The draft was reviewed by the cabinet committee and the education committees of the Senate and National Assembly. These committees invited experts for their input. The policy was finally presented on 27 March 1998.

EDUCATION POLICY, 2009

General Pervez Musharraf became the chief executive of Pakistan in October 1999 after a military takeover. He toppled the elected Prime Minister Nawaz Sharif whose government had announced a comprehensive education policy in 1998.

In 2001, the terrorist attack on 9/11 had far reaching implications for Pakistan. There was tremendous pressure on Pakistan to control terrorist activities especially through changes in education. Pakistan was funded extensively for this purpose. Pervez Musharraf benefitted from this situation and presented himself as a strong ally of the US in the war on terror. With these events in the background, a committee was constituted under the leadership of a retired bureaucrat, Javed Aly, to review the education policy and to reprioritize various targets. The process was divided into three stages, i.e. diagnostic stage, prescriptive stage, and policy implementation stage (GoP, 2009).

During the *diagnostic stage,* a literature review was done and green papers were prepared. A short study was planned to identify how many targets of the 1998–2010 policy were achieved. A number of consultative sessions and educational conferences were organized to gather views of different stakeholders.

During the *prescriptive stage*, meetings were held with education experts on specific aspects of policy, e.g. vision, literacy, non-formal education, childhood education, gender, *madrasah* education, technical and vocational education, and higher education. During this phase consultative meetings were held with organizations, and coordination was established with development partners.

The third stage was the *policy development stage* when a white paper was prepared in December 2006. The white paper was revised in the light of suggestions from different stakeholders in February 2007. Meanwhile Pervez Musharraf had to resign under tremendous public pressure in 2008. Thus the policy, after a review, was presented during the Pakistan Peoples Party's regime, headed by the Prime Minister, Yousuf Raza Gilani, in 2009.

In 2010 an important amendment was made in the Constitution of Pakistan as a new Article, 25A, was inserted after Article 25 of the Constitution, (w.e.f. 19 April 2010). According to the Article 25A, Right to Education, 'The State shall provide free and compulsory education to all children of the age of five to sixteen years in such manner as may be determined by law.'

SUMMARY

This chapter discussed the significance, rationale and planning process of an education policy for a country. It explained the major components of the policy, i.e. the identification of areas that needed attention, decisions on the measures to be taken, and the implementation process to achieve the targets. The chapter explained the planning process of each important educational policy document since 1947. Besides looking at the process of reaching a consensus the chapter highlighted the external and internal pressures and/or considerations that could influence the policymaking processes of each policy document.

Chapter 2

The Sociopolitical Context of Education Policies

Education policies in Pakistan were formulated, launched, and implemented in specific sociopolitical contexts within the country. It is thus important to familiarize ourselves with the particular milieu to appreciate the recommendations made in a policy and to understand the challenges posed to the processes of planning and implementation.

Pakistan came into being in 1947 as a result of a political movement seeking an independent country for Muslims. The initial problems of the young country included a lack of economic and human resources. Because of the migration of a number of educated and rich Hindus and Sikhs to India, there was a serious vacuum in the education sector in terms of financial and human resources. The literacy rate for India in 1947 was about 15 per cent (Bengali, 1999). This rate was even less for the areas that constituted Pakistan.

Against this dismal state of affairs, the Pakistan Educational Conference was held from 27 November 1947 to 1 December 1947, just three months after independence. The conference was given due importance as Quaid-i-Azam, Muhammad Ali Jinnah's message (Appendix-A) was read out in the conference and the minister responsible for education delivered a comprehensive speech. The conference worked with specifically designated committees. As expected, the conference grappled with a number of issues including the access of children to schools, the supply of teachers, the construction of new schools, state and regional languages, the medium of instruction, and the significance of Islam as part of educational objectives.

The conference recommended Urdu be the lingua franca (common language) of Pakistan. It also recommended that Urdu should be used as the medium of instruction in all the provinces. The DPI from East Pakistan opposed this suggestion. (The details of language recommendations can be seen in Chapter 8, *Language Issues*). What was important was the denial of state language status for Bangla, the language of the majority of the population of Pakistan. The recommendation of the conference regarding Urdu as a lingua franca was further strengthened by the following events.

In the first session of the constituent assembly in February 1948 it was proposed that members of the assembly may use English or Urdu during the proceedings of the assembly. An opposition member from East Pakistan moved a motion of amendment to also include Bangla as one of the Assembly languages besides English and Urdu, as it was the mother tongue of 56 per cent people of Pakistan. The motion was opposed by Prime Minister Liaquat Ali Khan and Chief Minister of East Pakistan Khwaja Nazimuddin, and was eventually defeated. The defeat of the motion ignited the feelings of Bengalis. This was followed by Jinnah's visit to East Pakistan where on 24 March 1948, Jinnah, in his speech (Appendix-C) at the University of Dhaka, elaborated on the issue of state language. He suggested that:

> For official use in this province, the people of the province can choose any language they wish. This question will be decided solely in accordance with the wishes of the people of this province alone, as freely expressed through their accredited representatives at the appropriate time and after full and dispassionate consideration.

But as far as state language was concerned Jinnah (Appendix-C) emphasised that 'There can be only one state language if the component parts of this state are to march forward in unison and that language, in my opinion, can only be Urdu.'

Besides the selection of a state language, the most important issue facing the policymakers was the medium of instruction. On the one hand was the language of the colonial masters, i.e. English, and on the other hand was Urdu, an identity symbol during the Pakistan movement. The third option was to use the languages of the majority of the population groups, i.e. Bangla, and Punjabi. Besides the linguistic question, the most important consideration for policymakers was to reflect on Islam and the teachings of Islam in educational documents, e.g. policies, curricula, and textbooks.

There was a feeling of discomfort among Bengalis in East Pakistan as their language was not given the status of state language. This sense of deprivation was further enhanced as the symbols of power, i.e. the capital, the president house, the prime minister house, the parliament building, the headquarters of the army, air force, and navy, the supreme court, and the civil services academy were situated in West Pakistan.

The nation was jolted when the founding leader of Pakistan, Quaid-i-Azam Muhammad Ali Jinnah, breathed his last on 11 September 1948, just a year after independence. His death was a serious blow to the young nation and a precursor to the political instability faced by the country in the following years. After the Quaid, Khwaja Nazimuddin became the Governor General of Pakistan. He was the first person from East Pakistan to assume the top slot of the government at the centre. Ironically it was he who had opposed the motion to use Bangla as an assembly language besides English and Urdu.

In March 1949, a resolution 'Aims and Objectives of Constitution' (Appendix-D), popularly known as the Objectives Resolution, was passed by the Constituent Assembly of Pakistan which was made a substantive part of the Constitution of Pakistan by a Presidential Order. This resolution was debated for five days in the assembly where some people voiced their disagreement with it (Appendix-E).

On 16 October 1951, Prime Minster Liaquat Ali Khan was shot dead when he was addressing a public meeting in Rawalpindi. His assassination created a serious vacuum of political leadership in Pakistan. Khwaja Nazimuddin assumed the position of Prime Minister as well. Later, Ghulam Muhammad, a senior bureaucrat, became the Governor General of Pakistan. Khwaja Nazimuddin, during his visit to East Pakistan, made a speech in Paltan Maidan on 26 January 1952, where he categorically announced that Urdu would be the only state language. This was a reiteration of the position taken by Jinnah in the 1948 speech at Dhaka (Appendix-C). Coming from a politician who belonged to Dhaka, the statement was shocking for the people of East Pakistan. The response was severe and swift. The unrest that was created by the defeat of the Bangla language motion suddenly turned into an aggressive outburst. On 21 February 1952, the students of the University of Dhaka took out a procession demanding the status of Bangla be uplifted to a state language. The procession was dealt with the might of state power, as the police opened fire and about seven students were reportedly killed. This was a sad incident with far-reaching implications.

The conspiracies in the corridors of power were active. Anti-Qadiani riots erupted in the Punjab. It was believed that the riots were encouraged by the Chief Minister of Punjab, Mumtaz Daultana, who was forced to resign by Prime Minister Khwaja Nazimuddin.

In March 1953, the first Martial Law was imposed in Lahore as civil administration failed to control the anti-Qadiani riots. Governor General Ghulam Mohammad, using his powers under the India Act 1935, dismissed Khawja Nazimuddin on 17 April 1953. He was replaced by Mohammad Ali Bogra, Pakistani ambassador to USA. In 1954 new elections were called for the provincial assembly of East Pakistan. The United Front, led by Maulvi Fazlul Haq won with a thumping majority, bagging 233 out of 309 seats. Maulvi Fazlul Haq was nominated the Prime Minister of East Bengal but the Governor General, in a strange move, sacked the Prime Minister. He also dissolved the East Bengal Assembly. Major General Iskander Mirza was appointed Governor of East Bengal in place of Chaudhary Khaliquzzaman.

In October 1954, the constituent assembly passed Hashim Gazdar's Bill amending Section 10 of the 1935 Act to curtail the powers of the Governor General. However, three days before the scheduled meeting of the assembly, Ghulam Mohammad dissolved the constituent assembly, allowing the incumbent Prime Minister Mohammad Ali Bogra to continue. In 1954, after prolonged protests by the Bengalis, Bangla was finally given the status of state language by the constituent assembly. This status of Bangla language was acknowledged in the 1956 constitution.

In 1958, Field Marshal Ayub Khan took charge of the government and became president of the country. He set up several commissions for different domains. The commission on education was set up in 1959. The country experienced extreme political instability after Jinnah's death with unexpected dissolutions and military coups making the political situation highly vulnerable. University campuses were centres of unrest and student unions were active in politics. This situation was not liked by the rulers, especially by military dictators. The commission's report (GoP, 1959) came during a military regime with issues of political and economic instability and students' unrest on campuses. In 1965, Pakistan and India were entangled in a war that lasted for 17 days, ending with the Tashkent Declaration. Zulfikar Ali Bhutto, who was a young minister in the cabinet of Ayub Khan, resigned from the cabinet and exploited the alleged 'secret deal' made in the Tashkent Declaration and mobilized the students. In 1966, a report was prepared to investigate the causes of students' unrest on campuses.

The 1966 report identified the politicization of campuses as an important cause of their unrest. It referred to weak university administrations that had failed to manage indiscipline and recommended giving students a role in decision-making forums. A series of protest processions were organized to demand Ayub Khan's resignation. After immense pressure from all sides, Ayub Khan gave up and resigned on 25 March 1969, but replaced himself with General Yahya Khan, instead of handing over the position to a civil government. The political unrest did not subside, especially since there was a strong movement fomenting in East Pakistan for more autonomy. Campuses were paralyzed by political chaos and the students were restive because of rising unemployment and political instability. The 1970 Education Policy was launched in this sociopolitical context. Besides other recommendations the policy proposed to set up teacher-students councils, creating employment opportunities for students, and providing transportation facilities to them. General elections were held in the country. The Awami League swept the elections in East Pakistan whereas Zulfikar Ali Bhutto's Pakistan Peoples Party emerged as the winning party in West Pakistan.

A parliament session was announced for 3 March 1971, but was postponed by Yahya Khan. Upon this Sheikh Mujibur Rahman announced a week-long strike. Ultimately the tension grew out of proportion and India announced its support for the Mukti Bahini (Bengali Liberation Army) leading to the 1971 war. As a result of this war East Pakistan became Bangladesh. Yahya Khan, who was considered one of the reasons of fall of East Pakistan, resigned on 20 December 1971 and Zulfikar Ali Bhutto became president of Pakistan. Bhutto came into power as result of his popular slogans of *roti, kapra, aur makan* (food, clothing, and shelter). As a champion of 'Islamic Socialism', he nationalized a number of industries.

Besides industries, Bhutto also nationalized all privately managed educational institutions in the country. The apprehension of politicking students could be the cause of this move, as through nationalization control could be exerted on the management and students. On the language front, serious ethno-lingual riots erupted in Sindh after the Sindhi language bill. Bhutto's Peoples Party claimed to be the party of students and the working class thus the 1972 policy was conscious of the issue of unemployment. Similarly, low salaries of college and university teachers was also a priority action point. The nationalization of educational institutions proved to be a highly controversial decision which was withdrawn later but not before it had a negative impact on the quality of education.

In 1977, Zulfikar Ali Bhutto announced general elections. All major opposition parties made an alliance named the Pakistan National Alliance (PNA). After the national assembly elections results were announced in Bhutto's favour, the PNA alleged rigging and boycotted the provincial assembly elections, launching massive protests against Bhutto which led to the imposition of Martial Law by the army chief General Zia ul-Haq on 5 July 1977. Since he had come into power as a result of the *Nizam-e-Mustafa* movement, Zia made it a point to Islamize all walks of life. He put Bhutto in jail on a murder charge and hanged him on 4 April 1979, following a controversial decision by the Supreme Court. Zia ul-Haq, who had assumed power with the promise of holding elections in ninety days, went back on his word and made himself president of the country.

The 1979 Education policy was prepared and launched by Zia ul-Haq's military regime. The overemphasis on Islamization was reflected in the policy. Zia's long dictatorial rule ended on 17 August 1988 when he died in a plane crash under mysterious circumstances. After the repressive era of Zia ul-Haq, students became active on campuses. Senate chairman Ghulam Ishaq replaced General Zia ul-Haq as president of Pakistan and held general elections. As a result of these elections Benazir Bhutto, chairperson of the Pakistan Peoples Party, became the prime minister of Pakistan on 2 December 1988. Her government could not complete it's tenure as President Ghulam Ishaq Khan dismissed Benazir Bhutto's government and dissolved the assemblies on 6 August 1990. In the 1990 elections, Nawaz Sharif won and took oath as the prime minister on 6 November 1990.

The 1992 Education policy offered detailed recommendations for improving the situation on campuses in terms of de-weaponizing them and establishing student teacher councils. The Nawaz Sharif government, however, was dismissed by President Ghulam Ishaq Khan in 1993.

As a result of new elections, Benazir became prime minister on 19 October 1993. Benazir could not complete her tenure as Farooq Leghari, President of Pakistan in Benazir's second term, dismissed her government on 5 November 1996. As a result of new elections Nawaz Sharif became Prime Minister in 1997. This time he enjoyed a two-third majority in the parliament which gave him extra confidence to embark upon long-term strategic planning. The Education Policy devised in 1998 was a part of that strategic planning. A useful document, Vision 2010, was prepared to plan things with long-term perspective. But the agenda remained unfinished as the army chief, General Pervez Musharraf, dismissed the Nawaz Sharif government on 12 October 1999.

During the regime of Pervez Musharraf, Pakistan came under tremendous pressure following 9/11, and his government survived by receiving financial aid which started arriving after his alignment with the US on the 'war on terror'. The 9/11 Commission Report recommended to help Pakistan 'improve' their education in order to combat terrorism and subsequently a large sum of money was given to the Government of Pakistan to bring changes in curriculum, textbooks, and teacher education programmes. Major focus was also shifted towards madrasahs and their alleged association with terrorism. To prepare a new education policy a team was organized under the leadership of a senior bureaucrat, Javed Aly, which put together the policy. However, as a result of new elections in 2008, Pakistan Peoples Party came into power and Pervez Musharraf had to resign on 18 August 2008 as a consequence of the restoration of judiciary movement. Thus the 2009 education policy which was prepared during the Musharraf era could only be presented after his departure.

Table 2 gives a summary of the education policies and their architects. It is interesting to note that out of eight education policy documents, four were prepared by military dictators. Most of the civil rulers who presented policies could not survive their tenure because of the dissolution of the assemblies.

Table 2: Policies and Rulers

Year	Policy Document	Ruler of the country
1947	Pakistan Educational Conference	Muhammad Ali Jinnah
1959	Commission on National Education	Field Marshal Ayub Khan
1969	Proposals for a New Education Policy	General Yahya Khan
1970	The New Education Policy	General Yahya Khan
1972	National Education Policy	Zulfikar Ali Bhutto
1979	National Education Policy	General Zia ul-Haq
1992	Education Policy	Muhammad Nawaz Sharif
1998	National Education Policy	Muhammad Nawaz Sharif
2009	National Education Policy	*General Pervez Musharraf/ Syed Yousuf Raza Gilani

*The Education Policy (2009) was prepared during Musharraf's regime but was presented later by the Gilani government as Musharraf had to resign in 2008.

Table 3 gives a summary of important social and political events which had a direct or indirect association with the educational policies, either in terms of their planning process or implementation phase:

Table 3: Important Sociopolitical Happenings

Year	Sociopolitical Happenings
1947	Pakistan came into being; Pakistan Educational Conference
1948	Constituent assembly does not approve Bangla as state language; Quaid-i-Azam announces in Dhaka that Urdu would be the only state language; Quaid-i-Azam dies
1949	Objectives Resolution passed by constituent assembly
1951	Liaquat Ali Khan shot dead
1952	Protests in East Pakistan to declare Bangla as a state language; 21 February: Police fire at the procession of students at Dhaka University killing seven students
1954	Constituent assembly approves Bangla as State language beside Urdu
1956	Bangla given the status of state language
1958	Field Marshal Ayub Khan takes over the government
1959	Commission on National Education
1965	War between Pakistan and India
1969	Yahya Khan takes over as Ayub Khan resigns under public pressure. Proposals for a New Educational Policy
1970	New Education Policy launched; General elections are held; Awami League in East Pakistan and Pakistan Peoples Party in West Pakistan emerge as majority parties; Parliament session called but then postponed by Yahya Khan; Large-scale protests in East Pakistan
1971	War between Pakistan and India; East Pakistan becomes Bangladesh; Bhutto becomes the chief executive as Yahya Khan resigns

Year	Sociopolitical Happenings
1972	Education Policy launched by Pakistan Peoples Party leading to nationalization of educational institutions
1977	General Zia ul-Haq takes over the government by dismissing the government of Zulfikar Ali Bhutto
1979	New Education Policy launched
1988	Zia ul-Haq dies in an air crash; Chairman senate Ghulam Ishaq Khan becomes the president of Pakistan; General elections are held in the country; Benazir Bhutto becomes the prime minister
1990	Benazir's government dismissed by President Ghulam Ishaq Khan; Nawaz Sharif becomes prime minister after new general elections
1992	National Education Policy launched by the Nawaz Sharif government.
1993	Nawaz Sharif government dismissed by President Ghulam Ishaq Khan; Benazir becomes the prime minister as a result of general elections in the country
1996	Benazir's government dismissed by President Farooq Leghari
1997	Nawaz Sharif becomes prime minister after the general elections
1998	National Education Policy launched by the Nawaz Sharif government
1999	General Pervez Musharraf dismisses Nawaz Sharif's government
2001	Twin towers in USA attacked on 11 September
2005	Musharraf government forms a committee to review education policy
2008	General Elections; Yousaf Raza Gilani becomes the prime minister; Pervez Musharraf resigns as president after tremendous public pressure
2009	Education Policy (2009) launched by the government of Pakistan Peoples Party.

Chapter 3

Education Policies: Vision and Ideology

There has been a growing realization in the recent past for the need to analyse and understand the phenomenon and dynamics of education with a sociological perspective (Siddiqui, 2012). It is through this perspective that we hope to get a fuller view of education, which is essentially a social phenomenon. It is important to understand that educational practices do not take place in isolation but are influenced, shaped, and in some cases, determined by certain ideologies (Apple, 1990). Thus, to bring a qualitative change in educational practices, it is important to recognize the relationship of ideology and education and the vital role ideology plays in the conceptualization and execution of education.

Before the role of ideology in the construction of social practices is analysed, it is pertinent to unpack how the term 'ideology' has been used in different periods of time with different connotations. In the past, the term 'ideology' had a negative connotation, but in contemporary times it is considered akin to the term 'philosophy'. Ideology, in simple words, can be defined as a set of beliefs. These beliefs are usually entertained at group levels. Ideology at group level can be contrasted with individual opinions in a society. A useful description is given by Eysenck & Wilson (1978) who refer to three levels, i.e. a specific opinion level, a habitual opinion level, and an attitude level. Ideology constructs the stereotypes that constitute *common sense* and are taken for granted in a society. These stereotypes are legitimized and supported by certain social institutions. Thus the ideology that has the backing of a powerful social institution becomes dominant in a society and has the potential to capture the minds of marginalized groups. It is this subtle hegemony of ideas which was first focused and elaborated by the Italian scholar Gramsci (1996).

The goal of education emanates from the philosophical, economic, and cultural considerations that drive the initiative of education. In the case of Pakistan, the overarching ideology of Islam remained present in the educational policies of Pakistan. This chapter attempts to focus on the stated goals of education policies during different historical periods since 1947. The vision of all the education policies seems to emerge from Islam, the official religion of the country. Without disturbing the religious vision, policies in different times had different preferences and positions.

PAKISTAN EDUCATIONAL CONFERENCE, 1947

The Pakistan Educational Conference that was organized in 1947, three months after the creation of Pakistan, was a gathering of top government officials where a message from Quaid-i-Azam Muhammad Ali Jinnah, was read out. In addition, the minister for interior, Mr Fazal-ur-Rahman, also responsible for education, gave a detailed speech where he discussed the philosophical considerations necessary for the educational system of Pakistan. The minister emphasized the need for reorientation of education in the light of Islamic teaching. He stated in his speech (GoP, 1947: 6) that:

> We have now before us the opportunity of reorienting our entire educational policy to correspond closely with the needs of the times and to reflect the ideals for which Pakistan as an Islamic State stands.

The conference (GoP, 1947: 21) recommended that the ideological basis of education be 'the Islamic conception of universal brotherhood of man, social democracy, social justice, and the cultivation of democratic virtues, i.e. tolerance, self-help, self-sacrifice, human kindliness, etc. and the consciousness of common citizenship as opposed to provincial exclusiveness.'

As far as the objectives of education are concerned the minister referred to three potential objectives of education, inclusive of the spiritual, social, and vocational and commented that the spiritual aspect of education was the most important one. He also considered illiteracy the country's most important challenge. On the whole, spirituality and morality deriving from Islam appeared to be the main virtues inspiring educational decision-making in the Pakistan Educational conference in 1947. The educational ideology was summed up in three points at the conference (GoP, 1947: 21):

(a) Education should be based on the Islamic concept of universal brotherhood of man, social democracy, and social justice.
(b) It should be compulsory for students to learn the fundamental principles of their religion.
(c) There should be proper integration of spiritual social and vocational elements in education.

COMMISSION ON NATIONAL EDUCATION, 1959

The 1959 Commission report (GoP, 1959), at the outset, mentioned its objectives being trained manpower, educated citizenry, national development, social justice, a sense of unity, nationhood, competent leadership, and a social welfare state. The commission report (GoP, 1959: 11) stated that,

> National unity and religious values have to be translated into deeds in a manner that all our citizens can accept them and join in the common effort. Islam teaches honesty in thought, indeed, and in purpose; it lays emphasis on social justice and active participation in the removal of distress and poverty.

Stating the need to inculcate patriotism among students the Commission (GoP, 1959: 117) proposed 'to provide a form of education which has its roots in the national culture and in Islamic values.' At another place, the Commission (GoP, 1959: 211) emphasized that, 'indeed Pakistan, to be true to her soul, should take inspiration from Islam, its principles, and ideology.'

The Commission proposed that Islamiat (the study of Islam) should be taught as a compulsory subject to all Muslim students at primary and middle levels. Some of the recommendations of the Commission (GoP, 1959: 212) included teaching students to read the Holy Qur'an (*Nazira*), making learning of the *Kalima* and *suras* for *namaz* compulsory for Muslim students, teaching stories and parables from the Holy Quran, the life of the Prophet (PBUH), and Muslim history. The Commission, however, proposed that religious studies beyond grade eight should be an optional subject.

PROPOSALS FOR A NEW EDUCATIONAL POLICY, 1969

The 1969 policy document stated in explicit terms that the education system should derive its inspiration from the state religion, Islam. The policy (GoP, 1969: 2) declared that, 'it must aim at providing a uniform and integrated system of education which seeks to impart a common set of cultural values based on the precepts of Islam.' The policy (GoP, 1969: 13) rejects outright the idea of secular values and emphasized that, 'to argue, therefore, that the set of cultural values to be imparted through the education system should be only secular in character is unrealistic. It must be recognized therefore that the unified system of education in Pakistan should be an Islamic one.' The policy proposed to accord high priority to Islamic research and incorporate its results into the normal curricula of our faculties of law, politics, economics, and other social sciences. The 1969 policy proposed to declare Islamiat as a compulsory subject up to class X. It is important to note that until then Islamiat was taught as a compulsory subject only up to class VIII and beyond that it was only an optional subject.

THE NEW EDUCATION POLICY, 1970

The 1970 Education policy listed the following areas of reform linked with goals and guidelines of educational development:

> The role of education in the preservation and inculcation of Islamic values as an instrument of national unity and progress.

> Reorientation of educational programmes in the light of the economic needs of the society particularly by shifting the emphasis to scientific, technical, and vocational education;
>
> Role of education as an instrument of social change and development and as a factor in the creation of a democratic social order by ensuring an equal access to opportunities of education.

The 1970 Report (GoP, 1970), like the Pakistan Educational Conference 1947 and the 1959 Commission Report, emphasized the provision of skills to the citizens in order to utilize human capital. According to the policy (GoP, 1970: 2), 'the ideological framework is provided by the basic values stressed in Islam including those of social justice, equality, and a democratic way of life, which are universal in character and also integral to the concept of Pakistan.' The policy felt the need to emphasise social and egalitarian aspects of education and to strive for quality education. Following is the detailed wish list stated in the 1970 policy (GoP, 1970: 2) in terms of goals, objectives, and the inspirational force behind them:

> The curriculum should be inspired by Pakistan's national objectives. The curriculum of elementary schools should be re-designed around basic linguistic and numerical skills and manual and productive work to suit the practical needs of everyday life. The aversion to manual work should be countered by relating the curriculum to the physical and social environment of children, which will make elementary education more responsive to the needs of society.

EDUCATION POLICY, 1972

The 1972 Educational Policy, unlike previous policy documents, provided a clear list of structured objectives. A number of these objectives, however, can be found in past policy documents (GoP, 1947; GoP, 1959; GoP, 1970). The Policy (GoP, 1972: 1) stated the vision of education as 'Ensuring the preservation, promotion and practice of the basic ideology of Pakistan and making it a code of individual and national life.' The policy proposed that curricula and textbooks would not contain any thing repugnant to, or inconsistent with, the cultural and ethical values of Islam.

EDUCATION POLICY, 1979

The 1979 Education policy launched during Zia ul-Haq's military regime was based on the Islamization of the educational system in Pakistan. Zia ul-Haq had dismissed the democratically elected government of Zulfikar Ali Bhutto. It is important to note that there was a public movement against Bhutto called the *Nizam-e-Mustafa* movement. The movement was largely influenced by right wing political parties gathered in the name of Islam. Zia ul-Haq exploited these sentiments and announced a number of measures to demonstrate his inclination towards religion. The 1979 Policy (GoP, 1979: 48) claimed that the national education policy was:

> ... mainly concerned with the promotion of Islamic values among the individuals and the social [society]. Inculcation of deep and abiding faith in Islam, development of Muslim nationhood and integration and cohesion of the society can be achieved by propagating the message of Islam and proper emphasis on the teaching of Islamiat and Arabic.

The 1979 Policy (GoP, 1979: 1) further explained the desired objective as:

> To foster in the hearts and minds of the people of Pakistan in general and the students in particular a deep and abiding loyalty to Islam and Pakistan and a living consciousness of their spiritual and ideological identity, thereby strengthening unity of the outlook of the people of Pakistan on the basis of justice and fair play.

As a strategic action the policy recommended to revise all the curricula with a view to, 'reorganizing the entire content around Islamic thought and giving education and ideological orientation so that Islamic ideology permeates the thinking of younger generation and helps them with necessary conviction and ability to refashion society according to Islamic tenets' (GoP, 1979: 2). The policy proposed to revise curricula and textbooks at all levels to ensure inclusion of adequate content on Islam, the ideology of Pakistan, and the promotion of national cohesion and integration. To ensure the desired method and practice of teaching, the policy proposed that teachers, besides possessing knowledge of subject matter and techniques of teaching, 'must also exhibit full commitment to the Ideology of Pakistan' (GoP, 1979: 62). The policy proposed Pakistan Studies and Islamiat as compulsory subjects from classes I till XIV and in professional colleges Urdu was made a compulsory subject for classes I till XII. The degrees of *madrasahs* were equated with MA in Arabic or Islamiat.

EDUCATION POLICY 1992

The 1992 policy was launched during the regime of Nawaz Sharif. In the foreword of the policy (GoP, 1992: III) the minister for education proposed to 'leaven the educational system with Islamic ethos and allow it to run through all its tributaries.' The policy suggested that the government's determination to introduce Islamic order in society brings the educational system into sharp focus.

The policy (GoP, 1992: 11) set the target 'to defend the ideology of Pakistan at the interface of international, social, political and economic development.' The 1992 policy was an elaborate policy document that offered a detailed set of objectives. The major emphasis of the policy (GoP, 1992: 11), however, was, '... to restructure the existing educational system on modern lines in accordance with the principles of Islam so as to create a healthy, forward looking and enlightened Muslim society.'

The policy proposed that Institutes of Education and Research should establish separate centres to carry out research on the contents of Islamic education for inclusion in courses at various levels, and on methods of teaching Islamic ideology.

EDUCATION POLICY, 1998

The 1998 Education Policy (GoP, 1998: 5), launched by Nawaz Sharif's government, stated the vision as under:

> The vision is to transform the Pakistani Nation into an integrated, cohesive entity, that can compete and stand up to the challenges of 21st Century. The policy is formulated to realize the vision of

> an educationally well-developed, politically united, economically prosperous, morally sound and spiritually elevated nation.

One of the major objectives of the policy (GoP, 1998: 6) was 'To make the Quranic principles and Islamic practices as an integral part of curricula so that the message of the Holy Qur'an could be disseminated in the process of education as well as training.'

EDUCATION POLICY, 2009

The 2009 Education Policy, which was presented during the regime of Pakistan Peoples Party, was largely prepared under the reign of Pervez Musharraf's government who had set up a committee to work on the preparation of this education policy. The policy (GoP, 2009a: 17) reproduced the following vision that was adopted by the ministry of education:

> Our education system must provide quality education to our children and youth to enable them to realize their individual potential and contribute to development of society and nation, creating a sense of Pakistani nationhood, the concepts of tolerance, social justice, democracy, their regional and local culture and history based on the basic ideology enunciated in the Constitution of the Islamic Republic of Pakistan.

One of the objectives of the policy (GoP, 2009a: 17) was:

> To play a fundamental role in the preservation of the ideals which lead to the creation of Pakistan and strengthen the concept of the basic ideology within the Islamic ethos enshrined in the 1973 Constitution of the Islamic Republic of Pakistan.

It is important to note that there is a complete section entitled Islamic Education in the policy (GoP, 2009a: 31) that begins with the following statements. 'The ideology of Islam forms the genesis of the State of Islamic Republic of Pakistan and its fundamental principles were defined in the Objectives Resolution of 1949.'

ANALYSIS AND DISCUSSION

Almost all education policies in Pakistan claimed to get inspiration from the ideology of Islam. It seemed to be a compulsive motivation for policymakers to refer to Islam as their vision, mainly for political reasons. The rationale of excessive references to Islam can be understandable on a political pretext as the case of Pakistan was fought on the premise of a country comprising Muslim majority areas. Resolve for reorientation of educational system in the light of an Islamic ideology was first reflected in the Pakistan Education Conference held in 1947.

We see the manifestation of Islamic ideology in education policies in different forms, e.g. reference to Islamic values, considering Islam as a source of inspiration for education, preparing curricula on the basics of Islamic principles, etc. In most of the cases emphasis was laid on inculcating Islamic values, i.e. brotherhood, social democracy, social justice, among the students. The interesting point, however, was that the set of values, according to the policy (GoP, 1969), could not be secular and had to be Islamic.

In some policies one can feel as if the Islamic ideology was introduced as a compulsion. Islamiat was initially offered as a mandatory subject up to class 8 but in the policies that followed it was declared a mandatory subject up to class 10. In Zia ul-Haq's education policy (GoP, 1979) Islamiat was made a compulsory subject even beyond class 10 and all the curricula were instructed to be redesigned on the principles of Islam. The prerequisite condition for hiring a new teacher was knowledge of Islam and the ideology of Pakistan.

During Zia ul-Haq's period, because of the Afghan War, *mujahideen* came from different countries to fight against Russia. They were encouraged at national and international levels to do so. The Afghan war brought an aggressive religious element into Pakistani society that acted as a pressure group and influenced the policymaking process. A recent example of such pressure can be cited about the education policy 2009. The policy was prepared in Musharraf's era. When its first draft was released it had no exclusive chapter on Islamic education. But under tremendous pressure from the religious components of society, a separate chapter titled Islamic Education was added to the final version of the policy.

SUMMARY

Vision plays an important role in setting the destination to be achieved. The vision informs the policymakers to identify targets and to decide on the measures to be taken to achieve the targets. The chapter discussed the stated goals of education policies launched during different periods of time in Pakistan. It is important to note that the vision of all the educational policies is linked with Islam, which is the religion of majority of the citizens of Pakistan. This emphasis grew during Zia ul-Haq's regime (GoP, 1979) but it also remained marked during Musharraf's era who claimed to be a champion of *enlightened moderation*, suggesting that a number of governments used religion as a rhetoric.

Chapter 4

Literacy

There is a powerful relationship between literacy and development. This correlation came to the forefront in the recent decades when the term *human capital* gained currency. The significance of education in terms of human development is manifested in the World Declaration on EFA, 1990 (www.unesco.org/org/education/efa/ed_for_all/background/jomtien_declaration.shtml), which states that, '... education is a fundamental right for all people, women and men, of all ages, throughout our world ...' but it is unfortunate that a number of people, mostly women, have been deprived of this fundamental right. According to the UIS (UNESCO Institute of Statistics) data, (http://www.uis.unesco.org/ev_en.php?ID=6401) there are an estimated 781 million illiterate adults in the world, about 64 per cent of whom are women.

In 1947, when Pakistan came into being, there were only 8,413 primary schools, 2,190 middle, and 408 Secondary schools, 40 colleges, and 2 universities in the areas constituting Pakistan (GoP, 1951: 5). The literacy rate for United India in 1947 at the time of the independence of Pakistan was about 15 per cent (Bengali, 1999). This rate was much lower for the areas that constituted Pakistan. Muslims lagged behind other ethnic groups in terms of modern education. For instance the literacy statistics cited in Ghafoor and Khan (1995: 20) in Rawalpindi district in 1912 are given in Table 4, which shows a vast gap between Muslims and other communities.

Table 4: Literacy Rate in Rawalpindi District in 1912

Religion	Literacy Rate (%)
Christians	85.1
Jains	33.1
Sikhs	29.1
Hindus	18.7
'Mohammadans'	2.1

It is important here to mention the other version on the state of literacy that suggested that, prior to the British rule, India had a far more comprehensive system of education that boasted educational opportunities in every village (Dharampal, 2000; Adam 1836, 1838; Leitner, 1882). To discredit the indigenous educational system, the British introduced an alternative system of education which was not only insufficient for the educational needs of large Indian populations but was also removed from indigenous culture and values. One direct outcome of this move was that the majority of the locally literate people were declared illiterate as they would not fit into the new definition of literacy.

When Pakistan came into being it inherited the problem of illiteracy. Different governments tried to grapple with this issue, focusing mainly on quantitative expansion of literacy. There have been a number of initiatives in terms of organizations, projects, and strategies to enhance literacy rate to meet the set targets.

PAKISTAN EDUCATIONAL CONFERENCE, 1947

The report on the Pakistan Educational Conference (GoP, 1947: 84) underlined the significance of literacy and suggested that, 'Literacy is a means to further education and must not be regarded as an end in itself.' The minister responsible for education, Mr Fazal-ur-Rahman, (GoP, 1947: 9) advised in his address that 'our first and foremost concern must inevitably be a determined and vigorous attack on the formidable problem of illiteracy and its evil consequences. It goes without saying that the existence of a large bulk of illiterate population constitutes a grave menace to the security and well-being of the State.'

The Conference (GoP, 1947: 9) recommended that 'the State in its own interests should provide to its boys and girls, universal, compulsory and free basic education which is the primary requisite of training in democracy.' Some major recommendations of the conference included the use of broadcasting, magic lantern slides, gramophone records, documentary films, and other scientific methods to help improve the literacy of masses. Provinces were to take early steps to introduce mass literacy in their respective areas, college students were to take part in the mass literacy campaign, a literacy centre for women was to be established, and teaching aids like cinema, radio, circulating libraries were to be greatly encouraged. The conference saw the need for the establishment of an adult literacy campaign in each province and recommended the allocation of 50 per cent of the amount allotted to adult education to be put towards adult literacy centres for women. Although Pakistan Educational Conference proposed a number of measures to enhance literacy, no specific date was given to achieve the literacy target. Most of these proposals could not materialize in the absence of a concrete work plan and political upheavals at the national level.

COMMISSION ON NATIONAL EDUCATION, 1959

The Commission on National Education that was set up in 1959 by Ayub Khan, besides other educational challenges, focused on the literacy issue as well. The Commission (GoP, 1959: 197) realized the menace of illiteracy and focused on the considered removal of illiteracy as a '... matter of crucial importance to Pakistan and one which will require a tremendous effort.' Evaluating the initiatives launched in the last three decades to enhance literacy, the Commission expressed its dissatisfaction on the outcomes of those initiatives. According to the Commission three major factors that hampered the literacy drive included lack of sufficient motivation, use of defective teaching techniques, and paucity of reading materials. The Commission proposed a literacy programme for primary education. The Commission (GoP, 1959: 202) proposed that, 'each child who joins school must continue for the full five-year programme, and gradually include all primary-aged children in this effort; it will mean that no new illiterates will be entering the productive (12–40) age group.'

The Commission appreciated the initiative of Village Aid, essentially focusing villages of the country, and recommended intensifying these efforts and setting up a centre similar to the Literacy Training and Production Centre at Lalamusa in East Pakistan. This centre was to have an education wing for the training of adult literacy workers and the production of the necessary reading materials. The Commission recommended that in urban areas of the country a programme similar to Village Aid should be undertaken by the Department of Social Welfare with the appropriate professional assistance from the education sector. The Commission referred to some approaches which had been tried and tested in other countries, including the use of school children as teachers in an effort to make their parents literate, the use of undergraduate college students as adult literacy teachers, and the use of one literate adult to teach another under the 'each one teach one' approach. The Commission recommended that the Ministry of Education should launch pilot projects for each methods and large scale programmes should be developed according to those methods that proved successful. The Commission recommended utilizing the services of women and *imams* (religious prayer leaders).

The Commission (GoP, 1959: 175) wisely cautioned that 'while making children completely functionally literate must remain a basic and constant concern at this level, we must remember that functional literacy in itself is not enough.' One important factor for the failure of literacy initiatives in the past was the lack of motivation. The Commission recommended that the programme to eradicate illiteracy should be based on economic motivation. The Commission showed its enthusiasm to eradicate illiteracy but proposed no deadline to achieve the targets.

PROPOSALS FOR A NEW EDUCATIONAL POLICY, 1969

The 1969 policy acknowledged that no real economic progress was possible without literacy. It referred to three advantages of literacy, namely providing a base for education, induction of social change in behaviour, and improvement in productivity. The policy (GoP, 1969: 19) observed that out of a 'total number of 20 million children in the age group 5–10, no more than 9 million (45 per cent) are enrolled in schools. The overall literacy in the country is no more than 20 per cent which is amongst the lowest in Asia.' The policy aimed to impart literacy to 68 million adults by 1980. It also realized that five years of education to a child did not prohibit the potential reversion to illiteracy. The policy thus proposed that the existing primary and middle stages of education should be consolidated into one 'elementary' stage to which a high degree of priority should be accorded so that illiteracy could be eliminated in the beginning. The policy observed that since a literacy program at the early level would take time to show its impact, crash programmes of literacy should be launched, focusing on adult illiterates and dropouts from schools. It also proposed the establishment of a National Literacy Corps comprising youth of 18 years and above who had passed their intermediate or higher examination, which should be administered by a young leadership. The policy also proposed the establishment of Adult Literacy Programmes, supported by the Literacy Corps, to realize the target of imparting literacy to millions of people by 1980. The Policy also recommended that future education policies should focus on elementary education.

THE EDUCATION POLICY, 1970

The 1970 Education Policy (GoP, 1970: 3) acknowledged at the outset that 'Pakistan today has one of the highest rates of illiteracy in the world.' The Policy observed that because of irregular attendance and a high dropout rate of children, they could not achieve the appropriate level of literacy. The policy (GoP, 1970: 4) proposed that 'the Provincial Governments should seriously consider adopting measures for compulsory school attendance up to 10 years of age.' Since the 1970 Policy was launched less than one year after the 1969 Policy, during the same regime of Yahya Khan, there were no changes as far as literacy initiatives were concerned. The Policy reiterated the claim of imparting literacy to 68 million adults by 1980. The Policy recommended that unemployed educated youth could be hired in the Literacy Corps (proposed in 1969 Education Policy). The major recommendations of the 1970 Policy included suitable measures by provinces for providing functional education to adults and school dropouts, provision of work-oriented basic education to unskilled employees by their employers for efficient performance, suitable institutional arrangements, including the establishment of a National Education Corps on a feasible basis, for implementing the literacy programme as a complement to the elementary education programme. The 1970 Policy claimed that the literacy rate, which was 24 per cent at that time, 'will rise to well over 35 per cent by 1982–83' and Pakistan is quite likely to attain '100 per cent literacy around the year 2010 if other important factors continue to remain constant.'

The Fourth Five-Year Plan (1970–1978) cautioned that mass illiteracy blocked economic and social progress. According to the plan the number of illiterates was rising in excess of 1 million persons a year. The Plan stressed the need to intensify efforts to obtain universal retention in primary institutions including drafting legislation to enforce regular attendance of children enrolled in classes I–V. It also stressed on one-year courses for the employees of public and private sector organizations set up by the employers.

THE EDUCATION POLICY, 1972

One of the objectives of this policy (GoP, 1972: 1) was to eradicate '... illiteracy within the shortest possible time through the universalization of elementary education and a massive adult education programme.' The policy declared that education would be free and universal up to Class X for all children throughout the country. The policy proposed to launch a National Service Corps between the ages of 17 to 23. According to the policy (GoP, 1972: 35), the youth would 'serve in the corps for a total period of one year after passing the Intermediate Examination. This service may be rendered either in one stretch or in short intervals during summer vacations and other free time.' Some proposed incentives for those joining this corps included a monthly honorarium, uniform allowance, preference in selection for admission to institutions of higher education, and for employment both in the private and public sectors, and the corps service period to be exempted from age limit restrictions of entry into services, etc.

The policy announced the establishment of the People's Open University to provide part-time educational facilities through correspondence courses, tutorials, seminars, workshops, laboratories, television, radio broadcasts, and other mass communication media. Another important feature of the 1972 Policy was the formation of the National Book Foundation. The professed purpose of the Foundation was to undertake the writing, editing, compiling, translating, printing, and publishing of both textbooks and reading material for schools, colleges, adults, and the general public at reasonable prices. The policy stated that, keeping in view the challenge of literacy, only state measures would not be sufficient. To make the literacy movement effective, voluntary participation by society was essential.

THE EDUCATION POLICY, 1979

The 1979 Policy (GoP, 1979: 25) at the outset acknowledged the enormous challenge of illiteracy faced by the country. 'Pakistan is among the countries of the world having the lowest rates of literacy. This has hampered the overall progress of the country.' The policy (GoP, 1979: 1) considered the provision of '... a minimum acceptable level of functional literacy ...' as one of its objectives. To implement its proposals the policy suggested total mobilization of community resources. In this respect, the policy took some drastic steps, e.g. opening mosque schools, *mohalla* (neighbourhood) schools, and village workshop schools. The policy pledged that 5,000 mosque schools would be opened during the Five-Year Plan period at the rate of approximately 1,000 schools per year. The students in the mosque schools would be taught by the *imams* (prayer leaders). The policy also proposed to establish 5,000 *mohalla* schools during the next five years. Such schools would be operative in those communities where no facilities for female education were available. The policy also recommended establishing 1,000 schools in the first phase with specially trained teachers where emphasis would be placed on indigenous agro-based trades and skills.

The policy (GoP, 1979: 25–6) recommended setting up a National Council on Adult Education with its nucleus at Allama Iqbal Open University, Islamabad. According to the policy, the Allama Iqbal Open University, through its multimedia delivery technology, would organize radio and television programmes, prepare special booklets and reading material for adults, and set up mobile operational units in the rural areas. The policy aimed to establish 10,000 adult literacy centres in the country. The policy intended to explore the possibility of recruiting a student volunteer corps, comprising senior students of BA/BSc, MA/MSc, to help launch this programme throughout the country.

On the recommendation of the 1979 policy, the Literacy and Mass Education Commission (LAMEC) was set up in 1981. The primary job of LAMEC was to come up with strategies to eradicate illiteracy through formal and informal means of education and promote functional literacy. The commission was asked to think of ways to integrate indigenous knowledge and vocational skill with literacy initiatives. In 1983 Zia ul-Haq announced a ten-point program for the promotion of literacy. Some of these points were overly ambitious, for example, he recommended that arms licenses, driving licenses, and similar other licenses and permits should be granted only to literate persons.

A year after the Sixth Five-Year Plan, a massive National Literacy Plan (1984–1986) was launched. The Plan, with Rs. 317.016 million funds at its disposal, took up the challenge of making 2.2 million persons literate in a period of two years (1984–1986). A number of projects were launched (Bengali, 1999: 13) including Afternoon School projects, Iqra projects, Razakar Muallim projects, Mosque projects, NGOs Volunteer Literacy Corps projects, *Sipah-e-Idrees* projects, Social Welfare Agencies Literacy projects, Literacy Village projects, Azafi Literacy Centres projects, Literacy Trade Centres on all the roads of the country, Open Air Schools under the shade of a tree, and Student's Literacy drives.

A very ambitious and unrealistic Literacy Ordinance was promulgated that barred any illiterate person from receiving a passport or a driving license. This ordinance, however, lapsed after 120 days. In the year 1985–86, a 5 per cent Iqra Tax was levied on all imports to finance education and literacy projects. The fate of this initiative will be discussed later in the discussion section of the chapter. As a follow up to the National Literacy Plan (1984–86), an initiative of Drop-in Schools 1986–89 was announced with the estimated cost of Rs. 208 million. It was decided to launch the project in nine districts. When the project was in its initial phase, it was replaced by the Nationwide Literacy Programme launched by the newly inducted Junejo government in December 1985. Interestingly the Literacy Programme was soon substituted by a new programme called Nai Roshni (New Light) Schools. LAMEC was assigned the job of implementing this programme for four years from 1986 to 1990.

THE EDUCATION POLICY, 1992

The 1992 Policy (GoP, 1992: 20) stated that 'The problem of illiteracy is formidable both in its size as well as in its complexity. From a socio-cultural perspective, the traditional prejudices against educating females still linger on, particularly in the tribal and rural milieu.' The policy in its preface acknowledged the dismal condition of literacy by referring to the 142nd position of Pakistan among 160 countries in terms of literacy. The policy set an ambitious target of increasing the literacy rate to 70 per cent by the year 2002. It proposed detailed strategies to realize this target. These strategies included:

- making primary education compulsory,
- reduction in dropout rates,
- literacy programmes through the provincial governments,

- NGOs handling local organizations with appropriate support from the Federal government,
- massive projects to raise the level of literacy among those who can only read the Holy Quran,
- a greater role for universities in training curriculum development and material development for literacy programmes and in the organization of student literacy corps,
- political leaders supporting the literacy effort by spearheading the formation of village development committees with literacy as their major concern,
- the full utilization of electronic and print media for motivating the public towards supporting the literacy effort,
- evening shifts in primary schools and the utilization of summer vacation to enhance the literacy effort,
- appropriate legislation to provide incentives for acquiring literacy,
- annual awards for meritorious work in the field of adult literacy at the national, provincial, and local levels,
- legislation to make funds allocated for the promotion of adult literacy non-transferable and non-lapsable,
- the National Education and Training Commission (NETCOM) acting as the main coordinating agency for adult education and literacy programmes, and
- creation of an Action Plan to implement the strategies developed by NETCOM with active participation of universities, particularly the Allama Iqbal Open University, NGOs, provincial government departments, and federal ministries in the social sector (GoP, 1992: 21–2).

The policy said that the concepts, procedures and targets as envisaged in the Social Action Program (SAP-11) would be adhered to. It claimed that the role of the Prime Minister's Literacy Commission had been enhanced for taking educational opportunities to the doorsteps of the deprived and underprivileged segments of society.

In 1995, during Benazir Bhutto's period, LAMEC was renamed as the Prime Minister's Literacy Commission.

THE EDUCATION POLICY, 1998

The Education Policy, 1998, underlined the significant role of literacy at individual and societal levels. The Policy (GoP, 1998: 28) reiterated 'Pakistan's international commitment to double the rate of literacy by the year 2000 cannot be accomplished without achieving universal primary education (UPE).' It resolved to raise the existing literacy rate of 39 per cent to 55 per cent during the first five years of the policy and 70 per cent by the year 2010.

The policy announced some ambitious plans to realize the target. Some of the major strategies (GoP, 1998: 21–3) included:

- launch of the Non-formal Basic Education Programme for 5.5 million primary school age children (5–9 years old) who were out of school,
- replication of the Asian Development Bank sponsored pilot project for 15–25-year-old rural women,
- creation of a Literacy Fund to finance the literacy movement in the country,
- launch of a National Literacy Movement on an emergency basis in every village, tehsil, and district,
- use of mosques for non-formal basic education to increase literacy,
- strengthening of the Prime Minister's Literacy Commission as a statutory body to enable it to discharge its functions effectively,
- local appointments in Non-Formal Basic Education Community Schools/Centres in consultation with the community barring political interference,
- consultation units to make the employees and their dependents literate,
- utilization of scouts and girl guides to work with communities especially with Non-Formal Basic Education Community Schools for enhancing literacy,

- increase in the number of Non-Formal Basic Education Community Schools/Centres to 82,000,
- upgrading of 25,000 Non-Formal Basic Education Community Schools to middle schools in far flung areas,
- establishment of a Literacy Corps comprising college, university students/teachers for literacy programmes during vacations,
- donation from *Khanqahs/Mazars* to the literacy fund, and
- use of electronic media for social mobilization and promotion of the cause of literacy.

In the 2000 World Education Forum, Dakar meeting (2000: 8) a number of countries gave their commitment to Education for All. One of the commitments was, 'achieving a 50 per cent improvement in levels of adult literacy by 2015, especially for women and equitable access to basic and continuing education for all adults.'

THE EDUCATION POLICY, 2009

The 2009 policy (GoP, 2009a: 18) stated as one of its objectives, 'To eradicate illiteracy within the shortest possible time through universalizing of quality elementary education coupled with institutionalized adult literacy programmes.' The policy proposed to develop a separate database for literacy. The policy suggested that because of the fragmented efforts, required results could not be achieved, thus literacy, along with various other streams of education, would be managed by one organization. The policy stated that adult literacy programmes would be strengthened through organizational structure, coordination, and enhancing budgetary allocation for this neglected subsection. The policy also aimed to develop a national literacy curriculum and identify instructional materials. The policy (GoP, 2009a: 39) in its action plans reiterates, 'Literacy rate shall be increased up to 86 per cent by 2015 through up-scaling of ongoing programmes of adult literacy and non-formal basic education in the country.'

ANALYSIS AND DISCUSSION

A critical analysis of the literacy initiatives reveals that the education policies and plans were generally unable to achieve the promised targets in the stipulated period of time. This is evident in Table 5 that gives an overview of the literacy targets and target dates set in the education policies and how these dates kept on shifting to the new target dates.

Table 5: Literacy Targets and Target Dates

Year	Policy/Document/Report	Target	Target Date
1947	Pakistan Educational Conference	No Specific Target	No Specific Target Date
1959	Commission on National Education	No Specific Target	No Specific Target Date
1970	National Education Policy	5 Million	1975
1972	National Education Policy	11 Million	1980
1979	National Education Policy	35%	1982–83
1992	National Education Policy	70%	2002
1998	National Education Policy	70%	2010
2009	National Education Policy	86%	2015

Table 6 gives the year-wise increase in literacy from 2001 onwards.

Table 6: Progress towards Goal 2 at the National Level (percentage)

Indicator	2001–2	2004–5	2007–8	2010–11	2011–12	MDG Target 2015
Net Primary Enrolment Rate (5–9 years)	42	52	55	56	57	100

Completion/ Survival rate grade 1 to 5	57.3	67.1	52.3	49	–	100
Literacy Rate (%) 10 years and above	45	53	56	58	58	88

Source: Pakistan Social and Living Standards Measurement (PSLM) Survey 2011–12.

The recent literacy rate in Pakistan, according to the Survey of Pakistan (GoP, 2014: 155) is 60 per cent; this is far lower than the target (70 per cent) set in 1998, which was to be achieved by 2010. The target of literacy (86 per cent) set by the 2009 policy could not be achieved by the 2015 target date. The most recent data regarding goal 2 is discussed in Chapter 16.

Why couldn't literacy policies achieve their targets? The primary reason was the lack of political will for education-related plans as literacy featured low in the priority list of different governments in Pakistan. The allocation for education in Pakistan is about 2 per cent of the total GDP, which is one of the lowest in South Asia. There was a lot of rhetoric in the policies along with some ambitious plans but they lacked the sustained financial support required to complete the task at hand. It is worth noticing that no financial allocation was made to promote literacy in Pakistan through the First Five-Year Plan (1955–60), the Second Five Year Plan (1960–1965), or the Third Five-Year Plan (1965–70). Consequently no specific targets with specific deadlines were set. In 2006–7 the allocation was 2.50 per cent of GDP and in 2007–8 this amount was reduced to 2.47 per cent of the GDP. In 2008–2009, the amount further came down to 2.1 per cent of the GDP. These declining figures allude to the ground realities where one can see a gaping chasm between professed ideas and actual deeds (Siddiqui, 2010).

The low priority given to education can be elaborated further with the example of the Iqra (reading) surcharge. In 1985, a 5 per cent Iqra Tax was levied on all imports in order to support literacy projects. About Rs. 66 billion was collected under the Iqra surcharge between 1985 to 1994. This was a substantial amount which could have financed a number of literacy projects but unfortunately this amount was diverted to non-developmental purposes. A legal case for the diversion of funds is still pending in the Supreme Court of Pakistan.

In 1951, the literacy rate was reported at 17.9 per cent. Interestingly after ten years, instead of going up, the literacy rate dropped to 16.9 per cent. A number of explanations could be given for this such as poor administration of the projects, lack of monitoring, and lack of funds, etc. Another interesting explanation emanates from the changing definitions of literacy. The definition established for literacy in 1951 was that a literate person is 'One who can read a clear print in any language.' It is important to understand that here *understanding* was not a condition, meaning that anybody who could recognize letters and could pronounce them would be considered literate. In 1961 a literate person was redefined as, 'One who is able to read with *understanding* a simple letter in any language.' Since the condition of 'understanding' was added to the definition, a large number of people who could recognize and pronounce the alphabet (for instance reading the Qur'an in some cases) without understanding were left out of the category of literates. The following modified table (Table 7) used in the UNESCO publication *Trends in Pakistan, Literacy* (2003) gives an idea of how the definition of literacy has changed over time in Pakistan.

Table 7: Changing Definitions of Literacy

Year	Definition of *Literacy*
1951	One who can read a clear print in any language
1961	One who is able to read with understanding a simple letter in any language
1972	One who is able to read and write in some language with understanding
1981	One who can read a newspaper and write a simple letter
1998	One who could read a newspaper and write simple letter, in any language

2018	Ability to identify, understand, interpret, create, communicate, and compute using printed and written materials associated with varying context

Source: UNESCO (2018).

The current definition of literacy given in the Ministry of Education' *Handbook on Literacy, Education and Gender, March 2004* is 'A person is considered literate if he/she can read and write with understanding a simple statement related to his/her life.' The World Bank defines literacy as 'the ability to read and write a simple statement about one's everyday life and do simple mathematical calculations.' It is interesting to note that if we apply the World Bank definition it would have negative impact on the literacy rate in Pakistan as the World Bank's definition includes mathematical calculations as a part of literacy.

The other potential problem with literacy numbers is the actual procedure of data collection. Usually a person would go to a house and ask for literate people and would jot down whatever is told to him or her. There is no way to confirm the information. The people involved in data collection are not professionally trained in data collection for research purposes. So the final outcome in the shape of literacy percentage apparently looks inflated (Siddiqui, 2010). The two other dimensions of literacy are a divide between males and females, and urban and rural areas. This divide is present in most countries but its nature is more acute in Pakistan.

A critical factor in the failure of policies is the unreliable data which is used in planning. For instance in 1992–93 four different literacy rates, 41.3, 34.0, 31.0, 35.0, (Ahsan, 2003: 274) were published in official documents. Usually the numbers are inflated in the government documents to demonstrate performance and, on the basis of that, ask for more funds from donor agencies.

Political interference in educational initiatives also had a negative impact on the educational initiatives. One example of such interference was the Nai Roshni Schools Project. Once the project was all set, a political decision was made that 30 per cent of the teachers would be appointed by the elected Members of the National Assembly (MNAs) and Senators and 30 per cent by the

Members Provincial Assemblies (MPAs), 10 per cent by the Prime Minister's quota and for the disabled and 30 per cent by LAMEC (Warwick, 1991). Consequently a potentially positive project suffered a serious setback because incompetent teaching staff was hired largely on the basis of political affiliations.

Another important factor responsible for the failure of policies was poor governance. An initiative was launched and without giving it time, it would be replaced by another initiative. This happened more conspicuously in 1980's where with quick succession more than a dozen initiatives were tried to enhance literacy. The ultimate result was that none of those initiatives could get the desired results.

A crucial factor responsible for the failure of policies is their inconsistency. There are a number of examples of such inconsistencies. In the 1969 Policy, the proposal of the National Literacy Corps was floated. In 1970, its name was changed to the National Education Corps. After two years in the 1972 Policy, the name was changed again to the National Literacy Corps. In 1979, a reference was made to the Student Volunteer Corps. In the 1992 Policy, the title of Student Literacy Corps was used and in 1998, this title was reduced to Literacy Corps. In the 2009 Policy, there was no mention of any literacy corps at all.

Similar to this was the case of the Literacy and Mass Education Commission (LAMEC), which was established in 1981. In 1989, this Commission was reconstituted with a different name, the National Education and Training Commission. In 1995, the name of the Commission was changed to the Prime Minister's Literacy Commission. Historically, new governments, for political reasons, tend to discard the names given by the previous administration and come up with new titles in order to dissociate the projects from them. One such example is the establishment of People's Open University by Zulfikar Ali Bhutto, which was changed by his arch rival Zia ul-Haq when he came to power in 1977. The new name was the Allama Iqbal Open University.

Besides tinkering with the names there were some serious inconsistencies in policies. Successive policies proposed using formal methods to complement the non-formal methods in order to raise literacy within the country (GoP, 1955; GoP, 1959; GoP, 1960; GoP, 1965). The Seventh Five-Year Plan (1988–93) completely rejects the non-formal approach for being more expensive and less effective. Referring to the non-formal initiatives of the Sixth Five-Year Plan, the Seventh Five-Year Plan (GoP, 1988: 252) stated, 'The Sixth Plan experience has shown that a shortcut to literacy is not only expensive but is hard to monitor. There is no substitute for formal education.' In the 1992 policy, the use of the non-formal approach along with the formal one was reinstated.

The issue of student dropout rates also played a negative role in the effort to promote literacy as a large percentage of students in Pakistan drop out of school before they reach grade 5, resulting in declining literacy figures. Subsequent policies did not focus on the issue of dropouts which kept on compounding the problem of low literacy. Fragmentation and lack of coordination between organizations also proved counterproductive. The 2009 policy (GoP, 2009a) stated that there was fragmentation in education, both at federal and national levels and there is no mechanism for developing a holistic view of the educational sector at the national level. The language factor also played an important role in the failure of policies. The non-formal basic education schools did not have any material to teach in the indigenous regional languages of Pakistan. The result was an extra effort required by the illiterate to study in a language which was alien to them.

Some of the initiatives taken to help enhance literacy were also not culturally sensitive. Teaching kits and accommodation for single female teachers were two glaring examples (Warwick et al., 1992). These initiatives consumed huge funds but miserably failed in achieving their objectives. Similarly the initiatives of mobile libraries and teaching techniques on wheels involving huge funds could not succeed.

There has been a constant tension between quantity and quality in all the policies and plans. In this tension, the ultimate winner, however, is quantity. Thus we see a number of initiatives proposed by the policies like, Mosque schools, Mohalla schools, *Nai Roshni* schools, Literacy Corps, and lowering the required qualifications for female teachers. All these initiatives were geared at crunching numbers but they certainly impacted the quality of teaching and learning. Another tension was between functional literacy and critical literacy. Most of the policies, however, focused on functional literacy.

SUMMARY

Literacy is considered to be an important step towards personal and collective socio-economic development. Almost all policy documents acknowledged the significance of literacy in the development of the country. When we talk of the relationship between education and development we need to realize that enhanced literacy numbers do not guarantee development. It is the quality of literacy that is very important. That is why we see that in some cases the numbers are inflated but we do not find the evidence of development in real life. Literacy, however, remained a challenge for policymakers due to social, cultural, and economic factors. The target dates set by one policy were moved farther by the following policy. The initiatives, at times, were numerous but uncoordinated. The sole objective of some initiatives was to enhance numbers. The policies could not offer ways for the provision of equal literacy opportunities irrespective of the divides of male/female, rich/poor and rural/urban. A critical analysis of the education policies reveals that the proposed measures could not achieve their targets in the stipulated periods of time as they were unrealistic, non-participatory, inconsistent, culturally alienated and lacked sustained political and financial support.

Chapter 5

Universal Primary Education

Education is considered to be an important condition for development. The gaps between developed and developing countries can be attributed to gaps of knowledge (World Bank Report, 1998–99). The significance of education in terms of human development is manifested in the World Declaration on Education for All (EFA) in 1990 (www.unesco.org/education/efa/ed_for_all/background/jomtien_declaration.shtml). It says, '... education is a fundamental right for all people, women and men, of all ages, throughout our world ...' Education is a powerful tool to help improve the quality of life and alleviate poverty. Keeping in view the central role of the knowledge economy in contemporary times, educational capital positively contributes towards the economic and social capital of a country.

At the time of Pakistan's independence, among other challenges faced by the newborn country, Universal Primary Education (UPE) was a major challenge. A large number of children did not have access to schools. Fifty per cent of enrolled students would drop out before they could reach class 5. Linked with this challenge was the issue of quality as the schools were not well-equipped with appropriate furniture and labs and there were not enough trained teachers available to teach in the classrooms. This chapter focuses on the challenge of Universal Primary Education (UPE) and critically analyses the initiatives recommended by the education policies and plans.

THE PAKISTAN EDUCATIONAL CONFERENCE, 1947

The Pakistan Educational Conference in 1947, through different specialized committees, identified important educational challenges, discussed them at length, and prepared recommendations in respective areas. The minister responsible for education, in his speech (GoP, 1947: 9), showed his resolve by stating, 'There is now general agreement that the State in its own interests should provide to its boys and girls, universal, compulsory and free basic education which is the primary requisite of training in democracy.' This urgent challenge required immediate and detailed planning. The Pakistan Educational Conference was organized in 1947, the year Pakistan got independence from British colonial rule. The committee on Primary and Secondary Education (GoP, 1947: 10) recommended that '... a national system of education be based on the strong foundations of free and compulsory primary education.' The Conference (GoP, 1947: 44) resolved that 'free and compulsory primary education be introduced for a period of 5 years which should be gradually raised to 8 years.' The other major recommendations of the conference included:

- pre-primary (3 to 6 years), primary (6 to 11 years), piddle (11 to 14 years) stages to be set up,
- state and provincial governments to organize teacher training courses and launch of crash courses to produce more teachers, and
- steps to bring the *madrasahs* into line with the existing system of general education.

The report emphasised maximum utilization of resources for basic education. It also recommended getting in touch with the United Nations Educational, Scientific, and Cultural Organization (UNESCO) to seek their advice on the abolition of illiteracy. Underlining the significance of Universal Primary Education (UPE), the conference claimed that the target of UPE would be achieved in twenty years, i.e. by 1967.

THE COMMISSION ON NATIONAL EDUCATION, 1959

The Commission on National Education, besides other educational challenges, focused on the UPE as well. The Commission acknowledged that 50 per cent of primary age group children were out of schools and the dropout rate in some cases was up to 75 per cent. The Commission (GoP, 1959: 174), reiterating the importance of universal education, stated, 'We believe the time has come for us to accept the implementation of universal compulsory education as a part of our national policy and for fixing a target date for this implementation, whatever be the difficulties and problems involved.' The Commission, however, realized that because of the paucity of economic resources it might not be possible to provide universal education immediately. The Commission, nevertheless, recommended setting a target to achieve UPE and then mobilizing efforts to achieve that goal. The Commission proposed that the first goal should be to make the five-year course a universal and compulsory one and to try to achieve this target in ten years. The Commission also proposed, to achieve the second target, to make eight years of schooling compulsory within fifteen years. The Commission recommended that the minimum number of working days for primary schools should be fixed at two hundred and the minimum working week for classes I and II be twenty-six hours and for classes III, IV, and V be thirty hours.

PROPOSALS FOR A NEW EDUCATIONAL POLICY, 1969

The 1969 Policy tried to differ from the previous policy documents and claimed that the existing policy attached a higher priority to secondary and higher education than to elementary education. The plan proposed to modify this policy by placing maximum emphasis on elementary education. The plan (GoP, 1969: 42) observed that, 'The enrolment of girls in primary schools is no more than 20 per cent of the total enrolment at that stage.' Some major recommendations of the policy (GoP, 1969: 27) included integrating *madrasahs* into the normal school system, and bringing the latter in line with ideological demands, integrating primary and middle schools into elementary schools, the complete reorganization of secondary education, making it a terminal stage for most of the students by imparting technical and vocational training to a majority among them, and effective decentralization of educational administration.

NEW EDUCATION POLICY, 1970

The aim of the 1947 conference to achieve UPE by 1967 was not realized in its stipulated target time. In 1970 a new education policy was announced that shifted the target date from 1967 to 1980. The Policy reiterated Pakistan's commitment for the goal of universal education. According to the Policy (GoP, 1970: 3):

> Pakistan is firmly committed to the objective of universal elementary education. This was accepted as a basic principle of State Policy in the Constitutions of 1956 and 1962, and the Karachi Plan of 1960 proposed a minimum of 7 years of compulsory, universal and free primary education as a target for 1980. The attainment of the goal, however, seems to have receded further and further with the lapse of time and Pakistan today has one of the highest rates of illiteracy in the world.

The major recommendations of the Policy (GoP, 1970: 4–5) included:

- high priority to universal elementary education up to class VIII with the aim to achieve universal enrolment up to class V by 1980, free education up to class V;
- provincial governments to consider adoption of measures for compulsory attendance up to class V for those enrolled in schools according to a phased plan beginning with those enrolled in class I;
- encouragement of enrolment of girls by establishing girls' schools wherever possible and by recruiting a larger number of female teachers, and
- redesigning the system of elementary education to ensure a purposeful selection of the knowledge and skills imparted, attitudes implanted, and the learning methods employed, so that those not proceeding to secondary education can be usefully employed in the economy of the local community.
- The plan emphasized the need to improve curricula, making them relevant to students' experiences and the need for trained teachers.

THE EDUCATION POLICY, 1972

The 1972 policy was announced by the democratic government of Zulfikar Ali Bhutto. The policy declared that education would be made free and universal up to class X for all children throughout the country. The policy (GoP, 1972: 3) envisaged that, due to limited resources, the target would be achieved in two phases. In the first phase, from 1 October 1972, education up to class VIII would be made free for boys and girls in both government and privately managed schools, and the latter would be suitably supported for the loss of fees incurred by them. In the second phase, starting from 1 October 1974, free education would be extended to classes IX and X in all schools.

The policy gave specific dates to achieve the target of Universal Primary Education. According to the Policy (GoP, 1972: 3) 'education up to class V will become universal for boys by 1979 and for girls by 1984. In a further period of three years, it is anticipated that elementary education will become universal up to class VIII, that is, for boys by 1982 and for girls by 1987.' As a result of this the Policy anticipated an increase in enrolment in primary classes of approximately 50 lakh children by 1980, raising the total enrolment from the present 46 lakhs to an estimated 96 lakhs over the period. Similarly it was estimated that in middle schools—classes VI–VIII—the expected enrolment increase over the period would be 23 lakhs. This would raise the total numbers from 10 lakhs to an estimated 33 lakhs by 1980. To deal with the challenge of increased number of students, the policy proposed the construction of 38,000 additional classrooms for primary classes to provide schools within easy walking distance from the children's homes. In addition, the policy proposed the construction of approximately 23,000 additional classrooms for pupils in classes VI to VIII. It was recommended that the primary schools, which had potential for growth, would be developed into elementary schools.

The policy (GoP, 1972: 6) envisaged that the universalization of elementary education would require about 2.25 lakh additional teachers. The existing teacher training institutes could provide about 75,000 teachers. The remaining 75,000 teachers, according to the plan, would be provided through the establishment of the National Literacy Corps and drawn from locally available unemployed persons, retired civil servants, ex-service men, etc., and university and college students. The policy announced the provision of free books to the students and a revision of curricula. On the issue of compulsory education the policy did not make any recommendation and proposed that since it was a complex issue with far reaching repercussions, it should be decided after debating it in the assemblies.

EDUCATION POLICY, 1979

The 1979 education policy observed a 7–8 times increase in the enrolment in primary education since independence. This was a significant accomplishment but due to rapid population growth, the absolute number of children of the relevant age group not enrolled in primary school, had increased. The policy (GoP, 1979: 5) stated that half of the school-going children were not going to schools. The enrolment in primary education was 32 per cent in Baluchistan, 52 per cent in North West Frontier Province (now Khyber Pakhtunkhwa), 59 per cent in Sindh, and 56 per cent in Punjab. The policy observed that about 50 per cent of those enrolled in class I dropped out by class V. The policy considered that there were out-of-school and school-based factors responsible for low enrolment and the high dropout rate. Extra-school factors included general poverty, low motivation of rural people to send their children to schools, uninviting rural conditions, sociocultural inhibitions towards education of females, and the malnutrition of children.

School-based factors included extremely poor conditions of school buildings, lack of equipment and teaching aids, shortage and absenteeism among teachers, inadequate supervision, poor communication facilities, the low morale of primary school teachers and their harsh treatment towards pupils, and unattractive school curricula and environment. The most important factor, however, was the financial factor as the allocation for education was less than 2 per cent of the total GNP.

Major recommendations of the 1979 Education Policy included:

- provision of facilities to attain universal enrolment for boys from the 5–9 age group by 1986–87;
- elimination of wastage to achieve 60 per cent retention rate by 1982–83 and 100 per cent thereafter;
- reconstruction and improvement of 17,000 existing primary schools;
- opening up of 13,000 new primary schools mainly in rural areas;
- establishment of 5,000 mosque schools for boys;
- provision of equipment to improve 12,000 existing schools;
- supply of textbooks to all students at the primary level;
- provision of 100 supplementary readers to each new primary school and two supplementary readers per student to existing schools;
- provision of at least one teaching kit to each existing and new primary school;
- carrying out a nationwide school-mapping exercise to evolve the process of school location planning, along with a nationwide survey to determine the repair needs of existing primary schools, and launch a programme for repairs of appropriate schools (GoP, 1979: 6–7).

EDUCATION POLICY, 1992

The 1992 policy, at the very outset, acknowledged that Universalization of Primary Education had remained a desired goal of successive policies and plans. This goal, however, could not be achieved for a number of reasons. The limitations which, according to the policy, obstructed universalization, included low female participation because of insecurity of female students, and distance of homes from schools; rapid increase in the population of the 5–9 age group; school drop-out rate of up to 50 per cent; lack of access to primary schools; unavailability of resources; inadequate school hours; and loss of opportunity cost.

The policy recommended the extension of basic education from class I-VIII, transformation of the present system of primary education into basic education, extension of the targets of the Social Action Plan (SAP) to provide for basic education, extension of the SAP to such urban areas as *Kachi Abadis* and slums in addition to rural areas.

The policy (GoP, 1992: 16) observed that the existing number of primary schools, including mosque schools, stood at 124,000 with an enrolment of about 11.5 million. By the year 2002, the population of the 5–9 age group would rise approximately to 22 million. To achieve universal primary education, additional space would be needed for 10.5 million students. This would require 107,000 new primary and mosque schools. Further, two-room buildings would be needed for 24,750 roofless schools and 20,000 one-room schools would also require improvement. The number of additional teachers required for this task would be 265,000. More recurring costs might be contemplated for subsidy on learning materials and expansion of the administrative and management machinery for primary education. The Policy envisaged that about 265,000 new primary school teachers would be trained and recruited.

The policy (GoP, 1992: 81) stated, as one of its objectives, 'To ensure 100 per cent participation of children in education at the primary level by the year 2002, and to eradicate illiteracy through formal and non-formal methods.' Thus in the 1992 Education Policy, the target date for UPE was further pushed to 2002.

EDUCATION POLICY, 1998

The 1998 education policy (GoP, 1998: 3) stated, as one of its objectives, 'To achieve universal primary education by using formal and non-formal approaches to provide a second opportunity to school drop-outs by establishing basic education community schools all over the country.' The policy referred to a number of issues that were impacting elementary education. Some of these issues included more than 5.5 million primary school age children

(5–9 years) left out of schools; a 45 per cent drop-out rate at the primary level; teacher absenteeism and lack of commitment and motivation; about one-fourth of primary school teachers were untrained; inadequate and poor quality learning materials; harsh and uncongenial teaching methods for learning and motivating of pupils; and lack of character-building exercises.

Some major objectives of the policy regarding UPE were to increase participation rates at the middle level from 46 per cent to 65 per cent by 2002–3 and 85 per cent by 2010; to enhance retention and completion of the primary education cycle for up to 90 per cent students (both boys and girls) by the year 2010; to ensure achievement of minimum level of learning for up to 90 per cent primary education students by the year 2010; to expand and strengthen the base for secondary education; to meet the basic learning needs of the child in terms of essential learning tools as well as the basic learning content; and to reduce the existing disparities to half by the year 2010. The policy (GoP, 1998: 1) resolved that:

> … by the year 2002–03, 90 per cent of the children in the primary age group (5–9) will be in schools and by the year 2010, the gross enrolment will rise to 105 per cent. Consequently, the promulgation and enforcement of Compulsory Primary Education Act will be possible by 2004–05.

THE DAKAR CONFERENCE

In the 2000 Dakar conference, Pakistan, being a signatory country, pledged to uphold the Millennium Development Goals (MDGs). One of the MDGs (http://www.un.org/millenniumgoals/education.shtml) was to 'Ensure that, by 2015, children everywhere, boys and girls alike, will be able to complete a full course of primary schooling.' An Action Plan for Education Sector Reforms (2004) was devised to meet the announced targets but, despite all action plan activities, the target of attaining UPE remained unrealized.

EDUCATION POLICY 2009

The 2009 policy stated one of its objectives as, 'To eradicate illiteracy within the shortest possible time through universalizing of quality elementary education coupled with institutionalized adult literacy programmes.' Some major recommendations of the 2009 policy (GoP, 2009: 19–20) included:

- affirmation of the goal of achieving universal and free primary education by 2015 and up to class 10 by 2025 for provinces and local governments;
- development of plans by provincial and local governments for achieving these targets, including intermediate enrolment targets and estimates of the required financial, technical, human, and organizational resources;
- promotion of equity through plans in education with the aim of eliminating social exclusion and promoting national cohesion;
- provision of greater opportunities to marginalized groups of society, particularly girls;
- achievement of the commitments of the Government of Pakistan towards Education for All (EFA) and MDGs;
- promotion of inclusive and child-friendly education;
- adoption of special measures to ensure inclusion of special persons in mainstream education as well as in literacy and TVE programmes;
- improvement of educational provision at all levels of Education by the governments;
- determination of National Standards for educational inputs, processes, and outputs;
- establishment of a National Authority for Standards of Education;
- permission for a provincial and local government organization having its own standards above the prescribed minimum;
- establishment of monitoring and inspection systems by provincial and district governments, to ensure quality

education service delivery in all institutions, and steps to make educational provision relevant for the labour market and for promoting innovation in the economy.

The overconfident tone of Education Sector Reforms (2004) could no more be seen in the National Education Policy (2009) where the approach to the issue appeared to be more realistic. According to 2009 National Education Policy (GoP, 2009a: 16):

> Pakistan's commitment to universal primary education by 2015 under EFA Framework appears elusive on current performance, as participation is low and drop-out rates continue to be high.

The policy declared that the government would commit to allocate 7 per cent of GDP to education by 2015 and necessary enactment shall be made for this purpose.

ANALYSIS AND DISCUSSION

A close look at the claims of the policies and plans regarding the target dates of achieving the target of UPE reveals a wide difference between rhetoric and reality. It is important to note how target dates were regularly shifted further in the ensuing policies. The initial target date to achieve the UPE target, from the Pakistan Educational Conference in 1947, was 1967. In the 1970 Education Policy the target date was shifted to 1980. In the 1972 Education Policy the target date for girls shifted from 1980 to 1984. In the 1979 Education Policy the target date for boys was shifted from 1980 to 1986–7 and the target date for girls shifted from 1984 to 1992. In the 1992 Education Policy the target dates were shifted from 1986–7 (boys) and 1992 (girls) to 2002. In the 1998 policy, the target date of 2002 was shifted to 2010. In the Dakar Conference, of which Pakistan is a signatory, the target date was shifted from 2010 to 2015. The most recent Education Policy (GoP, 2009) is not sure about achieving the target of UPE by 2015.

According to the report of Task Force on Education (2011) at least, seven million children were not in primary school. This is the second highest drop-out number of school children in the world. The report further revealed that 'Three million will never see the inside of a classroom at all.' These findings were disturbing, especially in the wake of numerous plans and policies targeting UPE since 1947. The report also tried to answer the important question, *when will provinces provide all children with their constitutional right to education, at current rates of progress?* The report has projected the dates for the achievement of target, summarized in Table 8.

Table 8: Province-wise Expected Dates for UPE

Province	Projected date
Punjab	2014
Sindh	2049
KPK	2064
Balochistan	2100

Source: Task Force on Education (2011).

The target, which should have been achieved by 1967 as envisaged in the Pakistan Educational Conference, is still an unrealized dream. Recently as an outcome of the 18th amendment, article 25 (A) was included in the 1973 constitution. According to this article (GoP, 1973: 15) 'The state shall provide free and compulsory education to all children of the age of five to sixteen years in such manner as may be determined by law.' This seems to be another promise added to the claims spread over sixty-four years of the history of Pakistan. Bray (1983: 175) summed up the ineffective initiatives by suggesting that, '... history of primary education since the foundation has told of objectives set but, alas, never reached.'

The target of Universal Primary Education remained an unfulfilled dream in Pakistan. The policies and plans did offer some ambitious proposals but they were not backed by the political will of the ruling governments. Money allocated for education was diverted to other non-developmental heads. This was particularly true for the Third Year Plan during the 1965 Indo-Pak War.

It is significant that in the past although there has been an overall increase of expenditure in education, the total expenditure at primary level has considerably decreased from 41 per cent in 1947–48 to 30 per cent in 1967–68. (GoP, 1970: 153). In most of the initiatives of UPE the whole emphasis seemed to be on expanding numbers. For this purpose, half-baked strategies involving poor school facilities, untrained teachers, substandard reading materials, and ineffective assessment techniques were used. One issue that the policies dealt with early on was to move up from class 5 to class 8 as target for Universal Education. The dilemma, however, was that even achieving the target of education up to class 5 remained a tough target. The constraints in the way of achieving this target were insufficient schools, which were devoid of physical facilities like proper buildings, furniture, and equipment for the labs. Besides the insufficient number of school and poor physical facilities available to schools, the related challenge was the non-availability of trained teachers. This problem was more serious in the case of female teachers. The issue of access was further aggravated because of the high dropout rate which was about 50 per cent for the initial years of independence of the country. A number of initiatives to cope with the challenge of UPE were proposed, e.g. integration of *madrasahs* with schools, mosque, and *mohalla* schools, short courses for teachers, lowering the educational qualifications for recruitment for female teachers, etc. (see details of such initiatives in chapter 4 on Literacy). Most of these initiatives were marred by lack of political will, lack of economic resources, unnecessary political interference, lack of monitoring and accountability systems, constant shifting of initiatives, political instability, and lack of consistency.

Besides these constraints, most of the policies and plans focused on the quantitative aspect of the challenge and proposed initiatives to enhance the number of students in schools. The result, therefore, was that though the numbers of UPE were inflated, the students didn't have the ability to justify the academic requirements of the respective level. Andrabi, et al. (GoP, 2007: iii) suggest that, '... the children perform significantly below curricular standards for common subjects and concepts at their grade level.'

Table 9, based on findings of Andrabi, et al. (2007), shows that by the end of class III, just over 50 per cent of children have mastered the Mathematics curriculum for class 1.

Table 9: What do Children Know in Mathematics

The Question	Percentage who answered correctly	Corresponding Class for Curriculum
4 + 6	89	K & I
36 + 61	86	K & I
8 – 3	65	K & I
5 x 4	59	II
238 – 129	32	II
Read and write the time (Clock shows 3:40)	24	II
384 ÷ 6	19	III
4 x 32	50	III
Fractions: ± 3/2	19	III
Read a diagram of a scale to answer which part is heavier	12	III
Fractions: 7/5	1	IV

Source: Andrabi, et al., (2007).

Another study by ASER (2018) revealed similar findings that student performance was far below the curricular requirement of the respective level. Table 10 reports the performance on reading English in levels 1 to 5:

Table 10: Class-wise Percentage of Children Who Can Read English

Class-wise % Children who can read						
Class	Nothing	Letters		Words	Sentences	Total
		Capital	Small			
1	31.9	28.6	28.6	10.9	0.0	100
2	15.9	25.8	31.2	25.8	1.3	100
3	12.7	12.8	29.4	40.3	4.8	100
4	12.5	5.5	16.0	38.5	27.4	100
5	9.6	3.5	9.4	25.2	52.3	100
6	11.2	1.6	4.5	19.3	63.4	100
7	10.6	1.0	2.4	13.7	72.2	100
8	10.7	0.9	1.6	8.8	78.0	100
9	10.6	0.8	1.0	4.8	82.8	100
10	10.7	0.6	0.7	3.3	84.6	100
How to read: 10.9% (10.9+0) Children of class 1 can read words						

Source: ASER (2018).

The findings of these studies are further supported by The Task Force on Education (2011) which reports that:

> … only 35 per cent of schoolchildren, aged 6–16, can read a story, while 50 per cent cannot read a sentence. The overall percentage of rural children in class 5 reading a class 2 text in Urdu/Sindhi was 52 per cent while for the English text it was 42 per cent. This meant that more than half of all rural children in class 5 in Pakistan were at least three grade levels behind.

All these findings raise questions about the quality of primary education being provided in our schools. They also suggest extra emphasis being laid on quantitative expansion at the cost of the qualitative aspect of education.

SUMMARY

This chapter focused on the theme of Universal Primary Education (UPE). Since the inception of Pakistan one of the most serious problems faced by the country was the access of children to schools. This problem was further aggravated with a high drop-out rate of about fifty per cent. Generally most of the education policies tried to tackle this challenge in a quantitative manner. A number of initiatives were announced like *masjid* schools, *mohalla* schools, and Nai Roshni schools to provide children access to education. A number of these initiatives, however, were political in nature and were not sustainable. This skewed approach towards dealing with UPE ignored the qualitative aspect of education. The result of the half-baked initiatives was poor academic achievements by the students. The chapter critically examined the deadlines set for each policy to achieve the target of Universal Primary Education and how the next policy always extended the deadlines.

Chapter 6

Higher Education

The relationship between education and the economic development of a country has been established through various research. This relationship can be seen in a number of countries in the South Asian region. In the World Bank report *Knowledge for Development* (1998–99), it was suggested that the knowledge gaps between the developed and developing countries lead to economic gaps between them. A more realistic view is stated in *Higher Education in Developing Countries* (2000: 19):

> Higher Education has never been as important to the future of the developing world as it is right now. It cannot guarantee rapid economic development. Higher education is important in the development of a society as the graduates are supposed to take up their jobs and get engaged in the process of development of country. Besides enhancing chances of getting good jobs, Higher Education facilitates the graduates to acquire an elevated social status in society.

In Pakistan, traditionally, intermediate was considered a part of higher education and thus it would come under the jurisdiction of universities. It was in 1954 that the Punjab University Act was amended and the intermediate stage was removed and assigned to a newly created Board of Secondary Education at Lahore. This practice was then followed in other parts of the country.

At the time of independence there were only two established universities situated in the Pakistani territory, the University of the Punjab in Lahore, established in 1882 and the University of Dacca (now Dhaka), established in 1921. A third university, University of Sindh, was established, in 1947, only a few months before the independence of the country. In the last three decades, most of the efforts at the donors' level have been directed at the strengthening of primary education in developing countries. No doubt, there have been some positive results of this approach, especially in East Asia. In Pakistan, higher education has been facing challenges which have impacted its quality and quantity. If we compare the number of students in higher education at the time of independence with the number of students enrolled in our universities and colleges today, we see a tremendous rise. Unfortunately we have not been able to cater to the increasing demands of students. Until the 1990s Pakistan was confined to a limited number of public universities and colleges responsible for imparting higher education. It was only in the mid-90s that universities in the private sector were given charters. This phenomenon gave a new direction to higher education in Pakistan. Since then progress has been made quantitatively.

According to the Economic Survey of Pakistan (GoP, 2012: 134) the number of universities has gone up to 139 and 'an enrolment of 1.60 million is estimated in 2012–13 in higher education (universities) over 1.32 million in 2011–12.' According to the HEC official website the number of universities and degree-awarding institutions is 177. Since colleges and universities are important in developing and preparing the students to serve the country, the issue of higher education has received constant but differential treatment by different educational policies prepared by various governments through the years.

PAKISTAN EDUCATIONAL CONFERENCE, 1947

At the Pakistan Educational Conference the minister for interior Mr Fazal-ur-Rahman stated that the role of universities was not to churn out degrees but to engage in the promotion of knowledge. He further stated that there was 'an urgent need for drastic reform' in higher education (GoP, 1947: 10). In his speech (Appendix-B) the minister proposed that universities:

> ... should cease to function as mere mechanical purveyors of knowledge in the form of cheap degrees. They are essentially homes for the promotion of learning and have a vital role to play in raising the moral and intellectual tone of society and of unfolding before it endless possibilities of human development.

During the conference, a separate committee was set up to discuss the issues related to university education and give recommendations. The committee realized the need of a coordinating body for the universities and proposed setting up a self-governing body to be named the Inter-University Board of Pakistan. Some of the functions of the proposed board stated in the report (GoP, 1947: 17) were:

- to exchange of information and opinion among the universities of Pakistan,
- establishment of relations with foreign universities on a reciprocal basis,
- equivalence of degrees and diplomas,
- coordination of activities,
- initiation of fresh developments in universities,
- maintenance of standards of teaching and examinations,
- coordination of research, and
- consideration of pre-university education in relation to university education.

Following is the resolution prepared by the committee and finalized by the conference (GoP, 1947: 19):

> It has been felt for a long time that the system of University education comprising the syllabi, curricula, examinations and teaching method is unsatisfactory and requires a thorough review in order to bring it into line with our educational ideals and needs. Such reviews have been undertaken in the past by various committees and commissions but few practical steps have been taken to implement their recommendations. The Committee strongly feels that we should without delay lay the foundation

> of our educational system anew and urge that Government and Universities should take immediate action towards that end.

It is important to note that the conference underlined the preferred objective of universities, i.e. promotion of knowledge. This was an early call for research in universities. The second important proposal, which was a little vague at that stage, was the need of an organizational body to liaison with universities. The third point emphasized the need of coordination with other universities through the exchange of teachers and the organization of extension lectures. These points were also reflected in the ensuing policy documents as well.

COMMISSION ON NATIONAL EDUCATION, 1959

The report of the Commission on National Education, 1959 dealt with the issue of higher education in detail. The commission (GoP, 1959: 15) appeared to be cognizant of the tension between quality and quantity as it recommended that '... higher education must prepare not only adequate numbers of persons to fill positions appropriate to modern conditions, but also offer education of quality.' To improve the situation in higher education the commission made three major recommendations:

- extension of the range of educational courses,
- provision of education to larger numbers of students, and
- improvement of the quality of the education.

The commission recommended that the objective of higher education should not be just equipping the students with knowledge and specialties. It should also assist the students to become educated human beings by,

> ... creating in them proper habits of work, a continuing desire for knowledge, initiative, an independence of thought, an understanding of the problems of society, a desire to help solve such problems, and a sense of honesty and fair play in dealing with others (GoP, 1959: 15).

The commission report, while acknowledging the quantitative expansion in higher education since 1947, expressed its concern about the negative impact on the quality as a result of expansion. According to the report (GoP, 1959: 16), 'This largely unplanned expansion has been at the expense of quality of education, which has deteriorated disastrously ...' The commission report recommended more accommodation, better equipment, trained teachers, improved conditions for teachers, more effective assessment systems, enabling conditions of study for students, more research, bachelor's degrees from two to three years and external examinations supplemented with internal examinations. The commission report was perhaps the most elaborate document that not only identified major issues related to higher education but also made achievable recommendations. The commission felt the need for a holistic improvement of higher education in terms of curriculum, pedagogy, assessment, research and physical resources at universities. The commission report was a complete road map of reforms in higher education. How far these recommendations were implemented can be seen in the latter part of this chapter.

PROPOSALS FOR A NEW EDUCATIONAL POLICY, 1969

The 1969 policy observed that there was a bias in the prevailing policies in favour of higher and secondary education and that primary education was given less attention. The policy (GoP, 1969: 4) recommended that '... for national development purposes, the first priority of education should be to create a literate society.' The policy, however, proposed to establish 3 new purely affiliating universities at Quetta, Multan, and Sargodha. The policy recommended to upgrade medical colleges, convert the agricultural colleges at Peshawar and Tandojam into full-fledged universities, establish a new agricultural university in East Pakistan, set up an new engineering university in Karachi, and establish two central universities, one in Islamabad and the other in East Pakistan. This policy shared for the first time a clear concept of the University Grants Commission with a detailed list of functions and powers.

EDUCATION POLICY, 1970

The 1970 Education Policy devoted a section to higher education. It is interesting to note that, like the 1947 conference and the 1959 commission reports, the 1970 policy also lamented the deterioration of higher education 'under the pressure of expansion'. Some of the major recommendations of the 1970 policy (GoP, 1970: 10–11) included:

- development of centres of excellence;
- constitution of fellowship scheme;
- reorganization of courses of study and curricula in line with national needs;
- establishment of two national institutes of modern languages;
- establishment of new universities and colleges;
- status of self-governing institutions for colleges with a long tradition of quality;
- benefits of Contributory Provident Fund along with Benevolent Fund and Group Insurance and provision of subsidized residential accommodation;
- establishment of university grants commissions, and
- high priority to residential accommodation for students particularly in the case of higher education.

THE EDUCATION POLICY, 1972

The 1970 Education Policy was presented in the context of political unrest when elections were being held. The following year, 1971, saw great political turmoil in East Pakistan (now Bangladesh) and war with India. Thus the implementation of the 1970 Education Policy was seriously jeopardized. Zulfikar Ali Bhutto became the chief executive in 1971 and during his regime a new education policy was announced.

The policy (GoP, 1972: 13) at the very outset stated that '... only 2 per cent of the population of the relevant age group is enrolled in institutions of higher education in the country, as against 50 per cent in USA and 25 per cent in Japan. More than 80 per cent of the students enrolled in the universities are studying arts subjects.'

The policy GoP, 1972: 13–15) made some major recommendations regarding higher education including,

- establishment of new universities to cover all parts of the country;
- establishment of the University Grants Commission;
- legislation to democratize the working of the universities;
- professional councils along the lines of the Pakistan Medical Council to be established for agriculture, law, engineering, etc.;
- establishment of centres of excellence;
- emphasis on science education;
- institution of a programme of National Professorships;
- Institution of National Research Fellowships;
- interest-free loans will be provided to talented students;
- library facilities to be set up in all educational institutions;
- representatives of students and teachers in the Library Committee of every institution, and
- creation of a National Service Corps between the age of 17 and 23.

A number of these recommendations were taken from the text of the 1970 Education Policy including setting up a University Grants Commission and centres of excellence. There was, however, an obvious tilt towards democratization of universities through participation of teachers and students on decision-making forums. A new initiative, that seemed to be a logical outcome of the 1971 war, was the creation of National Cadet Corps for compulsory training of students from ages seventeen to twenty-three. The policy, like all previous policies, highlighted the need for research in higher education.

NATIONAL EDUCATIONAL POLICY AND IMPLEMENTATION PROGRAMME, 1979

The 1979 Education Policy prepared and presented by the Zia government recommended drastic efforts to 'Islamize' education in Pakistan. The policy made some major recommendations in the domain of higher education.

- Setting up two women's universities, one at Lahore and the other at Karachi.
- Review of curricula and textbooks for higher education programmes in order to bring them in consonance with the ideology of Pakistan and principles of Islam.
- Establishment of the Academy of Educational Planning and Management to provide opportunities for training to vast numbers of administrators and supervisors.
- Strengthening of The Academy of Higher Education to provide pre-service and at least one in-service training facility to all the faculties of the universities and colleges once every five years.

The policy meant to Islamize the educational system of the country through curricula, textbooks, and teacher education. Two new universities, exclusively for girls, were recommended in order to provide female students an opportunity to study in a gender secluded environment. It is important to note that Zia ul-Haq's (GoP, 1979) was the only policy that mentioned 'implementation' in the title of the policy. This shows how important it was for the military government to use the tool of education to influence minds.

EDUCATIONAL POLICY, 1992

The 1992 Education Policy was prepared and presented by the elected government of Nawaz Sharif. The policy devoted a section to proposals for higher education. One can see the Islamic spirit of the 1979 policy in the 1992 policy document. Some major recommendations of the policy (GoP, 1992: 35–6) included:

- science and engineering laboratories in universities;
- allocation of special funds for research;

- provision of sizeable endowments to the universities to enable them to achieve financial self-sufficiency and financial autonomy;
- modernization of all curricula in order to accommodate new knowledge and new disciplines;
- restructuring and diversification of degree education;
- preparation of a ten-year programme for higher education development by the UGC in collaboration with universities, keeping in view the manpower needs for a growing industrial base in areas of science and technology;
- setting up of twenty new universities, four in the public sector and 16 in the private sector to meet the rising demand for higher education, and
- provision of competitive grants to institutions demonstrating high level of external efficiency.

The promises also included opening new universities, facilitation of research, modification of curricula, and preparation of a ten-year programme with the help of the University Grants Commission. The Nawaz Sharif government could not complete its tenure as, in 1993, the President, Ghulam Ishaq Khan, dismissed the prime minister and his government. Thus the implementation of the policy came to a halt with the dismissal of the government.

NATIONAL EDUCATION POLICY 1998–2010

In 1998, the second Nawaz Sharif government presented a new National Education Policy. The policy gave detailed recommendations for the improvement of higher education. Some major recommendations of the policy (GoP, 1998: 76–9) included:

- expansion of access to higher education to at least 5 per cent of the age group 17–23 by the year 2010;
- introduction of new disciplines or emerging sciences in the public sector universities;
- transformation of selected disciplines at major institutions into 'Centres of Advanced Studies and Research;'

- launch of three-year BA/BSc (Honours) course after BA/BSc in all colleges;
- provision of funds to improve buildings, libraries, laboratories and student support facilities of the degree colleges;
- revision of curricula of universities at all levels and their adjustment to the requirements of industry and to international standards;
- setting up search committees for appointment of vice chancellors;
- representation of industrialists on university authorities shall be encouraged, and establishment of technology parks and industrial research centres in the universities to achieve this goal;
- launch of local MPhil and PhD programs on a large scale in the Centres of Excellence (CoEs) and other university departments;
- introduction of the system of assessment of teacher performance for improvement of the teaching-learning process;
- introduction of methods of self-assessment by teachers;
- designing the mechanism of assessment pro-formas, to be designed with the help of the Vice Chancellors' Committee along with the present tenure system;
- introduction of a contractual system of appointment for teachers in the universities and colleges;
- initial appointment of a university lecturer at grade 18, a university professor at grade 21, and meritorious professors at grade 22;
- support of a goal-oriented quality research of applied nature related to pressing problems of socio-economic and industrial significance on priority basis;
- the funding of education shall be raised from the present 2.2 per cent to 4 per cent of GNP with enhanced allocations for universities;
- waiver of fee to poor and meritorious students subject to continuous good academic performance;

- appointment of a dean of students affairs in each educational campus for promoting and regulating the co-curricular activities of students;
- ban on all political activities on the campus in order to eliminate violence, and
- setting up a National Council for Academic Awards and Accreditation (NCAAA).

The list was exhaustive and ambitious. It is interesting to note that students unions, which were banned during Zia ul-Haq's military regime, remained banned during the civil governments of Nawaz Sharif and Benazir Bhutto. The policy recommended creating an office of dean of student's affairs to deal with the discipline problems of students. The policy laid emphasis on the need for research and revision of curricula. It referred to the role of educational management in universities and recommended the constitution of a search committee to select the vice chancellor of the universities on merit. A number of these recommendations such as research, revision of curriculum, and expansion of universities were as stated in the previous policies. The implementation process was again disrupted when Nawaz Sharif's elected government was dismissed by the Army Chief General Pervez Musharraf on 12 October 1998.

Pervez Musharraf's era saw the 9/11 attack on twin towers in New York, USA. As a result of that, external pressure was mounted on Pakistan but at the same time large funds were given to Pakistan to 'improve education' to bring an end to fundamentalism. Pervez Musharraf presented himself to the external world as a champion of 'enlightened moderation'. Massive programmes were launched to 'clean' the curricula of hate material. A team was set up to make a new education policy that held a number of consultative meetings to come up with a white paper on education. Finally an education policy was presented in 2009. Ironically the policy which was prepared by Musharraf could only be presented in 2009 during the Pakistan Peoples Party regime. The policy was significant because of its timing as there was tremendous international pressure to bring reforms in the educational system.

Some of the policy actions stated in the policy (GoP, 2009a: 58–60) included:

- increase in the higher education budget to 20 per cent with an enhancement of the total education budget to 7 per cent of GDP of the economy;
- competitive research grants for funding to ensure that the best ideas in areas of importance are recognized and allowed to develop;
- provision of opportunities for collaboration with the world scholarly community by both post-graduate students and faculty alike;
- institutionalization of a tenure track system of appointment of faculty members;
- faculty development award of doctoral and post-doctoral scholarships to meritorious students for pursuing their studies both in Pakistan and abroad;
- designing a Continuous Professional Development (CPD) programme for college and university teachers;
- development of quality assurance programmes by universities;
- ranking system of the universities on more broad-based parameters that directly point to the quality of learning;
- need-based scholarship programs to enhance equitable access to higher education;
- establishment of campuses of existing universities in second and third tier cities to facilitate the spread of higher education;
- recognizing the importance of social sciences in developing better social understanding;
- transmission of civic and cultural values and the potential to reduce conflict;
- universities shall pay greater attention to this area in their research function;
- introduction of integrated four-year bachelor degree programmes by universities;

- establishment of accreditation councils to allow accreditation of undergraduate programmes in the respective disciplines for which these councils are established;
- encouragement of research linked to local industry such as commerce and agriculture in order to support these areas through indigenous solutions and create linkages between academia and the market, and
- development of split-degree programmes in collaboration with foreign universities of good repute.

The policy focused on the quality of education with special reference to research. There was a manifold increase in the funding of the Higher Education Commission (HEC) which made it possible for HEC to grant funds for research projects and conference presentations. The recommendation of accreditation councils for different disciplines in the 2009 policy was a repetition of the same recommendation made in the 1998 policy.

ANALYSIS AND DISCUSSION

Higher education remained a constant theme in all the education policies with a difference in the degree of emphasis. In the 1947 conference some important recommendations, including the establishment of an Inter-Universities Board of Pakistan, were made but most of those recommendations could not be realized in the absence of a proper implementation plan and lack of sufficient funds. Similarly the 1959 Commission released a detailed report containing recommendations to improve the quality of education in Pakistan but the report did not have a solid political backing. The commission, for instance, proposed that the duration of degree programme should be three years instead of two years. This recommendation was implemented in 1960 only for one year but at the severe negative reaction of students throughout the country, the Government gave in and the proposal was withdrawn within a year and the degree programme was brought back to a two-year duration. We see a pendulum movement of the issue of higher education in the education policies of Pakistan. The proposals for a new educational policy lamented the fact that previous education policies were biased in favour of higher education whereas more attention should have been given to primary education. A similar complaint was raised in the Second Five-Year Plan. As a result we see the pendulum movement between primary and secondary education.

An important issue of academic freedom and democratization of universities was voiced in the 1972 Education Policy announced by the Peoples Party government. If we look at the quantitative expansion of universities we realize that there is a vast increase in the number of universities and degree awarding educational institutions. Quantitative expansion, however, is just one aspect of the issue.

A related problem is the quality of higher education. The quality issue includes physical facilities as well as the faculty, curriculum, and the actual dynamics of teaching. A look at the quality of available facilities in the institutions of higher education shows that generally the facilities do not match demand. Most of the buildings in the public sector are old and poorly maintained. The Higher Education Commission has become quite generous with its new pro-university approach. How the availability of funds is going to impact the physical side is yet to be seen.

The other aspect of quality is purely academic. This aspect refers to questions like: What is the quality of the faculty that is available to the institution? How useful and relevant are the syllabi of courses being offered? What kind of knowledge is being generated in the classroom and the labs? Keeping in view the significance of the teaching faculty, a lot is expected from it but Pakistan's academic dynamics seem to be largely barricaded by political interest and most of the faculty available in the universities does not come up to the high standards set by the world's universities.

The process of hiring teaching faculty is also questionable. In many cases, these decisions are influenced by political pressure at various levels. Though there are written rules about the eligibility of candidates applying for different teaching positions, these conditions may be bent as and when required. A related aspect of the problem is the relatively low salaries of the teaching faculty in the public sector and bureaucratic sanction on academic freedom of the faculty. As a reaction to this, a number of teachers, instead of strengthening their academic base in the institutions they work for, engage themselves in teaching assignments in various other institutes. Consequently their academic performance is affected negatively. This situation is not very encouraging.

Research is considered to be the most powerful source of creating knowledge. The state of research at our higher education institutions is miserable. The number of PhDs available in academic institutions is far from satisfactory and very few faculty members are engaged in meaningful research. Paucity of resources is just one aspect of the problem. The real issue, however, is lack of motivation. In the absence of a strong research tradition in higher education, we are promoting the kind of education that supports the status quo, as it does not permit any fresh ideas, and blocks the way to a positive change at the societal level.

A quick look at the syllabi of programmes that we are offering at the higher education level and their execution in the classrooms would reveal that these programs cannot prepare the students to meet the challenges of the new millennium. This situation raises a legitimate question; can the kind of higher education being promoted ensure the results attached with higher education worldwide, i.e. a rise in living standards, enhanced productivity, and alleviation of poverty?

In the contemporary competitive world just acquiring a degree is not enough. What is required is the relevant knowledge which could be of real use to the market. Economic development that used to revolve around manufacturing is now centred on knowledge, a development that is vibrant and relevant. Is knowledge a vibrant entity in our classrooms? The answer to this question can be found in our dull and drab teaching dynamics and memory-oriented assessment system. This system can only produce students who are very good at memorizing and reproducing what they have been told. Expecting creativity from them is asking rather too much from them. This does not mean that there is no talent in our country as the same students excel in creative output when they go abroad. The point is that a kind of disabling environment is being provided in the majority of Pakistan's educational institutions.

In Pakistan, while the access to higher education in public universities is not very difficult in terms of financial requirements, the rapidly changing world poses a much bigger challenge for us. The real challenge is not only to attain the quantitative target, but to impart higher education that ensures the economic development of Pakistan and paves the way for raising our standards of living, not just in terms of provision of physical facilities but for attaining the values of mutual respect, tolerance, peace, and harmonious social coexistence. This kind of target can only be achieved by bringing revolutionary changes to ensure better planning, more funding, enhanced physical facilities, ongoing monitoring, meaningful research, qualified and competent faculty, relevant syllabi, effective classroom dynamics, and better educational governance.

SUMMARY

This chapter explained the link between higher education and national development. It critically analysed different policies in terms of their initiatives on higher education. In Pakistan a very limited segment of the population has access to higher education. The chapter highlighted the inconsistent policies regarding allocation of funds to higher education and further discussed the quantitative expansion of the universities, but at the same time raised some questions about the frequency and quality of research output of the university and its dissemination in terms of publication in world-class journals.

Chapter 7

Female Education

Article 26 (1) of the Universal Declaration of Human Rights (UNO, 1948: 5) states that 'Education shall be free at least in the elementary and fundamental stages. ... Technical and professional education shall be made generally available and higher education shall be equally accessible to all on the basis of merit.' It is unfortunate that a number of people, mostly women, have been deprived of this fundamental right. According to the most recent UIS data, (http://www.uis.unesco.org/ev_en.php?ID=6401) there are an estimated 781 million illiterate adults in the world, about 64 per cent of whom are women.

According to the World Bank report *Gender Equality and Development* (2011: 5) '... in Pakistan, children whose mothers have even a single year of education spend one extra hour studying at home every day and report higher test scores.' Almost all the important educational policy documents since 1947 have acknowledged the significance of female education and set targets to enhance it and reduce gender gaps. Education policies in Pakistan have consistently included the objective of increasing female access to education and reducing the gender gap. Article 34 of the Constitution of Pakistan requires that 'steps shall be taken to ensure full participation of women in all the spheres of national life'.

This chapter offers a critical analysis of the policies pertaining to female education. In the process the chapter will discuss the economic, social, cultural, and religious factors that have made female education more challenging.

THE PAKISTAN EDUCATIONAL CONFERENCE, 1947

The Pakistan Educational Conference, 1947 made a special committee on women's education. The terms of reference for the women's education committee included:

- suggesting means for surveying the facilities for women's education in Pakistan;
- chalking out a programme for women's education at all stages with the syllabus of studies suited to the needs of the country;
- suggesting a programme of adult education with special provision for *purdah*-observing ladies;
- considering the desirability of having separate women's educational institutions after the primary stage;
- suggesting ways and means for popularizing vocational education among women;
- considering the arrangements for the training of women teachers for pre-primary and nursery schools, and
- considering any other related matter.

Some of the major proposals of the conference dealing with female education included surveys by the education departments of the provinces in Pakistan and collection of all factual statistical information about the present facilities available for various grades of women's education in their respective provinces. The conference also proposed that:

- primary schools could be co-educational or otherwise according to local needs;
- there should be separate schools for girls at the secondary stage and domestic science and home-nursing should be introduced as compulsory subjects in the curriculum;
- as far as practicable, separate colleges be established for girls such as two women's medical colleges in East Pakistan and West Pakistan respectively;
- more educational facilities in the form of scholarships;
- properly equipped boarding houses and conveyance for female students;

- liberal stipends and scholarships for girls desiring to take up courses in subjects like nursing, commerce, radio engineering, etc. (GoP, 1947: 15–16).

The Conference also proposed efforts to enlist the active help and cooperation of the public, especially of industrialists, businessmen, and *zamindars,* in establishing adult literacy centres for women both in towns as well as in the rural areas; they were to be persuaded to earmark a certain percentage of their profits towards the establishment and maintenance of such centres for their women employees and tenants. Furthermore first-aid, home-nursing and hygiene were to be made compulsory in the higher stages of secondary education; 50 per cent spending was allotted for adult literacy centres for women; women would be encouraged to receive vocational training; a sufficient number of first-rate Teachers Training Institutes for Women would be established to impart special training in the teaching of nursery and primary classes; all the nursery and pre-primary schools were to be staffed entirely with properly trained female teachers; 'Industrial Homes' were to be established where women could receive training in various types of vocations to enable them to earn their livelihood; appointment of female experts were to be made on the Joint Committee to draw up the syllabi for secondary, high school, and university education; universities were to consider starting a University Nursing Training Corps and a University Officers Corps for Women.

THE COMMISSION ON NATIONAL EDUCATION, 1959

The Commission on National Education (GoP, 1959: 189) acknowledged the importance of women's education by suggesting that, 'Unless a mother is educated, there will never be an educated home or an educated community.' The commission (GoP, 1959: 189) emphasized the equality of implications of its proposals by suggesting that:

> … women need education just as Pakistan needs educated women, and it is the purpose and nature of this education that concerns us

> here. It should be clearly understood that the reform and expansion of education at all levels dealt with in other chapters of this report have been proposed with the needs of both boys and girls, men and women in mind.

The recommendations of the 1959 commission (GoP, 1959: 195) included the provision of equal facilities in terms of quantity and quality for the education of boys and girls, female teachers for girls and boys for the first three classes and for exclusive subjects at the secondary school level; introduction of subjects of particular interest to girls such as elementary home craft, tailoring, weaving, cookery, and child care; girls should be guided either into secondary schools or into vocational schools after class eight; offering courses suited to their aptitude and interests; special courses for girls dealing with secretarial work, the operation of telecommunication and electronic equipment, and the driving of light and heavy vehicles in the technical and vocational domain, diversion courses in commercial subjects such as typing, stenography and book-keeping, food technology including dietetics, catering and canteen management; textile design and interior decoration at high school level; introduction of a home economics departments in colleges for girls at the higher education level; special provision for the training of women in secretarial work and office management and in the fields of book-keeping, accountancy, and commercial banking, along with courses in nursing and fine arts in commercial colleges; clean and comfortable accommodation for girls living in a boarding house with provision of wholesome food; university student participation in an organized national programme which, in the case of girls, would involve nursing or adult education or training in civil or military defence.

THE PROPOSAL FOR A NEW EDUCATIONAL POLICY, 1969

The 1969 policy (GoP, 1969: 42) at the outset acknowledged the significant role of women's education by stating that, 'It is from his mother, more than from anyone else, that a child acquires his values for life. To have a nation of educated mothers could itself be considered a worthwhile aim of an education policy.' The policy lamented the fact that at the primary level girls' enrolment was not more than 20 per cent and at a higher level this percentage was even lower. The policy held economic and social factors responsible for the low school enrolment of girls. Most parents consider that a girl's education is not a good investment and similarly for social reasons would not send their daughters to schools where they are taught by male teachers alongside male students. According to the policy, the aims of the proposed policy would be difficult to achieve unless a breakthrough was made in women's education. The policy proposed free education of girls up to class eight in order to deal with the economic restraints of the parents. As for the social restraints, the policy proposed that separate school buildings should be made for girls. Also the number of female teachers should be increased by giving them certain incentives like free transportation, housing assistance, and special pay for difficult assignments.

THE EDUCATION POLICY, 1970

The 1970 Education Policy acknowledged the significant role of women education in national development. According to the policy (GoP, 1970: 4), 'A very low enrolment of girls has contributed to a low enrolment ratio of the total elementary age-group children. Parents are often reluctant to send their daughters to co-educational schools with male teachers.' The policy recommended separate schools for girls and boys in order to address resistance from parents to send their girls to co-education schools. It was also recommended that the requirements for hiring female teachers should be relaxed in order to enhance their chances of employment. The policy proposed condensed courses in both general and professional education for women teachers and a comprehensive programme of in-service training of women teachers. The policy also proposed availability of part-time training arrangements, and correspondence courses. The 1970 policy, like the 1969 policy, did not devote a larger section for the women education.

THE EDUCATION POLICY, 1972

In the 1972 policy, education for girls and boys was declared free up to class 10 and it was announced that Universal Primary Education for girls would be achieved by 1984. The Policy observed that parents would feel reluctant to send their daughters to schools where male teachers taught. Like the 1970 policy, the 1972 policy reiterated the recommendation to enhance the number of female teachers. The policy promised to equalize access to education through the provision of special facilities for women including establishing special sports and recreation centres for women.

It was recommended to convert comprehensive schools into schools for talented children in each district. Women would be given opportunities to read the Holy Qur'an and skills such as sewing, knitting, embroidery, child care, nutrition, and poultry keeping.

The policy (GoP, 1972: 23) observed that, 'At present, the proportion of women teachers in primary schools in Pakistan is less than 30 per cent as against 71 per cent in USSR and over 75 per cent in USA'. The policy realized that male teachers are considered offensive by some parents of female students. It was thus proposed to gradually replace male teachers in primary schools with female teachers and that recruitment conditions may be lowered for female candidates who would like to join the teaching profession. These recommendations were to cope with the challenge of a shortage of female teachers.

EDUCATION POLICY, 1979

The 1979 Education Policy (GoP, 1979: 20), known for its agenda to Islamize the educational system, approached the issue of female education by stating that, 'Despite the fact that Islam provides equal opportunities for the education of men and women, female education in Pakistan has been grossly neglected.' The policy observed that only 33 per cent of female children of the relevant age group attended primary schools and the drop-out rate, particularly at the primary level, was greater among females than males. One major factor of the low female education was the unavailability of qualified female teachers.

The major recommendations of the 1979 Education Policy (GoP, 1979: 21–2) included:

- Special efforts to expand and improve facilities for the education of females;
- laying of solid foundations at the primary level to achieve universal education among females by 1992;
- recruitment of 30,000 female teachers for primary schools during the next five years;
- introduction of education as a subject in a sufficient number of intermediate colleges;
- establishment of 5,000 *mohalla* schools to impart literacy and selected home management skills to girls and, depending upon the success of the programme, development of primary education facilities for girls around this structure;
- attempt to increase enrolment of girls at the secondary stage from the present benchmark of 400,000 to 650,000;
- improvement of facilities for the teaching of science and introduction of home economics subjects;
- provision of liberal scholarships and loans exclusively for the female at all levels of education;
- construction of 6,000 female teachers' residences mostly in the rural areas to attract potential female teachers to the teaching profession;
- construction of a boundary around 10,000 existing primary schools for female children;
- provision of science laboratories, hostel seats, and provision of books in adequate numbers;
- appropriation of a greater share to the education of females in all other programmes envisaged under primary education, secondary education, non-formal and adult education, vocational and technical education, teacher education, higher and professional education and other provisions of the policy;
- expansion of the scope of post-graduate courses, including home economics for higher education, and

- establishment of two women universities, one in Lahore and the other in Karachi.

EDUCATION POLICY, 1992

The 1992–2002 Education Policy (GoP, 1992: 18) acknowledged the challenge of female education, 'Social, cultural and economic factors have put off the women participation rates. For improvement of female education, innovative approaches, both in the formal and non-formal sectors, are clearly warranted.' The policy recommended the provision of special incentives to enrol and retain girls in schools. It also suggested the use of distance learning to increase women's access to education. The policy recommended:

- special incentive-oriented programmes in areas where women participation was low, to enrol and retain them in schools;
- use of distance education programmes, for example, the women's matric programme designed by the Allama Iqbal Open University (AIOU), to be used for the education of women and setting up a national network of male and female vocational training centres and vocational high schools;
- establishment of quality institutions (model schools) for the education of talented rural males and females;
- ensuring participation of the talented rural females and males by providing a large number of indigent scholarships for all levels of education; and
- motivation campaigns through print and broadcast media.

The 1992 policy was followed up by The National Plan of Action for Women in 1996 which recommended reducing gender gaps at all levels in order to remove gender stereotype from educational curricula and to promote a positive image of girls and women. Two Millennium Development Goals (World Education Forum, 2000: 8) that deal with female education are stated below:

Goal 2: Ensure that, by 2015, children everywhere, boys and girls alike, will be able to complete a full course of primary schooling.

Goal 3: Eliminate gender disparity in primary and secondary education preferably by 2005 and in all levels of education no later than 2015.

The Education Sector Reforms (GoP, 2004) reiterated the intent of maximizing equal opportunities and reducing the gender gap at all levels of education.

THE EDUCATION POLICY, 1998

The 1998 policy (GoP, 1998: 25), underlining the role of women's education, stated that 'Education and empowerment of girls and women are key factors contributing to social development, well-being and education of present and future generations. Certainly, it is more expensive and costly to keep a girl illiterate and uneducated than educating her.' The policy (GoP, 1998) emphasized measures for the full participation of women by ensuring that all the boys and girls desirous of entering secondary education, get access to schools. The policy envisaged the retention and completion of the primary education cycle up to 90 per cent students (both boys and girls) by the year 2010. To achieve this target the use of non-formal education was emphasized. It proposed functional literacy and income generation skills for rural women of the 15–25 age group. It was proposed to establish one or more women universities with campuses in the provinces. The policy recommended relaxing the age limit for female teachers and giving them incentives to join the profession.

THE EDUCATION POLICY, 2009

The 2009 National Policy of Education (GoP, 2009a: 66) observed that '... females and pupils in rural areas face systematic disadvantage at all levels of education.' According to the policy,

(GoP, 2009: 67) females are particularly under-represented in rural areas (36% versus 43% for urban areas), a feature that also holds for secondary education (35% for rural and 48% in urban areas). The policy announced equal access to education through the provision of special facilities for girls and boys alike and that greater opportunities would be provided to marginalized groups of society, particularly girls. Special literacy skills programmes were recommended to target older child labourers, boys and girls (fourteen to seventeen years). Food-based incentives programmes were promised to increase enrolment and improve retention and completion rates, especially for girls. The policy promised expansion of provisions, particularly in the rural areas and of schools dedicated for girls. According to the policy all boys and girls would be going to school by the year 2015.

The Gender Parity Index (GPI), commonly used to assess gender differences, is the value of an indicator for girls divided by that for boys. A value of less than one indicates differences in favour of boys, whereas a value near one indicates that parity has been more or less achieved. Despite improvements, it is evident that girls continue to face significant disadvantage in access as they reach adulthood. The National Education Policy 2009 (GoP, 2009a: 16) quotes the GPIs in different years which does show improvement but still shows a gap that needs to be filled to achieve equality of access between girls and boys. The policy recommended that, in order to increase the number of female teachers, the maximum age limit should be waived for female teachers.

Table 11: Gender Parity Index

Year	Primary	Secondary
2001	.72	.73
2005–6	.82	.77
2007–8	.85	.77
2016–17	.87	.81

Source: AEPAM (2018).

ANALYSIS AND DISCUSSION

In the contemporary world where human capital is increasingly becoming crucial, female education is considered to play a vital role in national development. Pakistan has been struggling with problems related to access, dropout rates, and quality of education. Despite a number of education policies and plans the educational outcomes could not be improved to a satisfactory level. According to the Global Competitive Index (GCI) cited by the National Education Policy, 2009 (GoP, 2009a: 12) Pakistan's score on health and primary education is 108, lagging behind Bangladesh (90), China (55), India (93), Malaysia (42), and Sri Lanka (36). It is important to note that the higher the number, the weaker the performance.

The challenges of female education lie in multiple directions including access, quality, dropouts, and less visibility in the work force. The most serious challenge faced by Pakistan at the time of its independence was the large illiterate population, especially women. In 1947, 85 per cent of the population of Pakistan was illiterate (Bengali, 1999). Out of 15 per cent of literate people the percentage of women was dismal. There were a number of factors that deterred students from entering schools. These factors were economic, social, religious, and psychological. Most parents did not have sufficient economic resources to send their children to schools and in the case of girls it was perceived that there were no economic returns if they went to school, as they would eventually marry and leave them. On the other hand boys, after getting education, would earn and support them. Socially, in those times (1940s), formal education for girls was not considered as important. Most of the girls who managed to get into school would be allowed to receive only a primary education. On a religious count, a number of girls who observe *purdah* would not be very comfortable with male teachers who would be teaching in primary schools where female teachers were not available. Psychologically, parents' preferred not to send their daughters to a distant school, which was a big constraint for girls. Apart from distant locations, some schools did not have boundary walls and thus were not considered safe for girls. All these socio-economic, religious, and security related factors deterred a large number of girls from going to school.

The education policies did identify the social problem and proposed separate schools for girls. Such a proposal had some practical difficulties in terms of implementation. The challenge was difficult because of the paucity of economic, physical, and human resources to build separate schools for girls. One difficulty was the economic resources that were required to build separate houses. A nascent country that was struggling because of the lack of funds could not afford to build new schools exclusively for girls. The second difficulty was the lack of human resources, i.e. teachers. There was great dearth of teachers and many schools were understaffed. The lack of qualified female teachers was another challenge that remained a focal point for all the education policies.

The education policies tried to attract female children to school and proposed initiatives like mosque schools and *mohalla* schools. Such initiatives did help enhance the number of literate female students but the quality of education was questionable. A related strategy recommended by education policies was to enhance the number of female students through distance education. Distance education was considered to be an efficient mode of education in developed countries. The purpose of setting up the People's Open University was to have a distance education university on the model of UKOU (United Kingdom Open University). The university did make education accessible for girls who could not leave their homes and those who lived in remote areas of the country where there were no schools.

To deal with the lack of sufficient female teachers, education policies proposed certain measures dealing with incentives and lowering of requisite qualifications for potential female teachers. In the 1979 policy (GoP: 1979), the construction of 6,000 schools was proposed. The idea of constructing residences for single female teachers did not succeed because of the sociocultural reasons, as the teachers did not prefer to live alone in these residences. Most of these residences were either not occupied or were vacated soon after occupation.

To recruit more female teachers to meet the demand in girls' schools, a number of policies proposed lowering the recruitment requirements for female teachers. Similarly the maximum age limit was waived for female teachers to retain some female teachers in schools. In the Seventh Five-Year Plan (1988–93), it was proposed that average candidates could be appointed as teachers. Such measures, though proving helpful in meeting the demand for female teachers, did not have a positive impact on the quality of education.

A number of proposals made in various education policies focused on offering women specific courses, e.g. tailoring, weaving, cookery, fine arts, home economics, nursing, etc. This was a skewed perspective of female education. The problem appeared to be certain assumptions working in the minds of policymakers regarding a fixed role of women in society. It was interesting to note that the committee on women's education proposed to establish two medical colleges one each in the eastern and western wings of Pakistan but wording was changed from 'immediately' to 'as soon as possible' (GoP, 1947: 46). The Conference proposed scholarships to bring female students towards education but discussed little of the sociocultural forces of resistance which, at that time, were hindering the growth of female education.

An important and relevant problem is that of non-utilization of a number of female professionals such as doctors and engineers, who, after successfully completing their professional degrees, do not undertake professional work. After marriage they find it difficult to practice their profession. In most cases, they are not allowed by their husbands and in-laws to enter the workforce. Consequently women spend most of their time in housework with children but that labour is not recognized as a job and there are no wages attached to homemaking. Thus quantitative expansion in female literacy rate is not sufficient. There is also a need to create socio-economic spaces for females on the market place.

SUMMARY

Female education is one of the major challenges the Pakistani education system faced since 1947. Social, economic, religious, and security reasons were responsible for the low female literacy rate in Pakistan. There were insufficient schools and a shortage of trained teachers. The chapter discussed three important domains of female education, access, quality, and visibility in the work force, with respect to initiatives proposed by education policies. It is interesting to note that every policy document, in theory, acknowledged the rationale of female education but the gap between male and female literacy persisted. Initiatives like *mohalla* schools, mosque schools, *Nai Roshni* schools, etc. tried to increase the number of female literates but such initiatives overlooked the qualitative aspect of literacy. Quality was also compromised when the minimum requirements for teachers were lowered and the maximum age limits for female teachers was waived. The education policies generally failed to realize the related issue of the invisibility of educated women in the paid workforce of society.

Chapter 8

Language Issues

A major challenge faced by the education policymakers in Pakistan was the issue of language and its central role in the process of learning and achievement of educational pursuits (Rahman, 1996; Siddiqui, 2010, 2011). Besides an instrument of communication and educational access, language is also an identity marker at personal and societal levels (Rahman, 1996; Mansoor et. al, 2004; Siddiqui, 2010, 2014). The role of a national identity was quite evident during the Pakistan Movement, at a time when different languages were being displayed as distinguishing markers for different sets of population in United India; for example, Urdu was associated with Muslims. Language remained a contested issue even after the independence of the country, giving birth to a number of questions.

What should be the state language of the country? What would be the status of English, the colonial language? How would the provincial/regional languages be conserved and promoted? What language should be used as a medium of instruction? Which languages should be compulsorily taught in educational institutions? All these questions kept popping up in the educational policies of Pakistan. This chapter critically reviews the responses to language related issues offered in education policies.

PAKISTAN EDUCATIONAL CONFERENCE, 1947

In the Pakistan Educational Conference held in 1947, Fazal-ur-Rahman delivered an important speech. It is pertinent to study the section of his speech dealing with English, Urdu, and Provincial/Regional languages. Talking of Urdu he claimed that '... it has shown an extraordinary vitality and sensitivity both as an instrument of communication and as a vehicle for the expression of the subtlest shades of thought and the most ethereal flights of fancy' (GoP, 1947: 11). This was a clear indication that Urdu would be given a special status in the national structure. Later in his speech he alluded to the attributes of Urdu and deemed it fit to be the lingua franca in Pakistan. According to him (GoP, 1947: 11):

> The facility with which it can borrow and assimilate words from foreign languages, its historic affiliations with Persian, Arabic, Sanskrit and English and its high creative output in prose and poetry constitute to my mind unassailable grounds for its establishment as the 'lingua franca' of Pakistan.

As far as English was concerned, there was a mention of '... the injurious effects of making an alien language the medium of instruction' but in the same wake the inevitable role of English was acknowledged. 'Besides, from purely self-regarding motives we should not easily throw away a language which gives us so easy an access to all the secrets of Western science and culture' (GoP, 1947: 11). The question of the role of English kept recurring in the education policies. The conference also underlined the significant role of provincial/regional languages. It was suggested (GoP, 1947: 11) that:

> We in Pakistan must provide the maximum scope for growth to our provincial languages not merely as media of instruction but also as instruments for the dissemination of the culture they embody without at the same time sacrificing the unity of our common culture.

The conference, which lasted for five days, made committees to deliberate on issues important for education. The committee that deliberated on the issue of language and medium of instruction reported that:

> ... the institution of common language was essential to the maintenance of the new nation of Pakistan. The Committee agreed that the common language should be Urdu. Some members of

> the Committee suggested that Urdu should not only be the common language for Pakistan but it should also be the medium of instruction in each Province. Other members of the Committee, however, felt that the question of medium of instruction should be left to each Province to decide according to its requirements but that Urdu should be the second compulsory language in schools. The Committee was inclined to support the second view. The D.P.I. East Bengal, however, felt that Urdu should not be the compulsory second language and should be one of the options (GoP, 1947: 21).

This rather long quote is reproduced here in order to appreciate that the resistance to the imposition of a certain state language issue emerged even during the initial years of Pakistan. This later turned into a powerful language movement. The committee also considered the question of English and suggested that 'as a transitional measure it should be retained as a compulsory language at the school stage' (GoP, 1947: 21).

COMMISSION ON NATIONAL EDUCATION (1959)

The report of the Commission on National Education (GoP, 1959: 289), which had a detailed section on language issues, observed that:

> Urdu and Bengali have now been officially declared to be the National languages of Pakistan, and therefore the question of their adoption in place of English in the educational system is no longer a matter of debate.

The commission recommended that the national language should gradually and progressively replace English as the medium of instruction at all levels (GoP, 1959: 290). We can see more rhetoric and less commitment as the commission talked about the status of national languages, English, and provincial languages. According to the 1959 Commission Report (GoP, 1959: 290):

> Even when this has been done, it will still be necessary for our young men and women to learn English as a compulsory language

> from class VI onwards to the degree level. ... We therefore recommend that English should be taught as a compulsory language from class VI to XII in schools and at the graduate level.

The commission believed that, '... a period of approximately fifteen years will be needed to replace English as the medium of instruction in a large number of subjects taught at the university level' (GoP, 1959: 295). According to this, English should have been replaced by the national language by 1974 but like many other educational targets, e.g. literacy, universal education, and female education, this target date also passed without bringing any significant change in the linguistic scenario.

PROPOSALS FOR A NEW EDUCATIONAL POLICY, 1969

The 1969 Education Policy criticized the social gulf being created and perpetuated on a linguistic basis. The policy (GoP, 1969: 3) commented that:

> Not only does the use of English as the medium of instruction at higher levels perpetuate the gulf between the rulers and the ruled, it also perpetuates the advantages of those children who come from the well-to-do families, and results in a colossal waste of human resources which could be developed to a far greater extent if instructions were to be given in national languages.

According to the policy, the government had decided in 1954 to introduce the national languages into official use by 1974 but because of the lack of preparation it could not happen. The policy recommended pursuing a definite programme of conversion of official languages. The policy proposed to reduce the teaching of English by changing the medium of instruction at all levels of education to the national languages. The policy (GoP, 1969: 15) committed that, 'as a consequence of this determined effort it should be possible to introduce Urdu as the official language in West Pakistan and Bengali in East Pakistan by 1974 and to introduce both the languages in the Central Government of Pakistan by 1975.'

THE NEW EDUCATION POLICY, 1970

The New Education Policy, 1970, underlined the educational, social, and political role of language in a society, acknowledging the potential role language can play in national development and cultural identity. The issue of using Pakistan's mother tongue was discussed at a theoretical level by suggesting the criteria for selecting the medium of instruction. The criteria given by the policy (GoP, 1970: 18) included that the language selected as a medium of instruction should have the ability to, '(a) help students acquire knowledge as effortlessly as possible; (b) communicate with clarity and objectivity; and above all; (c) stimulate critical and creative thinking.' The policy links the change of medium of instruction at a higher level with the replacement of English for official purposes.

The policy (GoP, 1970: 19) suggested that, 'Both of these interlinked issues need, therefore, to be examined together, and, their full implementation worked out so that the changeover is easy and smooth.' It is important to note that this condition was not easy as the tradition of official correspondence in English was well established in the offices and preparations for 'official Urdu' were not made. The policy referred to the Pakistan Provisional Constitution Order that envisaged the establishment in 1972 of a commission to examine and report on the question of the replacement of the English language for official purposes. The policy recommended that the commission should be set up forthwith to examine the question of the changeover from English to the national languages for official purposes and also that of complete switchover to the national languages as media of education.

EDUCATION POLICY, 1972–1980

In 1971, Pakistan lost East Pakistan, where the Bangla language was predominantly used and the 1972 policy reflected the changed circumstances. There was no elaborate section devoted to language issues in the 1972 policy. Surprisingly, there were no directions given in the policy for the medium of instruction. However, there was a reference to the significance of provincial languages. The policy suggested that (GoP, 1972: 15) '... for national cohesion, it is necessary for the people of one region to understand the language and literature, social structure and customs, attitudes and motivations of the people of the other regions.'

The policy (GoP, 1972: 15) recommended to '... establish a department for undergraduate study of the language, literature and culture of the various regions of Pakistan. For research and postgraduate studies of the language, literature and culture of the people of Pakistan, a National Institute of Pakistan Studies will be established at Islamabad University.' Besides reference to provincial languages, there were no guidelines given on the medium of instruction issue which had always been a hot topic in Pakistan's educational system. According to Aly (2007: 79), the policy adopted a position of benign neglect on the medium of instruction and made no reference to language.

CONSTITUTION OF ISLAMIC REPUBLIC OF PAKISTAN, 1973

The 1973 constitution of Islamic Republic of Pakistan contains provisions for language rights for the citizens of Pakistan. According to this article (GoP, 1973: 16) 'Subject to Article 251 any section of citizens having a distinct language, script or culture should have the right to preserve and promote the same and subject to law, establish institutions for that purpose.'

The constitution (GoP, 1973: 148) also clearly mentions that, 'The national language of Pakistan is Urdu, and arrangements shall be made for its being used for official and other purposes within fifteen years from the commencing day.' According to this the arrangements should have been made by 1988 but there were no serious and consistent efforts made to this effect.

The constitution contains the following articles for the promotion of Arabic, English, and the provincial languages:

> The state shall endeavour, as respects the Muslims of Pakistan: To make the teaching of the Holy Qur'an and Islamiat compulsory,

> to encourage and facilitate the learning of Arabic language and to secure correct and exact printing and publishing of the Holy Qur'an (GoP, 1973: 17).
>
> Subject to clause (1), the English language may be used for official purpose until arrangements are made for its replacement by Urdu (GoP, 1973: 148).
>
> Without prejudice to the status of the National language, a provincial Assembly may by law prescribe measures for the teaching, promotion and use of a provincial language in addition to the national language (GoP, 1973: 148).

It is important to note that even in the presence of the provision the provincial assemblies did not work for the promotion of local languages. Only recently did the provincial assembly of Khyber Pakhtunkhwa legislate for the promotion of local languages.

NATIONAL POLICY, 1979

The National Educational Policy (1979) reflected the cultural, linguistic, and religious preferences of Zia ul-Haq who was the military ruler at that time. He tried to Islamize education in Pakistan and vowed to promote the national language, Urdu, as a medium of instruction (GoP, 1979: 2). English medium schools were instructed to use Urdu as a medium of instruction. In 1979, class I started with Urdu as the medium of instruction to matriculate in 1989. Urdu was given much importance by promoting it as a symbol of Muslim identity. The English language was dubbed as a legacy of colonialism and was maligned in the 1979 policy (GoP, 1979: 59) which stated that:

> ... it has been decided that all Pakistani 'English medium schools' throughout the country will be required to adopt Urdu or an approved provincial language as the medium of instruction. The nomenclature 'English medium schools' will be abolished.

This decision was, however, reverted later and English again became the medium of instruction. Besides the extra emphasis on Urdu, the policy suggested ways to promote Arabic. The 1979 policy gave elaborate directions in terms of medium of instruction at various levels and the use of Urdu, English, and provincial languages at various levels with certain conditions. The emphasis, however, was on the promotion of Urdu.

Some important recommendations of the policy (GoP, 1979: 60–1) included:

- Starting April 1979 all students admitted to class I in all English medium schools will undergo instruction through the medium of Urdu or an approved provincial language, which will be progressively introduced in successive grades thereafter.
- Primary education will be imparted in the national or an approved provincial language depending upon the choice of the provincial governments.
- A provincial government may run educational institutions in the approved provincial language. In such institutions, Urdu will be a compulsory subject from class III onwards.
- English will be taught as a compulsory second language from class VI onwards in all the schools.
- The national language will be used as alternate medium of instruction at the college and university levels progressively. Complete switchover to Urdu as a medium of instruction will be accomplished in a phased manner in a period of 5–7 years.
- The decision to introduce the national language at the professional and university education level as medium of instruction will be based on preparations made in this regard in due course.
- Teachers in the existing English medium schools will be permitted to teach through the medium of Urdu or an approved provincial language.
- Existing textbooks in the English medium schools in subjects other than English will be replaced by those written in Urdu or an approved provincial language.
- No new English medium school will be established throughout the country.

- The task of standardization of terminology will be undertaken on an urgent basis.
- Writing of Urdu books in scientific, professional, and technical subjects will be encouraged. Selected books in various crucial subjects will be translated for adoption in universities and colleges.
- In schools where the national language is the medium of instruction, one of the regional languages will be taught from class III onwards.

The most drastic shift in the 1979 Education Policy was turning the existing English medium schools into Urdu medium schools by allowing the teachers to teach in Urdu medium and replace the existing textbooks in English with those in Urdu or an approved provincial language.

EDUCATION POLICY, 1992

The 1992 Education policy was launched by a civil government after a long tenure of military dictatorship. According to the policy (GoP, 1992: 16) 'The medium of instruction as may be determined by the provinces, shall be either the approved provincial language, the National language, or English.' The policy (GoP, 1992: 25) recommended that, 'At tertiary level, English may be the medium of instruction for science and technical subjects.'

THE EDUCATION POLICY, 1998

The policy (GoP, 1998: 5) reproduced the following paragraph from the 1973 constitution that dealt with the promotion of Arabic, the language of the Holy Quran:

> To make the teachings of the Holy Qur'an and Islamiat compulsory, to encourage and facilitate the learning of Arabic language, and to secure correct and exact printing and publishing of the Holy Qur'an to promote unity and the observance of the Islamic moral standards.

It was proposed by the policy that examinations like Graduate Record Examination (GRE) and Test of English as a Foreign Language (TOEFL) of USA, the National Testing Service (NTS) should provide for testing of all interested candidates twice or thrice a year.

EDUCATION POLICY, 2009

The 2009 Education policy was designed during Musharraf's era but was revisited and approved by the Pakistan Peoples Party Government. The policy laid emphasis on the promotion of English. It suggested that English, being a globalized language, was important for international competition. The policy (GoP, 2009a: 27) considered English as one of the factors responsible for educational inequality in Pakistan. The policy stated:

> A major bias of the job market for white collar jobs appears in the form of the candidate's proficiency in the English language. It is not easy to obtain a white collar job in either the public or private sectors without a minimum level proficiency in the English language. Most private and public schools do not have the capacity to develop the requisite proficiency levels in their students. English language also works as one of the sources for social stratification between elite and non-elite. Combined with employment opportunities associated with proficiency of the English language the social attitudes have generated an across the board demand for learning English language in the country.

Musharraf made a conscious effort to offer a vision of 'enlightened moderation', which had a symbolic importance after the 9/11 incident, in order to present a softer look of Pakistan to the outer world. It was during Musharraf's regime that English was declared a compulsory subject from KG 1 up to the higher levels. A number of practical steps were recommended in the policy (GoP, 2009a: 28) to implement the pro-English initiatives. The Education Policy 2009 focused on the significance of English as a language of globalization and offered a number of measures to promote English. Some major recommendations of the policy (GoP, 2009: 28) regarding language included:

- development of a comprehensive plan of action for implementing the English language policy in the shortest possible time;
- paying particular attention to disadvantaged groups and regions lagging behind;
- inclusion of English (as a subject), Urdu, one regional language, mathematics along with an integrated subject in the curriculum from class I onwards;
- choice of medium of instruction given to the Provincial and Area Education Departments up to Class V;
- English as the medium of instruction for science and mathematics from class IV onwards;
- option of teaching mathematics and science in English or Urdu/official regional language for five years, and after five years teaching these subjects would be in English;
- provision of opportunities to children from low socio-economic strata to learn English, and
- development of a comprehensive school language policy in consultation with provincial and area governments and other stakeholders.

ANALYSIS AND DISCUSSION

Pakistan, having a colonial past, had a choice to opt for the language of its imperial masters, i.e. English as its state language, or the language of the majority of the population, i.e. Bangla. Neither of the two choices was exercised; rather a third option was made in favour of Urdu because of an emotional association with it. Another stated reason for the selection of Urdu was its intelligibility in various part of the country. It is important to note that Urdu was the mother tongue of only a small minority in Pakistan, constituting about 6 per cent of the total population.

The initial education conference recommended Urdu as the lingua franca of Pakistan. It was also recommended that Urdu be used as a medium of instruction in all the provinces. The DPI from East Pakistan opposed this suggestion. It is important to note that Bangla, the language of the majority of the population of Pakistan was denied the status of state language. The recommendations of the conference regarding Urdu as lingua franca were further strengthened by the following events.

In the first session of the constituent assembly in February 1948 it was proposed that members of the assembly may use English or Urdu during the proceedings of the assembly. An opposition member from East Pakistan moved a motion of amendment to also include Bangla as one of the Assembly languages besides English and Urdu, as it was the mother tongue of 56 per cent people of Pakistan. The motion was opposed by Liaquat Ali Khan and Khwaja Nazimuddin and was eventually defeated. The defeat of the motion ignited the feelings of the Bengalis. This was followed by Jinnah's visit to East Pakistan where on 24 March 1948, Jinnah, in his speech (Appendix-C) at the University of Dhaka, elaborated on the issue of state language. He emphasized that 'There can be only one state language if the component parts of this state are to march forward in unison and that language, in my opinion, can only be Urdu.'

Besides the selection of state language, the most important issue for policymakers was that of the medium of instruction. On the one hand was the language of the colonial masters, English, and on the other hand was Urdu, which had been an identity symbol during the Pakistan Movement. The third option was to use the languages of the majority of the population groups, i.e. Bangla, and Punjabi. The decision was made in favour of Urdu as the lingua franca of Pakistan.

The largest ethnic groups living in Pakistan at the time of independence were Bengalis and Punjabis. There were four important differences between the languages and attitudes of these two majority ethnic groups. Firstly Punjabi had relatively more linguistic affinity with Urdu than Bangla. Secondly, Punjabi, compared to Bangla, had no strong tradition of acting as an academic language. Thirdly, a majority of the urbanized Punjabis preferred Urdu over Punjabi as a language of communication in their families and finally, a large number of Punjabis were part of the military, an important domain of power in Pakistan. As a result, they did not experience political deprivation and thus felt no need to insist on the Punjabi language. The case of Bangla was quite different as it was an established academic language used by their speakers with pride. Bangla, unlike Punjabi, had no affinity with Urdu in terms of its vocabulary and script (it is, however, pertinent that before the British Raj, Bengali was written in the Arabic/Persian script as Urdu is). Unlike Urdu, which is written from right to left, Bangla is written from left to right. Besides, Bengalis had a strong sense of deprivation as all the sources of power, e.g. the capital, the presidency, the prime minister, the headquarters of the army, navy, and air force were situated in West Pakistan.

This background is important to understand the two distinct responses to the declaration of Urdu as the state language. The overwhelming majority of the population demanded Bangla be declared the state language. Protests and rallies were organized against the status of Urdu as the sole state language. On 21 February 1952, the students of the University of Dhaka took out a procession demanding Bangla as a state language. The procession was dealt with through force and a number of student protestors were killed by police fire. In 1954, the Constituent assembly passed the resolution to give Bangla the status of state language beside Urdu and it was in 1956 that Urdu and Bangla were considered as the state languages.

A critical review of the education policies reflects that the language issue was not given priority and thus suffered in the absence of proper language planning. The initial omission of Bangla as one of the state languages had serious repercussions on the political scene of the country. We witnessed a prolonged debate on the issue of the medium of instruction. Promises were made at governmental level for the promotion of Urdu as a national language. Unfortunately these promises were not followed up by any serious efforts to empower Urdu to become an official language. Similarly the major power domains of Pakistan, the military, judiciary, and bureaucracy, remained 'no go areas' for

Urdu, whereas English was considered key to enter these domains of power. Declaring Urdu the state language of the country in 1948, therefore, had no adverse effect on the social status of English.

The major role of English as a language of power had multiple effects on the educational domain of Pakistan. A number of rulers made political statements in favour of Urdu without taking concrete steps, i.e. introducing it in the domains of power. With this meaningless lip-service in favour of Urdu by the political rulers, we see the emergence of some scholars who vehemently opposed English and English medium schools. This opposition that could be based on good intentions, but it ignored the global role of English in terms of jobs, higher studies, and trade. We see this tension between adherence to national linguistic heritage and a compelling desire to reach out since 1947.

Similarly the other local languages spoken in provinces like Punjabi, Sindhi, Pashto, and Balochi were either ignored or considered inferior. This attitude was manifested in the lack of institutional support given to these languages. A case in point is Punjabi, which is the mother tongue of about 50 per cent of the citizens of Pakistan. Punjabi is not taught as a subject at school level. Thus children of Punjabi families cannot read or write in their mother tongue and are literally cut off from the rich literary heritage of their language. To a lesser extent this is true of other Pakistani languages like Balochi, Pashto, and Sindhi as well.

Unfortunately in Pakistan the two competing schools of thought vehemently reject the opposition. One school of thought is in favour of Urdu and other local languages, and does not see any role for English in the country. The other school of thought, in favour of English, considers Urdu and regional languages insignificant and irrelevant in the global scenario. Since the second school of thought is in power, we see that the local languages are either ignored or undermined. There is no institutional support provided to them and they have been subjected to a slow death. The painful fact is that a majority of students who are being educated in English medium schools in Pakistan find it difficult to read a book written in their own mother tongue. They do not even know how to count in Urdu or in their mother tongue. The reason is obvious; they are exposed to English primers first and then to any other reading material. They start learning the English alphabet before they learn any alphabets of their national language or mother tongue.

English is an important contemporary language and its rejection could in fact be depriving the students with low socio-economic status of a passport to the enhanced opportunities of success in life. We must learn English but it should not be based on the rejection of local languages. Rather we should be striving for a balance between English and local languages. Such balance could only be achieved if our national and local languages are given respect and validation through institutional support. This would mean introducing these languages in primary classes as a subject.

The significance of exposing students to their own native languages is not just to provide them an extra linguistic tool for communication but to help them remain associated with the roots of their culture of which language is an important manifestation. As discussed earlier, a number of educational policies were presented during different governments but there was no comprehensive document that could be called a language policy. Excerpts from different documents do refer to certain claimed objectives but they did not enjoy institutional support. There is a serious need to carve out a policy that is realistic in nature and makes an attempt to preserve local languages and culture as well.

We see a lack of seriousness and commitment on the issue of language at the state level. That is why the promises made in favour of Urdu and provincial languages were not realized. In 1959, the Commission on National Education (GoP, 1959: 295) stated that '... a period of approximately fifteen years will be needed to replace English as the medium of instruction in a large number of subjects taught at the university level.' Similarly in the 1973 Constitution (GoP, 1973: 148) it was promised that 'The National language of Pakistan is Urdu and arrangements should be made for its being used for official and other purposes within 15 years from the commencing day.'

Both targets remain unachieved. A major factor was the lack of practical measures and follow-up. Another factor was the lack of continuity of policies. We see some drastic and at times adverse decisions by different governments. For instance Zia ul-Haq's military regime's direction was to replace the existing English medium schools with Urdu medium schools and it was also decided that no English medium schools would be established in the future. Similarly during Musharraf's era, another military dictator in the history of Pakistan, schools were instructed to teach English from grade one. These two examples lead to a third factor, i.e. lack of consultation with the stakeholders. The outcome is lack of ownership that ultimately results in poor implementation.

Keeping in view the significance of the language issue, proper planning based on reliable linguistic data needs to be done. A commission on languages should be formed which would give recommendations to the parliament. The language policy should be designed as a result of a consultative process, keeping in view national as well provincial aspirations. Arrangements should be made on a consistent basis to ensure the promotion, growth, and empowerment of national and provincial languages. Language policy needs to realize the pragmatic need of English as a global language together with the cultural identity linked with national and provincial languages. The vitality of a language is often linked with the academic support it gets from educational institutions. It is important that provincial languages be taught as a subject in schools. Similarly Urdu needs to be associated with the domains of power in Pakistan. These practical steps may help enhance the prestige of Urdu as a national language.

SUMMARY

Language plays an important role as an identity marker at individual and national levels. It is also a cohesive force for the effective administration of a country. Besides being an important cultural constituent, the role of language in the educational system of country is vital. The issue of language remained a hot topic during different times in the history of the country. This chapter examined language issues in the different education policy documents of Pakistan. The chapter discussed the question of state language, the exclusion of Bangla, the Bengali language movement, and acknowledgement of Bangla as a second state language of the country. The chapter also looked at the question of the medium of instruction in schools with special reference to Urdu and English medium schools. The roles of regional and indigenous languages were also discussed. The chapter identified the gaps between rhetoric and reality of various claims and promises.

Chapter 9

Technical and Vocational Education

Technical and Vocational Education (TVE), two close but different streams of education, were usually treated as one in most of the education policy documents. The realization of the significant role of technical education grew after the Second World War. This realization was further strengthened when, as a result of the 1947 Partition, many good technical institutions became inaccessible as they were situated in India. There was no organized system of technical education in place in 1947 (GoP, 1955). It was due to this realization that in the 1947 conference organizers formed a subcommittee to deliberate on the issues of technical education.

On the recommendations of Council for Technical Education, two technical high schools were established in Karachi and Dhaka. Similarly, two polytechnic institutions were also planned to be set up in both these cities. One common point among all the policy documents was that they considered technical and vocational education vital for the development of the country.

PAKISTAN EDUCATIONAL CONFERENCE, 1947

The Pakistan Educational Conference acknowledged, at the outset, the crucial role of technical education. According to the conference report (GoP, 1947: 9):

> Living as we do in an age dominated by science with its ever increasing tempo of technological development we cannot afford to neglect the problem of technical education. The dire consequences which have flowed from this neglect in the past, our all-round industrial backwardness, the primitive state of our agricultural

> economy, our helpless dependence on foreign countries for technical personnel—are all too obvious.

The policy made some important recommendations to improve the technical and vocational education in the country. Some recommendations of the 1947 conference (GoP, 1947: 1) included:

- establishment of a Council of Technical Education in order to survey the field of technical education in Pakistan and to make suggestions for its improvement;
- grant of liberal stipends and scholarships for girls desiring to take up courses and subjects like nursing, commerce, radio engineering, etc. and thereby encourage vocational educational training among women;
- consultation of the Messrs Abbott and Wood report on Vocational Education in India for the duration, scope, and content of courses of training and the syllabi of the various technical institutions, and
- no rigid distinction between adult education in the strict sense and technical, commercial, or art instruction or to regard the latter as falling outside the sphere of the former.

The easiest approach for many adult students was considered to be through subjects of a vocational character. Vocational education was the first consideration in any plan of educational reconstruction, along with a proper integration of spiritual, social, and vocational elements.

THE COMMISSION ON NATIONAL EDUCATION, 1959

The 1959 Commission Report, which was a comprehensive policy document on education, considered technical and vocational education important for national development. The report (GoP, 1959: 151) acknowledged that:

> Technical education is at the moment receiving great emphasis in all countries and it is proper that we should profit from experience

> elsewhere. We must fully develop the skills of our manpower if we are to achieve national self-sufficiency and materially raise our standards of living.

The Commission made elaborate recommendations for technical and vocational education. Some recommendations of the 1959 commission (GoP, 1959: 166) included:

- integration of technical education within the educational system;
- diversification of the curriculum of general education in schools by including practical courses in technical subjects, agriculture, commerce, and home economics;
- curriculum of technical and vocational schools should include courses in social studies and humanities;
- a common course be established for all students through the middle stage, after which the first diversion of students from general to vocational and technical schools be made;
- second diversion after Class X when the students may join polytechnics and technical institutions;
- establishment of a network of vocational schools throughout the country with the aim of training students who have manual skill and show an aptitude for craft work, for apprenticeship schemes in industries;
- arrangements to set up more technical institutes for the next five years for producing 7,000 technicians annually in various fields;
- establishment of model factories, in all development schemes, with up-to-date production methods in well-planned workshops, and
- putting all technical institutions, other than those administered by universities, under the control of the Directorate of Technical Education in the Department of Education.

PROPOSALS FOR A NEW EDUCATIONAL POLICY, 1969

The 1969 policy document lamented the fact that no more than 4 per cent students, at secondary level, were opting for technical and vocational education. Two of the stated aims of the policy (GoP, 1969: 8) documents were to 'attract some of the best talent of the country into the teaching profession and (b) reorganize secondary education incorporating a massive shift towards technical and vocational training.' A massive shift was proposed towards vocationally and technically oriented education in the country. The policy document claimed that by 1980 technical and vocational education would be provided to 60 per cent of the students. The policy document recommended establishing a separate directorate for Technical and Vocational Education in each province.

THE NEW EDUCATION POLICY, 1970

The 1970 policy, like the previous policy documents (GoP, 1947; GoP, 1959; GoP, 1969), underlined the significance of technical and vocational education. At the outset, the policy (GoP, 1970: 11) stated, 'Pakistan's goals of national development clearly warrant a much higher priority to be assigned to science and technical education than has been done in the past.' The policy (GoP, 1970: 12) made some major recommendations for the technical and vocational education including:

- establishing a coordination unit at the Ministry of Education;
- diversifying education from the secondary level upwards with a separate stream for technical education at the various levels;
- making arrangements for (a) curriculum development, (b) counselling and guidance service, (c) practical training programmes in cooperation with industries, and (d) coordination at the national level;
- development of at least one science high school in each subdivision and one science college in each district as centres of excellence, either by developing existing institutions or by establishing new ones;

- supplementing the government's efforts to establish technical institutes with similar efforts on the part of industrial concerns individually or through consortia;
- short-term, sandwich, and extension courses in various trades for various kinds of semi-skilled/skilled workers and technicians as well as refresher courses for teachers in vocational subjects in schools that offer vocational courses;
- emergency teacher training programmes in selected centres in the vicinity of industries, conducted by teachers recruited within and outside Pakistan, to meet the present and anticipated demand.

EDUCATION POLICY, 1972

The 1972 policy was important as a number of educational institutions were nationalized by the Peoples Party government. The policy was presented after the 1971 Indo-Pak War. The policy recommended a number of measures for the improvement of technical and vocational education. Some of the major policy recommendations (GoP, 1972: 17) included:

- conversion of polytechnics into technical colleges;
- encouraging students to undergo two years of industrial training/experience after completing a 3-year diploma course;
- provision of a variety of programmes covering new areas of technology which require urgent attention for modernization and development;
- a massive programme of technical education in all the high schools and general colleges;
- assistance to technical colleges/institutes to develop new areas of technology;
- assistance to some of these colleges/institutes to offer specialized instruction in technologies of critical national importance leading to the degree of masters of technology, and
- development of institutions into centres of excellence in certain specialized technologies.

EDUCATION POLICY, 1979

The 1979 Education Policy, launched in Zia ul-Haq's regime, acknowledged the significance of technical and vocational education. Some major recommendations of the policy include:

- constitution of advisory committees with representatives of trade and industry to keep the training responsive to the changing market requirements;
- encouragement of all the technical and vocational institutions to generate funds for supplementing their resources by producing saleable goods during training;
- establishment of small production units with technical and vocational institutes under a phased programme;
- introduction of evening programmes in technical and vocational institutes for the benefit of the community, wherever needed;
- establishment of separate vocational schools for dropouts of the school system;
- standardization of equipment for various levels of technical and vocational institutes;
- introduction of a mechanism for standardizing, testing, and certifying technical and vocational skills required through formal, non-formal, or traditional system of training in consultation with trade and industry;
- on-the-job supervised training for diploma and bachelors of technology students and enacting legislation for providing this training in industrial organizations;
- enactment of undertakings, encouraging teachers of polytechnics and technical colleges to provide consultancy and advisory services to the industry;
- invitation to personnel from industries to advise these institutions on production methods, and
- establishment of teacher training colleges for the teachers of technical and vocational institutes (GoP, 1979: 38).

EDUCATION POLICY, 1992

Like all previous policies the 1992 Education Policy (GoP, 1992: 31–2) highlighted the importance of technical and vocational education. The promises made by the policy (GoP, 1992: 31–2) to improve the technical and vocational education included:

- consolidation of the existing polytechnics and diversification of their teaching programmes through the introduction of selected high technology disciplines;
- introduction of a parallel stream of vocational high schools so that one such school for males at tehsil level and one for females at district level is located in line with the needs of the area;
- establishment of a network of colleges of high technology offering study programmes leading to graduate and postgraduate degrees in the country wherever feasible;
- conversion of some of the existing degree colleges into colleges of higher learning and technology;
- regulation of industrial training for engineering and technology graduates through legislation;
- provision of opportunities to polytechnic graduates for higher studies at home and abroad, and
- establishment of a national council of technical and vocational education.

EDUCATION POLICY, 1998

The 1998 Education Policy (GoP, 1998: 55) underscored the significance of technical and vocational education by suggesting that 'Rapid economic growth demands a mixture of skilled workers, tradesmen, technicians, technologists, engineers, and research and development scientists trained in areas linked with national development requirements and needs of the industry.'

The 1998 policy (GoP, 1998: 60–2) made some important recommendations including:

- establishment of a National Council for Technical Education to regulate technical education and to coordinate efforts of various departments in the field;
- reflection of communication skills, safety and health measures, and entrepreneurial skills in the curricula;
- strengthening of institution-industry linkages to enhance the relevance of training to the requirements of the market;
- improvement of evaluation and accreditation;
- provision of in-service training to improve quality of teachers;
- introduction of a pre-service teacher training programme of BEd (Technology) to provide trained instructors for polytechnics and vocational institutes;
- establishment of new institutions to improve spatial coverage and access to TVE;
- introduction of evening shifts in the existing institutions where demand exists;
- increase in access to TVE through distance education and other non-formal modes;
- introduction of technical education as a separate stream of education in general schools at appropriate level, preferably as an evening shift;
- introduction of emerging technologies such as telecommunication, computer, electronics, automation, petroleum, garments, food preservation, printing and graphics, textile, mining, sugar, and technology, etc. which are greatly in demand on the job market in selected polytechnics;
- making computer education a compulsory component of the curriculum of technical education and establishment of computer laboratories with related facilities in all the polytechnic institutes and colleges of technology;
- introduction of continuing education programs based on a modular approach in different institutions;
- motivation of senior teachers of TVE through financial incentives to develop teaching learning resource material;
- provision of opportunity for further education to be provided to the graduates of polytechnic institutes/colleges of technology;

- modernization of programmes of instruction in commercial training institutes and introduction of a diploma program in 'Office Management and Commercial Practices', broadening the base for technical and vocational education;
- thorough introduction of a stream of matric (technical) on pilot basis and establishment of vocational high schools, and refurnishing and modernization of laboratories and workshops to provide conducive teaching-learning environment.

EDUCATION POLICY, 2009

The 2009 Education Policy (GoP, 2009a: 53), which was largely prepared by a committee during Musharraf's regime, was presented in 2009 by the government of the Pakistan Peoples Party. Some major recommendations about technical and vocational education included:

- institutionalization of inputs of all stakeholders like the industrial/agricultural/service sectors & business community to ensure their inclusion in all current and future reforms of TVE to enable the sector to meet market needs;
- development and standardization of skills curriculum at national level;
- development of the TVE curriculum in standardized modules for each trade to eliminate differentials across various training institutions and to provide opportunities to the trainees for horizontal/upward mobility along with help in assessment and certification of apprentices in non-formal sectors for their entry into formal vocational/technical sectors;
- extension of TVE according to the need of the area, i.e. tehsil, district, and division, offering skills-based vocational training courses, relevant to the local labour market to the graduates of literacy programmes by the National Education Foundation, provincial/area literacy department/directorate and relevant NGOs;

- commissioning of a study to evaluate failures of vocational training intervention at school level to make more realistic recommendations, including cost requirements, for making it part of general education up to secondary school level;
- focus of technical & vocational education institutions on agro-based vocational skills to deal with both agriculture and livestock;
- flexible curricula for vocational education for adaptation as per requirements of local market including contingencies for future changes in the market;
- teacher training in the industries during vacation period every year for improvement of technical know-how on technological changes;
- introduction of a commerce stream under technical education and vocational training regimes;
- establishment of a university of technology at the national level, and strengthening Public Private Partnerships (PPP) in this area, and
- registration of BTech technologists by the Pakistan Engineering Council.

DISCUSSION AND ANALYSIS

It is important to note that almost all policy documents did acknowledge the significance of Technical and Vocational Education (TVE) but in certain policies, e.g. the 1959 Commission on National Education, TVE was overemphasized. Tall promises were made but only a few of them could be implemented. For instance the 1947 Conference recommended establishing two polytechnic colleges in Karachi and Dhaka, but only one polytechnic college was set up in Rawalpindi which was not mentioned in the policy document.

There were some core challenges faced by the policymakers. One major challenge that the policies grappled with was the disconnect between TVE and general education. Starting from the 1947 Pakistan Education Conference report, almost all policy documents reiterated the resolve to integrate general and technical education but we still see a wide gap between these two systems of education.

Another major challenge faced by TVE was its societal perception of those engaged in technical education. Usually students with average scores would opt for technical courses. Thus TVE did not enjoy a high social status. National policies, despite identification of this issue, could not take effective steps to tackle this problem.

A number of policy documents referred to the apparent disconnect between technical courses and the demands of industry. In this regard two things were important: firstly, TVE was not keeping pace with the changing demands of industry and secondly, as a result of this, TVE courses were not job-oriented. Consequently in some areas there was surplus manpower and in some areas there was a shortage of skilled workers.

The Pakistan Educational Conference in 1947 recommended setting up a council for technical education. This should have been a permanent body to recommend and monitor initiatives for TVE but after it was assigned the task of conducting a survey about TVE, it apparently became dysfunctional, which is why the 1998 Education Policy made a recommendation to set up a National Council for Technical Education.

A related issue with TVE was the lack of higher education facilities for those who completed their diplomas from polytechnics. Unlike general education, where students could get a bachelors, masters and PhD, in TVE students would get stuck after the diploma. This was a major reason for the frustration of TVE students.

Some of the above issues were identified by the policy documents and certain recommendations were also made to meet the challenges but the policies could not be turned into reality because of the poor implementation process. As a result some major challenges of TVE are still unresolved.

SUMMARY

Technical and vocational education, though different from one another, have been treated as one in the education policies of Pakistan. The chapter discussed the importance of technical and vocational education in a developing country like Pakistan. It attempted to analyse the policies announced from time to time with regard to technical and vocational education. The chapter alluded to the problem that there is not a very positive image of those who join vocational and technical education in society and there exists a gulf between technical and general education. A number of policies hinted towards this gap and recommended to expose students to interdisciplinary subjects.

Chapter 10

Special Education

Special education deals with physically and mentally challenged persons. There have been varying disagreements about defining disability. National Policy for persons with disabilities (GoP, 2002: 1) defines disability as, 'A person with disabilities means who, on account of injury, disease, or congenital deformity, is handicapped in undertaking any gainful profession or employment, and includes persons who are visually impaired, hearing impaired, and physically and mentally disabled.' According to the policy, (GoP, 2018: 4) the special children in Pakistan can be divided into categories mentioned in the table.

Table 12: Distribution of Disparities among the Defined Population of Disabled Persons

Disability	Per Cent
Physically Handicapped	18.93
Mentally Handicapped and Insane	14
Multiple Disabilities	8.23
Visually Impaired	8.6
Hearing Impaired	7.43
Others (Not classified but included as disability)	43.37

Source: GoP (2018d)

The challenge of special education becomes more difficult in the absence of appropriate facilities for special learners and the social stigma attached with any disability. This would also mean that in some cases the parents would not disclose the disability of their children. This chapter looks at the important education policy documents and their response to special education challenges. It is worth noticing that in the Pakistan Educational Conference in 1947, that lasted for five days and deliberated on educational issues at length, there was no discussion about special education.

COMMISSION ON NATIONAL EDUCATION, 1959

It was in the 1959 Commission report that the issue of special education was addressed for the first time. A separate chapter entitled 'The Education of Handicapped Children' was devoted to this purpose. The term used for special children in the report was 'handicapped children'. The nature of the term was described in the report (GoP, 1959: 257) as:

> Handicapped children are those who suffer from physical or mental defects, whether congenital or acquired, which keep them from ready participation in educational and vocational pursuits. Typical of these are the blind and the deaf mutes, but there are also the crippled and the delicate, the subnormal and the maladjusted, who deserve special consideration in our educational planning.

The commission (GoP, 1959: 257–8) made the following recommendations for the education of special children:

- The doctor and the psychologist must share with the educator the responsibility for helping these children to achieve at least some degree of productive activity and a satisfactory adjustment to their environment.
- In almost all of these cases the educator must combine the provision of general education with vocational education so that the individual may be equipped to earn his own living and trained to live contentedly within the limits of his handicap.
- It is in the nature of the case that such children must have a great deal more individual care and attention than others, and that they cannot be provided for adequately in the regular school system.

- Partnership between the government and representatives of social organizations, to set up agencies specifically for the care of the several types of handicapped persons. With branches in local centres this partnership would be able to establish the required institutions and keep alive the interest of sympathetic people in the needs of the unfortunate.
- The need to develop more schools for special children in localities where they can be of greater service and where the public is ready to cooperate in philanthropy and charity.
- Government must provide the funds and take responsibility for the training of teachers who will serve in institutions for the handicapped. This training must be highly specialized and for the time being will have to be carried on by experts brought in for the purpose from other countries.
- Initially, there should be in our country at least one centre for the training of teachers for the blind and another for the training of teachers for the deaf and mute.
- To take over such a programme our personnel will have to be sent abroad for training and specialization.
- The main effort for the care of the handicapped should come from the community, financed in large measure by the charitable inclinations of the people, and managed by the cooperative work of philanthropic organizations and the government, with the latter lending stability and soundness to the programmes as they develop.

Proposals for the New Educational Policy, 1969 and the New Education Policy, 1970 strangely do not have any mention of special education.

EDUCATION POLICY, 1972

The 1972 Education Policy (GoP, 1972: 1, 11, 26, 39) dealt with the issue of disability and made the following recommendations about special education:

- Equalizing access to education through the provision of special facilities for women, underprivileged groups, and mentally retarded and physically handicapped children and adults in all areas in general and the backward areas in particular.

- Handicapped Children's Education Committees will be established by the education councils of each province. They will be responsible for the education, protection, institutional care, rehabilitation, and employment of these children.
- In order to provide them with the opportunity to become productive and self-reliant citizens, arrangements for special education for handicapped children will be made by opening new schools and strengthening the existing ones. For this purpose, the work already carried out by various philanthropic voluntary organizations/institutions will be duly encouraged and suitably coordinated with the efforts of the government in this field.
- To assist in the formulation, implementation, and evaluation of education policies and practices, consultative and policy-planning education councils will be set up at the national, provincial, district, and institution levels. They will include elected representatives of national and provincial sssemblies and local bodies, citizens of various shades of opinion from different walks of life interested in education, and representatives of teachers, students, and relevant government departments and other agencies. The functions of these councils will, *interalia,* include the following:
  - to formulate and recommend changes and developments in educational policy
  - to oversee the implementation of the policies adopted from time to time
  - to assess and evaluate the overall educational progress in their respective spheres
  - to initiate and support educational research and disseminate its findings
  - to harness and mobilize the latest educational techniques and resources for the improvement of education.
- These Councils will have standing committees for various specific areas of activity including special education. A

provincial education council will also be established for special education.

EDUCATION POLICY, 1979

The 1979 policy devoted a full chapter on special education, entitled 'Education of the Handicapped'. The policy made some important recommendations for special education and special children. One reason for the emphasis on special education could be that the policy was launched by Zia ul-Haq, whose own daughter was a special child. The policy (GoP, 1979: 28) stated the gravity of the problem at the outset:

> Handicapped children suffering from physical or mental defects who deserve special consideration continue to suffer from utter neglect. It is estimated that handicapped form nearly 4 per cent of our total population but there are great many more in the society for many of them are kept sheltered within their parents' homes and are not reported.

The policy (GoP, 1979: 28–9) undertook to:

- survey existing facilities for the education of the handicapped in all four provinces.
- identify institutions which have the potential of becoming national institutions.
- develop National Demonstration Pilot Projects for Education of the Disabled and Handicapped.
- develop projects for identifying needs for strengthening existing institutions for the disabled.

The policy further stated that 'the above activities will be kept under review for purposes of evaluating, modifying, and renewing them in the light of experiences and feedback from the implementation of the Pilot Projects and the existing institutions. Funds for this purpose will be provided by the Federal Government. The educational programmes for the handicapped children will include:

- Provision of general education together with the vocational education of the right type so that the individual does not grow up as a burden on the resources of the nation but can be directed into productive activities.
- Presently, there is only one school in Pakistan to train teachers for the Deaf and Dumb Schools. The government will provide at its own expenditure and accept responsibility for the training of teachers to send them to the institutions for the handicapped. One teacher training institute for the Deaf and Dumb will be opened in Sindh and another for [the] Blind in the Punjab.
- Negotiations will be made with the foreign aid agencies for procuring equipment, expert advisory services, and training requirements for the staff of the institutions of Special Education.
- The experience of the countries with sound facilities in special education shows that the actual care of handicapped children is often suitably and effectively performed by the medical and educational services of private philanthropic organizations. The efforts of the benevolent organizations will, therefore, be supported, supplemented and coordinated by the government in opening more schools in the communities and strengthening the existing ones. Active involvement of Health, Social Welfare, and Industry will be sought to prepare and launch integrated programmes for the handicapped.
- The curricula and syllabi of special education will be brought in conformity with the needs and requirements for the present day.
- An amount of Rs. 23 million was allocated for the development of Special Education during the next five years. The anticipated expenditure should not exceed the Plan provision. Further, the governmental efforts would be supplemented through the cooperation of external agencies (GoP, 1979: 29).'

THE DECADE OF 1980s

The year 1981 was important for special persons in Pakistan on two counts. Firstly, it was declared the International Year of Disabled Persons, bringing disability-related issues to the limelight at a global level. Secondly, in 1981, an ordinance was promulgated for the employment and rehabilitation of disabled persons. The United Nations announced the Decade of the Disabled (1983–1992), underlining the need to formulate an effective strategy to cope with the challenges faced by special persons. The Decade of the Disabled motivated countries to reorganize their efforts to take on the challenge of disabled persons. The first national policy for the rehabilitation of the disabled was launched in 1986 and it underscored the provision of services to special persons and an effective mechanism for implementation. In 1985 a separate directorate had been established to look after the affairs of model schools or special education in the country. In 1988 the policy was revisited in terms of distinct categories of disabilities including mental disability, visual impairment, hearing impairment, physical disability, multiple disabilities, and not classified. In 1999, The National Policy for Special Education came out, emphasizing the need of continuous efforts for the rehabilitation process which was the central agenda of the 1986 policy. The policy, besides recommending some motivation benefits for special persons, called for a fundamental change in the attitude of the masses towards persons with special needs and emphasized the role of media in influencing and constructing the public attitude.

THE 2002 NATIONAL POLICY

In 2002 the National Policy on the issues of disability was released. This was first comprehensive policy document focusing on issues related to physically and mentally challenged persons. The report offered vision, guiding principles, and strategies to realize the set objectives. The thrust of the policy was to integrate and coordinate scattered efforts for a positive impact. Some major recommendations of the policy included research and development, advocacy, vocational training and employment, education and training programmes, and design of building and parks in order to cater to the needs of special persons. In 2006, the National Plan for Action emphasized the components of access, inclusion, and equalization. The plan proposed short-term targets along with long-term targets. The short-term targets included establishment of a data bank, strengthening of disability prevention programmes, mechanism for early detection, provision of care at schools, expansion of vocational training, and promotion of inclusive education. The long-term targets included provision of a conducive physical environment in public and private buildings and a more effective implementation of social security laws.

In 2008, the Special Citizen Act (GoP, 2008) was promulgated. It aimed to provide access to persons with special needs to public places, allocate seats in public transport, and to create provision for wheelchairs on footpaths. In 2009, a Special Citizens (Rights to Concessions in Movement) Act (GoP, 2009b) was promulgated in order to provide concessional rates to special persons in all public and private modes of transport.

EDUCATION POLICY, 2009

The 2009 Education Policy, which dealt with other educational issues in detail, did not pay much attention to Special Education in the country. The policy (GoP, 2009: 18) made two major recommendations for special education:

- To equalize access to education through provision of special facilities for boys and girls, underprivileged, marginalized groups, and handicapped children and adults.
- Special measures were to be adopted to ensure inclusion of special persons in mainstream education as well as in literacy and TVE programmes.

ANALYSIS AND DISCUSSION

A critical study of the education policies reveal that special education was absent from the policy documents in the initial years of Pakistan. It was in the report of the Commission of National Education (GoP, 1959) that the issue of disabilities was discussed at length. It was in this document that a definition of special children was given, which were termed as handicapped children. The emphasis, however, was more towards the medical side of disability and the cultural aspects were undervalued. The recommendations of the 1959 Commission report, however, could not be realized in the absence of a proper plan of action. The 1969 Proposals for A New Educational Policy and the 1970 Education Policy surprisingly ignored the topic of disability and special education. This shows the inconsistency between policies that a topic which was taken seriously in one policy (GoP, 1959), is not even mentioned in the following policies (GoP 1969, GoP, 1970). The 1972 policy offered some radical recommendations to improve special education practices including the establishment of consultative and policy-planning councils to be set up at national, provincial, district, and institutional levels. Like many good ideas, this one was not realized either.

The 1979 policy, which was announced during the regime of General Zia ul-Haq, had some concrete recommendations for special education and for the people with special needs. This policy was different from other policies as it had a detailed plan of implementation embedded in the policy. Another important difference was the political will of the government led by General Zia ul-Haq whose own daughter was a special child. There was an exclusive chapter devoted to special education. The policy announced the allocation of Rs. 23 million for the development of special education during the next five years. It also expressed the resolve of the government to seek cooperation from external agencies. This was a real booster for special education which was brought to the attention of policymakers through the 1959 Commission of National Education and the 1972 Education Policy.

We see some positive happenings in the eighties for the advocacy and improvement of lives of persons with special needs, e.g. the declaration of 1981 as an International Year of Disabled Persons, the 1981 ordinance of employment and rehabilitation, the UN declaration of a Decade for the Disabled (1983–1992), the establishment of a separate directorate of education, the policy for the rehabilitation of the disabled, and a revision of the policy in 1988. Most of these initiatives were triggered by international agencies working for special education. These initiatives did contribute to the quantitative and qualitative improvement to some extent but a large part of the agenda in special education is still unfinished.

There were a number of factors that posed constraints in the implementation process. The first and foremost was a lack of reliable data. Another reason was the varying definition of disability. A factor that influenced the reliability of data was the hesitation of parents to share their children's disabilities with others. The third factor responsible for unreliable data was the defective methods used by untrained people to collect the data. Thus in the absence of reliable data the assessment process, which is a vital part of a policy, could not take place.

A number of good recommendations could not be put to practice because of the paucity of funds, absence of political will, lack of consistency and lack of proper legislative support. Though a number of policies underlined the significance of awareness about the issues relating to disabilities and persons with special needs, we see lack of a consistent and effective awareness from the media and other sources, in order to influence public opinion to appreciate the needs of special persons.

Another point which is highlighted by various policies is the need to bring persons with special needs to the mainstream. This is a challenging task for which consistent efforts are required. Such education will not only help the persons with special needs to gain confidence but also prepare people to appreciate their special needs and live without any bias. We see a quantitative expansion of institutions for special education which is certainly a positive contribution of public and private sectors but such institutions need to be strengthened in terms of qualitative improvement, e.g. curricula, teaching materials, and pedagogy.

Besides improvement of educational institutions, the policy emphasized the need for training parents. Parents should be given seminars and workshops for greater awareness about the nature of disabilities and requisite skills required to deal with emotional needs of their children.

SUMMARY

Special education is crucial for physically and mentally challenged students. The chapter discussed the rationale of special education in society in order to include special children in the mainstream population. It is important to note that the first education conference in 1947 did not mention the term special education but we see the recommendations in the 1959 Commission report for 'handicapped' children. The policies in the following years also announced initiatives in the domain of special education. The 1979 policy focused on special children and announced some practical measure for mainstreaming them. The two-pronged challenge that the policies faced was that on the one hand there was not much awareness among parents about the physical and mental challenges of their children and on the other hand there was a serious dearth of facilities for special children's education.

Chapter 11

Religious Education and *Madrasahs*

Religious and *madrasah* education has deep roots in the Indo-Pak subcontinent. Some famous centres of these *madrasahs* represent different sects of Islam, e.g. Deobandi, Barelvi, and Ahl-e-Hadees. Besides these three main branches of *madrasahs*, the Shias have their own *madrasahs*. Interestingly all these *madrasahs* have *Dars-i-Nizami*, though their curriculum and textbooks may vary. The British brought a parallel educational system to the subcontinent and since the British education system was more pragmatic in terms of government jobs, it gradually became more popular. After independence, one important question was where to place *madrasah* education vis-à-vis modern education.

The role of *madrasahs* took a new turn during the first Afghan War in the 1980s when *mujahideen,* mostly educated from *madrasahs,* were given money, equipment, and training to fight against the USSR in Afghanistan. *Madrasahs* were brought under close scrutiny after the 9/11 incident in 2001 as terrorism was supposedly linked with the inflexible education of *madrasahs.* It is important to note that the post-Afghan War discourse about *madrasahs* is critical of their curricula and pedagogies associated with them (Ahmed, 1993; Nayyar, 1998; Rahman, 2004). This, however, was not the case in United India where *madrasahs* used to cater to the educational needs of a large number of Muslims (Khalid, 2004). Most of the *madrasahs* would not only charge no fee but also provide food and shelter to the poor students. This chapter critically analyses the religious education and role of *madrasahs* as reflected in the education policies of Pakistan.

PAKISTAN EDUCATION CONFERENCE, 1947

The conference, apart from discussing other important educational challenges faced by Pakistan, also deliberated on religious education. The conference (GoP, 1947: 38) resolved that 'religious instruction should be compulsory for Muslim students in schools. Attendance at religious instruction should be compulsory or Muslim students in colleges. The same facilities may be provided for other communities in respect of their religions should they so desire.' As far as *madrasah* education was concerned the conference recommended that the provincial and state governments be asked to take steps to bring *madrasahs* in line with the existing system of general education. Bringing *madrasah* education in line with general education was important not only in terms of exposure to contemporary subjects but also in terms of enhancing job/life chances of students. This, however, was not an easy task for two reasons. Firstly there was a wide gap between the curricula of *madrasahs* and schools and secondly there was resistance by *madrasah* administrations who considered the general school system a symbol of imperialism.

OBJECTIVES RESOLUTION

In March 1949, a resolution 'Aims and Objectives of the Constitution', popularly known as the Objectives Resolution (Appendix-E), was passed by the Constituent Assembly of Pakistan which was made a substantive part of the Constitution of Pakistan by a presidential order. This resolution was debated for five days where non-Muslim members of the assembly expressed their concerns (Appendix-F). This resolution is a significant document that became an integral part of the Constitution of Pakistan and impacted the ideological vision of education policies.

COMMISSION ON NATIONAL EDUCATION, 1959

The commission report (GoP, 1959: 44) recommended that '... the educational system in Pakistan should be inspired by Islamic ideology emphasizing among many of its characteristics those of universal brotherhood, tolerance and justice.' The commission devoted one exclusive chapter to *maktab* and *madrasah* education. Following is the summary of the recommendations (GoP, 1959: 287):

1. The curricula of *maktabs, madrasahs* and *dar-ul-ulooms* are overloaded with courses in religion and allied subjects, without any regard to the needs of such studies as mathematics, science, social studies, and humanities.
2. At the elementary stage, education must be broad based and the curricula of *maktabs, madrasahs* and *dar-ul-ulooms* should make due provision for subjects of study which will give their students some training for the vocational or professional courses they may later choose to follow. At the higher levels these institutions must present Islam as a dynamic and progressive movement which can endure through changing times. The dynamic spirit of Islam can be imbibed only if Islam is presented in every age in the light of the latest advances of science, philosophy, economics, and contemporary history.
3. As these institutions have themselves become conscious of the need for change, they should not find it difficult to adapt their curriculum to the requirements of our complex society and present Islam in a way that is acceptable to the rational mind. The 1959 Commission report reiterated the need to revisit the curricula of *madrasahs* and bring in subjects that are contemporary and useful. The report hoped that the change would not be difficult but in reality it was not an easy task because of the rigid stand of *madrasah* owners who preferred to stick to same old curricula and would not allow space to accommodate contemporary subjects.

PROPOSALS FOR A NEW EDUCATIONAL POLICY, 1969

The proposals for A New Educational Policy referred to the conflicting educational systems, modern versus classical, in Pakistan. According to the 1969 proposals (GoP, 1969: 1):

> Remote as these Madrasahs are from the trends of secular education, they have also been found wanting in serving the needs of Pakistan. In view of this it is necessary to re-structure completely [the] educational system in light of the present day national requirements.

The 1969 proposals suggested that Islamiat be made a compulsory subject up to class X and an optional subject beyond class X. It was also recommended that universities should be engaged in Islamic research. For *madrasahs*, the 1969 proposal recommended that '... the teaching of mathematics and science subjects should be introduced in 'madrasahs' and special programmes should be undertaken to train their existing teachers to teach such modern subjects.' (GoP, 1969: 3). The 1969 proposal also addressed the issue of equivalence of degrees of *madrasahs* and other educational institutions and proposed that, 'equivalence should be established between the various stages of *madrasah* education and those of modern education, so that the products of *madrasahs* can obtain all those jobs which, at present, are available only to those who have had modern education.'(ibid). Another important recommendation was setting up a Madrasah Education Board to regulate *madrasahs*. It is important to note that such a board was working in East Pakistan but *madrasahs* in West Pakistan were working without a board. The 1969 proposal also recommended that the new education policy should nationalize the missionary schools as they were responsible for emergence of a secular class.

THE NEW EDUCATION POLICY, 1970

The policy (GoP, 1970: 14) stated that there were over 4,000 *madrasahs* in East Pakistan. The breakup of these *madrasahs* is given in Table 13:

Table 13: *Madrasahs* and Levels of Education

Number of *Madrasahs* in East Pakistan	Level of courses offered
3,000	Primary level courses
1,000	Secondary level courses
A few *madrasahs*	Kamil or college level courses

According to the 1970 policy (GoP, 1970: 14) there were 4,000 *madrasahs* in East Pakistan with 600,000 students, whereas in West Pakistan there were about 700 *maktab* type institutions and only a few higher level *madrasahs*. The policy claimed that eminent *ulema* and principals and teachers were amenable to the reorganization of *madrasahs* to one of the streams of national education with a proper board of administration in each province for designing their curricula, conducting examinations, and preparing textbooks. The policy shared that transition needed caution and thus both the provinces suggested forming committees to look into the challenges of the transition phase. The reorganization of the courses needed to be done without impairing their distinctive character as institutions of Islamic learning. The policy also observed that as a number of *madrasahs* are run privately, any reorganization should be made in a persuasive manner instead of through an executive directive.

The 1970 policy also made some recommendations for general religious education, such as giving religious instruction an important place in general education, redesigning curricula to reflect Islam as a dynamic force of unity and progress, strengthening of Islamic departments in higher education institutions to produce students well-versed with religion as well as responsive to the challenges of the contemporary world and *madrasahs* to be developed and standardized without impairing their distinctive character as institutions of Islamic learning.

The measures recommended by the 1970 policy (GoP, 1970: 15) also included committees in the provinces to suggest how the curricula and the courses of studies in *madrasahs* should be revised with a view to:

(i) establishing an equivalence between the courses offered in *madrasahs* and in institutions of general education, and
(ii) enabling their products to be assimilated in the economic life of the nation; and examine the question of strengthening the organizational set-up and giving a statutory status to the Madrasah Education Board in East Pakistan and the development of institutional arrangements for the same purpose for the provinces of West Pakistan.

THE EDUCATION POLICY, 1972

The 1972 policy was launched after Bangladesh had emerged as an independent country and was no more a part of Pakistan. More than four thousand *madrasahs* situated in East Pakistan (Bangladesh) were now excluded from future policies. The policy (GoP, 1972: 37) made the following recommendations for *madrasahs* and religious education:

1. The study of Islamiat will be compulsory for Muslim students up to class X. Steps will be taken to ensure that the curricula and textbooks for all stages do not contain anything repugnant to, or inconsistent with, the cultural and ethical values of Islam. It will also be ensured that the study of Islamiat does not remain an isolated item in the school curriculum but that the values and the spirit of Islam are woven into the entire warp and weft of our educational fabric.
2. The chief aim of religious instruction will be to enable the students to develop a positive way and code of life which combines into itself the rich heritage of our past and fulfils the hopes, aspirations, and ideals of our future. In promoting this objective, a great burden of responsibility will devolve on parents to provide, inside the home, suitable training and environment to serve as a base for the development of proper religious attitudes in the minds of their children.
3. The new educational radio and televisions channels will devote substantial time to the recitation of the Holy Qur'an

and its translation. Educational institutions run by religious societies may continue to function provided they comply with the regulations governing the operation of privately-managed schools/colleges.

4. Status quo will be maintained in respect of institutions imparting exclusively religions instruction such as *maktabs, madrasahs, dar-ul-ulooms*, etc. run by Muslims and similar institutions run by any other religious denomination.

It is important to note that the recommendation of revisiting curricula of *madrasahs* and including subjects of modern education made in 1947 report was still a dream to be realized. The 1972 policy stated that that no change would take place and the status quo would prevail in case of *madrasahs* and missionary educational institutions.

NATIONAL EDUCATIONAL POLICY AND IMPLEMENTATION PROGRAMME, 1979

The 1979 policy was significant because Zia ul-Haq had decided to islamize the educational system of Pakistan. The 1979 policy came up with enthusiastic recommendations about religious education and *madrasahs*. The policy stated that *maktabs*, *madrasahs*, and *dar-ul-ulooms* would no longer be neglected as they used to be in the past and all the facilities and concessions which were available to the students of other institutions would be extended to their students as well. One major recommendation was the recognition of *asnad* (degrees) of the *madrasah* for the purposes of higher education and the affiliation of *madrasahs* with education boards. To take up these major recommendations it was proposed to set up a high-powered national committee. The proposed committee (GoP, 1979: 44–5) would undertake the following:

- Constitution of study groups for exploring the possibilities of creating a *madrasah* board for standardization and uniformity of teaching and certification;

- making recommendations about the possibilities of introducing common curriculum in primary schools and *maktabs;*
- to undertake a comprehensive survey of all the *deeni madaris* by levels of teaching, classification, and available facilities;
- to make recommendations regarding the integration, improvement and modernization of curricula;
- to assess the needs of these institutions and make recommendations to the government for grants, scholarships, and loans;
- to evaluate existing programmes and suggest methods and means to introduce the element of skill development, and
- to conduct a survey of the existing physical facilities and make recommendations for critical/marginal inputs to improve these self-financing institutions.

EDUCATIONAL POLICY, 1992

The major recommendations of the 1992 policy (GoP, 1992: 15) on the strategy for religious education included:

- pre-service and in-service training to disseminate Islamic teachings in classroom;
- moral education based on Islamic values as a main theme of the Islamic curricula;
- the work and contribution of Muslim philosophers as a compulsory part of the teaching of Islamic curricula;
- emphasis of educational institutions on character building, high moral values, and societal development, based on the injunctions of the Qur'an and Sunnah;
- a second PTV channel to disseminate information about the worldview of Islam and Islamic values;
- Institutes of education and research to open separate centres for undertaking research on the contents of Islamic education for inclusion in courses at various levels, and on methods of teaching Islamic ideology;

- preparation of video cassettes of special lectures by high ranking Islamic scholars and scientists would be prepared and broadcast through electronic media;
- emphasis on the Holy Qur'an along with detailed commentary at secondary and post-secondary levels, and
- implementation of recommendations of the Commission on Islamization of Education after approval of the parliament.

NATIONAL EDUCATION POLICY, 1998–2010

As we see in all the education policy documents since 1947, the biggest challenge for the state remained making general and *madrasah* education amenable to each other. The 1998 policy (GoP, 1998: 14) recommended:

> ... the establishment of Deeni Madaris Board for uniform standards of *Deeni* Madrasah education through registration, standardization of curricula and examination system, equivalence of *asnad* (degrees), award of foreign scholarships, grant-in-aid and financial assistance by the government.

The policy also promised the establishment of model *dar-ul-uloom* at divisional levels to absorb the graduates of *madrasahs*. The existing Sheikh Zayed Islamic Centres at Lahore, Karachi, and Peshawar Universities were promised to be converted to *madrasahs* by introducing *dars-i-nizami,* along with modern subjects as well as technical and vocational subjects.

The policy (GoP, 1998: 15) recommended that, in order to integrate the general education with *madrasah* education, subjects like English, mathematics, general science, economics, and Pakistan studies should be included in the curricula of *deeni madaris* and their *asnad* at matric, intermediate, and graduate levels shall be equated with formal education. All the willing *madrasahs* would be provided suitable financial assistance for payment of salaries to the teachers. The policy also recommended that the students of affiliated *madrasahs* shall be given the same facilities and concessions which are available to the students of formal education.

NATIONAL EDUCATION POLICY, 2009

The 2009 policy was launched one year after the exit of Pervez Musharraf, though it was largely prepared during Musharraf's regime. The issue of *madrasahs* had come to the limelight after the 9/11 incident in 2001 and large scale reforms were made to de-radicalize the *madrasahs*. For such reforms, substantial aid was given to Musharraf government by the US government.

The 2009 policy, like the previous policy documents, confronted the challenge of compatibility of *madrasah* education with general education. The policy recommended the introduction of formal subjects, including market-oriented and skills-based subjects, to *madrasah* education to enable the children graduating from *deeni madrasahs* to have more employment options. The policy (GoP, 2009: 34) recommended the establishment of a *Madrasah* Education Authority with the following mandate:

- provision of an opportunity for all existing and future *madrasahs* to excel and enhance the services they already provide to the nation;
- provision of funds for education and socio-economic welfare of students;
- infrastructure and equipment for improvement of existing facilities;
- further training to enhance skills of teachers;
- support in vocational training to equip students to generate income, and
- advice and assistance in streamlining policies, objectives, and syllabi to give graduates a competitive edge in the job market and for placement in institutions of higher education.

ANALYSIS AND DISCUSSION

Religious education and *madrasahs* go far back in the Islamic tradition of learning. Over time we have seen different denominations in Islamic practices, namely Sunnis and Shias. There are further subdivisions among the Sunnis, such as Deobandi, Barelvi, and Ahle-Hadees. Each of these major denominations has its own *madrasahs*. Historically the differences in some areas of beliefs and practices could lead to friction but on the whole *madrasahs* were not linked with violence as they are viewed in recent times. The popularity of these *madrasahs* was due to a number of factors, i.e. religious, social, and economic factors. Those who were interested in religious education had the option of going to a *madrasah* in or around their neighbourhood. Since acquiring religious education would mean attaining a prestigious social status, in terms of following and influence, it was socially imperative to go to a prestigious *madrasah*. Besides religious and social reasons there was a major economic factor to join a *madrasah* as this would mean free lodging and bedding. Thus *madrasahs*, because of the religious, social, and economic reasons, emerged as an important social institution that could influence societal trends and perpetuate certain ideas and beliefs. It was this significant position of *madrasahs* that always compelled rulers deal with them tactfully.

During the Afghan War the *madrasah's* role was redefined by important stakeholders as *mujahideen* (religious fighters) were funded and encouraged to fight against Soviet forces in Afghanistan. The *mujahideen* were given money, weapons, and training to take part in the war (Cooley, 2000). It is during this war that the Taliban (literally meaning students or seekers of knowledge) were created and used to win the war. The scenario changed when after the war the Taliban, who were once lauded as heroes, were disowned by the United States of America. After the 9/11 incident in 2001, *madrasahs* were brought under close scrutiny. According to the 9/11 Commission Report (2002: 367), 'Millions of families, especially those with little money, send their children to religious schools or *madrasahs*. Many of these schools are the only opportunity available for an education, but some have been used as incubators for violent extremism.'

In almost all the education policies there is mention of Islamic studies being a mandatory subject. In the 1947 report of the Pakistan Education Conference, Islamiat was recommended as a compulsory subject whereas *madrasah* curricula were encouraged to include modern subjects. Revisiting the *madrasah* curricula and exposing the *madrasah* students to modern subjects was a continuous demand of almost all the education policies (GoP, 1947; GoP, 1959; GoP, 1969; GoP, 1970; GoP, 1992; GoP, 1998; GoP, 2009a). This recommendation to change curricula was based on the observation that the *madrasah* curricula were outdated and the textbooks which were being taught had little relevance to contemporary realities (Nayyar, 2004; Rahman, 2004).

The 1959 Commission on National Education observed that the *madrasah* curricula were overloaded with subjects which had no direct relevance to the students. This impression of disconnect was also mentioned in the 1969 document Proposals for a New Educational Policy suggesting that *madrasah* education was not only divorced from secular education but is also not fulfilling the needs of the country.

The social and economic prestige of *madrasahs* was affected because of the changing times and certification of knowledge by modern educational institutions and the requirements of degrees for jobs and higher education. The Proposals for a New Educational Policy (1969) raised the issue of equivalence of *madrasah asnad* (degrees), which was reiterated by the 1972 education policy. The issue, however, was resolved in the 1979 Education Policy where not only were *asnad* equated with degrees but it was announced that all facilities and concessions given to the other students must be given to *madrasah* students as well.

Besides outdated and unrevised reading material, pedagogical practices are also oriented towards a one-sided teaching method. Students are encouraged to conform and there is little space for disagreement or discussion. Bridging the gap between *madrasah* and modern education was a common recommendation of almost all the education policies. The 1959 Commission report was hopeful to see such union but over time it was realized that the task was not that easy as it was thought. In the 1972 Education policy it was admitted that status quo would be retained in respect of institutions imparting exclusively religious instructions.

According to Ahmed (1993) large numbers of *madrasahs* belong to four major subdivisions of Muslims, e.g. Barelvi, Deobandi,

Ahl-e-Hadees, and Shia. There are four boards to deal with the *madrasahs* registered with them. These boards included Wafaq ul Madaris, Multan (for Deobandi *madrasahs*), Tanzeem ul Madaris (for Barelvi *madrasahs*), Wafaq ul Madaris, Faisalabad (for Ahle-Hadees *madrasahs*), and Wafaq ul Madaris (for Shia *madrasahs*). These boards are responsible for registration, curriculum design, textbook recommendations, and conducting exams. It is important to note, however, that there are a number of *madrasahs* are not associated with any of the boards mentioned. A number of education policy documents (e.g. 1969, 1972, 1979, 1998, and 2009) stressed the need of a Central Board for *madrasahs* to monitor and control them. Despite recommendations in education policies there is no central board of *madrasah* education to administer *madrasahs* of all sects. Thus the major aspects regarding *madrasah* education revolving around integration, improvement, and modernization are still to be realized.

SUMMARY

Religious education and *madrasahs* were part of the traditional education in United India. One major advantage for the students going to *madrasahs* was free education, boarding, and lodging. Besides, there were social and religious reasons to opt for *madrasah* education. The chapter showed how religious education has always been one of the major objectives of the education policies of Pakistan. There was an early call (GoP, 1947) to bridge the gap of *madrasah* education and general education. But it remained a challenge for the different governments because of the different nature of curricula, textbooks, pedagogical, and assessment practices and the fixed mindset of important stakeholders. The role of *madrasahs* went under tremendous change during the Afghanistan war. The scrutiny process of *madrasahs* gained momentum after the 9/11 incident. There had been attempts to revisit the curricula of *madrasah* and bring all *madrasahs* under one board but a lot of work still needs to be done.

Chapter 12

Curricula and Textbooks

The concept of curriculum-building, as understood by decision-makers in the field, places primacy on creating a document that reflects the course of studies in terms of the content and activities to be covered in a stipulated period of time. This notion is not only incomplete but misleading as well. The direct outcome of such a notion is that every new government that embarks upon the task of educational reform immediately announces the re-engineering of curricula. The finalization of new curricula also implies that all educational problems are taken care of. The basic flaw in this approach to curriculum-building is that the implementation side is totally ignored (Siddiqui, 2010). Decision-makers tend to forget the important fact that it is the actual execution of curricula and not just the planning of them that truly makes a difference.

While reflecting on the term 'curriculum' we need not just look at the list of contents but at the teaching materials, procedures, and evaluations as well. Connelly and Clandinin (1988: 1) suggest that:

> Curriculum is often taken to mean a course of study. When we set our imaginations free from the narrow notion that a course of study is a series of textbooks or specific outline of topics to be covered and objectives to be attained, broader and more meaningful notions emerge.

Almost all the education policies of Pakistan acknowledged the significance of curriculum as an important component of education. In the following pages we will see the major recommendations by the policy documents of Pakistan.

PAKISTAN EDUCATIONAL CONFERENCE, 1947

The Pakistan Educational Conference, 1947 considered curriculum an important component of quality education. The conference proposed to prepare curricula for earlier classes so that girls and boys should be exposed to practical and academic subjects. The conference also recommended introducing domestic science and home nursing as compulsory subjects in the curriculum. The conference also alluded to the issues of equivalence of degrees and diplomas and the standardization of curriculum and syllabus. The conference proposed to design curricula which were relevant, interesting, intelligible, and situated in indigenous socio-economic conditions.

COMMISSION ON NATIONAL EDUCATION, 1959

The 1959 Commission on National Education discussed curricular issues in detail. Some major recommendations of the Commission (GoP, 1959: 175–6) regarding curricula included:

- courses taught to the child aged five plus to ten plus, should naturally be adapted to the mental abilities of this age group;
- curricula should include courses in simple science and social studies which will give the child an introductory knowledge of the world around him;
- curriculum construction and revision needs to be done with reference to evolving social and individual interests;
- teachers in Pakistan rely too much on centrally prepared textbooks and do not exercise sufficient initiative in finding material for their lessons in the resources of their village and the community around them;
- manual work, including gardening, home-making, and repairing school grounds, should be made compulsory in the primary school so as to nourish the habits of cooperative work and a sense of responsibility;
- there must be a strong emphasis on the proper learning of the National language at the primary stage.

The commission also made some major recommendations with respect to textbooks. According to the commission (GoP, 1959: 131):

- Textbooks should be prepared by a team comprising a practicing teacher, subject specialist, language specialist, and an artist for illustrative material.
- Textbooks should be prescribed in all subjects up to class XII.
- Appropriate education authorities should undertake the preparation of textbooks and acquire their copyrights.
- Education authorities should also control the printing and publishing of textbooks in respect of price, paper, format, and illustrations, self-publishing or using publishers who have sufficient resources in terms of technical staff, distribution, and production of books of good quality at the most economical prices.
- Libraries should be established by education authorities containing a wide sample of foreign textbooks, periodical literature containing articles relating to school publications, and reference material in the several subjects included in the school curriculum.
- The Ministry of Education should set up a Textbook Board as a small, autonomous body with representatives from the provinces, which would work through textbook committees operating within the sphere of each education authority, to establish policies for the preparation, printing, and publication of textbooks; and use a portion of the funds from the sale of textbooks to publish (i) reference and research material, (ii) guidebooks for teachers, and (iii) supplementary material relating to textbooks.

PROPOSALS FOR A NEW EDUCATIONAL POLICY, 1969

The 1969 policy document proposed a uniform national structure of education from the elementary level to the university; the standardization of the syllabi and courses for each class for adoption throughout the country, with variations allowed for regional and local colour; and the development of a range of standard textbooks, not by one but by several authors, together with back-up material to be studied as side-reading. It was also proposed to set up committees of scholars, writers and educationists to draw up the standard courses and syllabi so that printing and distribution of books and reading material may be completed in time for the 1970–71 session.

EDUCATION POLICY, 1970

The 1970 policy stated that the curriculum should be inspired by Pakistan's national objectives and curricula at all levels should be redesigned by designated curriculum committees. The curricula of elementary schools should aim to establish basic linguistic and numerical skills and also feature manual and productive work to suit the practical needs of everyday life. The policy recommended setting up a Bureau of Curriculum Development for the continuous evaluation of curricula and coordination. The policy also encouraged the development of more than one textbook on a subject and permission to private publishers to publish textbooks approved by the textbook boards. The Commission also recommended setting up libraries in schools and in communities.

EDUCATION POLICY, 1972

The 1972 Education Policy recommended that curricula be relevant to the nation's changing social and economic needs and compatible with the basic ideology of the country, endorsing a massive shift from general education to more purposeful agro-technical education. The policy proposed to strengthen and reorganize the National Curriculum Bureau and establish the Curriculum Centre Province to review and update curricula for all stages of education. It promised revision of curricula for elementary and secondary stages to eliminate overloading, emphasize learning of concepts and skills, and encourage observation, exploration, experimentation, practical work, and creative expression through representative committees of specialists, lecturers, practicing teachers, and curriculum research experts.

The policy recommended establishing the National Foundation for Book Production in order to undertake writing, editing, compiling, translating, printing, and publishing both textbooks and reading material for schools, colleges, adult students and the general public. The policy announced adequate provision for well-equipped libraries to be established in all educational institutions. The 1972 Policy made some important recommendations for textbooks including provision of free textbooks and writing materials to primary school children, and provision of adequate library books, educational toys, and other audio-visual aids to all schools.

EDUCATION POLICY, 1979

The 1979 Education Policy contained an exclusive chapter entitled 'Curriculum and Textbooks'. The policy aimed at Islamizing education, and adjusting curricula was considered an important means to do so. The policy stated that curricula, textbooks, and instruction would be revised to ensure that 'Islamic ideology is protected, the concept of nationhood is reflected, and high academic standards are maintained.' The policy also emphasized the need to reorganize the Textbook Boards to improve their efficiency, and create an effective liaison between the National Book Foundation and the Textbook Boards. Some major recommendations of the 1979 (GoP, 1979: 56–7) policy related to curriculum and textbooks included:

- the revision of entire curricula and textbooks to ensure inclusion of adequate content on Islam, the ideology of Pakistan, the promotion of national cohesion and integration;
- undertaking evaluative studies of the existing curricula;
- the introduction of integrated curricula and textbooks in class I and II;
- the preparation of supplementary reading materials for children and teacher guides;
- provision of laboratory equipment and instructional aids;

- the constitution of a Standing Committee of the National Education Council on Curriculum and Textbooks;
- the review by the Ministry of Education of all the textbooks prescribed by the English medium schools;
- requiring prior approval of textbooks and auxiliary materials by the Ministry of Education;
- examining the possibilities of introduction of common textbooks in selected subjects at different levels;
- the reorganization of Textbooks Boards to improve the quality of textbooks and to ensure their in-time availability; and
- the development of adequate facilities for printing, storage and distribution.

EDUCATION POLICY, 1992

The 1992 policy (GoP, 1992: 8) acknowledged the significant role of the curriculum in educational development and proposed:

- starting a new cycle of curriculum development at all levels of education;
- bringing about cognitive compatibility between one level of curriculum and the next;
- eliminating unnecessary overcrowding of subjects in curricula;
- allowing the production of textbooks in the private sector with the possibility of different books to be prescribed by different institutions;
- encouraging enquiry, creativity, and progressive thinking through project-oriented education;
- relating vocational curricula to the employment market;
- reinforcing linkages among curriculum development;
- reinforcement of textbook writing, teacher training, and examinations;
- introducing a special mathematics course for students studying social science;

- improving teaching of languages in order to enhance communication skills;
- improving teaching of social sciences in content and quality; and
- introducing the teaching of Islamic philosophical thought at secondary and tertiary levels.

The 1992 policy (GoP, 1992: 25) further proposed actions to improve the quality of textbooks. Some of these actions included:

- revision of textbooks to incorporate new knowledge;
- coordination of curriculum development and book development;
- adoption of workshop technique to develop new books;
- provision of incentives to teachers for producing new and attractive learning materials;
- making use of audio, video, and print media;
- expansion of the scheme of textbook banks to include all educational institutions;
- approval of multiple textbooks for each course;
- launch of special development projects for improving the libraries in schools, general and professional colleges and universities;
- provision of matching grants to communities to set up libraries for the use of the common public; and
- separate budget for books and journals in the annual budget of each educational institution.

EDUCATION POLICY, 1998

The 1998 Education Policy contained a separate chapter entitled 'Curriculum and Learning Materials'. The policy proposed that the curriculum should be based on two principles, (a) provision of compulsory core subjects to give every pupil the knowledge useful for a developing society, and (b) inclusion of additional subjects and training to prepare the student for a definite career. The policy proposed that the curriculum for the secondary stage would aim at stimulating problem-solving and independent thinking. Supplementary teaching/reading and other educational classroom materials would be prepared based on the relevance of various concepts to life. The policy realized the problem of the monopoly of provincial textbook boards over production and distribution of textbooks. The policy (GoP, 1998: 44–5) observed that:

> The textbooks are written in a very traditional manner. Due to the absence of healthy competition, the Boards have not considered the possibility of introducing innovation in their production. It is time to give new orientation to the whole process. In the first instance, the entire style of writing textbooks will be transformed. In order to perform that operation effectively, the Ministry of Education will design models for evaluation of textbooks in selected disciplines at secondary level and conduct a model trial. The tried out textbooks will then be handed over to the private publishers and the Provincial Textbook Boards for designing their textbooks accordingly.

The 1998 policy suggested integrating technical education into general education gradually and carefully, starting with limited number of technologies.

EDUCATION POLICY, 2009

The Education Policy 2009, in the wake of 9/11, proposed major changes in the national curriculum. Some of the proposed recommendations of the 2009 policy (GoP, 2009: 45) included:

- reflection on important social issues;
- provision of more room for developing the capacity for self-directed learning, the spirit of inquiry, critical thinking, problem-solving, and team-work;
- standardization of curriculum and textbook review processes;
- involvement of professional councils like Pakistan Medical and Dental Council (PM&DC) and Pakistan Engineering Council (PEC) in consultations for relevant curriculum development;

- emphasis on the fundamental rights guaranteed to the citizens of Pakistan in the curriculum;
- making environmental education an integral part of educational syllabi;
- promoting the use of Information Communication Technologies (ICTs) in education;
- giving awareness about emerging trends and concepts such as school health, prevention education against HIV/AIDS and other infectious diseases, life skills education, environmental education, population and development education, human rights education, school safety and disaster and risk management, peace education and inter-faith harmony, detection and prevention of child abuse;
- infusing school health education and school safety in the curriculum;
- introducing entrepreneurial studies to develop entrepreneurial and business skills in students of general education;
- an ongoing feedback and evaluation mechanism; and
- introducing the matric-tech scheme at secondary level.

TEXTBOOKS AND LEARNING MATERIALS

A comprehensive document entitled *National Textbook and Learning Materials Policy and Plan of Action* was prepared in June 2007. The rationale of this exercise was stated as:

> Improvement in the quality of education at all levels through better quality textbooks at affordable prices and other learning materials for promoting Pakistan as a knowledge-based society … Choice and competition are major forces in achieving this objective. Choice on the part of the buyer promotes acquisition of knowledge, empowerment and participation. Competition on the part of the producer leads to a wider variety of products, improved quality, availability and better prices' (GoP, 2007: 18).

The 2009 Policy (GoP, 2009: 46–7) proposed some important actions with regards to the textbooks including:

- introduction of a well regulated system of competitive publishing of textbooks and learning materials;
- transformation of textbook boards into competent facilitating, regulating, and monitoring authorities;
- formation of a provincial/area committee comprising representatives of the education authorities, textbook boards, the private sector, teachers, and other stakeholders to select and prescribe textbooks for use in public schools in their respective province or areas of jurisdiction;
- private sector schools shall be free to use from amongst the books authorized by the respective textbook board;
- provision of assistance in capacity development for the national and/or provincial publishing industry to become competitive players in an expanded education publishing market; and
- assurance by the government for the availability of quality paper at reasonable cost for printing of textbooks.

ANALYSIS AND DISCUSSION

The curriculum issue has been discussed in all the major policy documents of Pakistan. The 1947 policy document flagged some important issues regarding curriculum. There are some themes which recur in most of the policy documents. Almost all the policies, with varying degrees of emphasis, recommended that Islam should be the guiding principle of curricula and textbooks. In the 1970 policy the guiding principle was 'national objectives' which remained an unexplained and abstract notion. The 1979 policy was conspicuous because of its extra emphasis on Islamizing curricula, textbooks, and teacher education. The influence of this policy could be seen for a long time in the curricula and textbooks (Riaz, 2011). Pervez Musharraf's era prepared a draft policy which didn't have a separate chapter on Islamic education. Following protest and pressure of the religious sects, a separate chapter on Islamic Education was added in the final draft of the policy.

The compatibility of curricula with the mental level of students was another point of concern for education policies. This issue was first raised in the 1947 conference as the conference emphasized that curricula should be cognizant of the mental capacity of students. This point was flagged again by the report prepared by the 1959 Commission on National Education.

The relevance of curriculum is another theme which was discussed by some major policy documents. One level of relevance is the inclusion of themes, topics, and courses that are contemporary. In the 1947 conference, it was recommended to include the subjects of special interest for girls. In the 2009 Education Policy, a recommendation was made to include subjects highlighting important emerging issues, such as environmental education, life skills based education, and HIV/AIDS, etc. The other level of relevance is the link with an indigenous context. This concern is also highlighted by subsequent education policies. A third level of relevance is the practical nature of curricula. This point was underscored at the 1947 conference and later the commission highlighted the practical aspects of education and recommended hand crafts. Such emphasis on hand crafts was a hallmark of the series of *Nai Taleem* (New Education) schools opened and patronized by Gandhi in United India. The practical nature of curricula was also emphasised by the 1969 Proposals for a New Educational Policy.

The issue of standardization is another aspect of curricula which has been a point of concern for different education policies. The 1947 conference recommended having standard curricula for all classes. This concern resurfaced in the 1969 Proposal for a New Educational Policy. The process of preparation of curriculum seems to be another theme in most of the education policies. The 1970 policy recommended establishing a Bureau of Curriculum to look after the activities related to curricula. The 1972 education policy recommended further strengthening the Bureau of Curriculum.

Most of the education policies in Pakistan emphasize just one aspect of a curriculum, i.e. the preparation of a document for which committees are formed and experts are gathered. But what about the real curriculum that is used every day in the real setting? There seems to be less emphasis on this aspect, i.e. the construction of curriculum as a result of interaction among teacher, materials, students, and school milieu. Do we have proper teacher education programmes which focus on developing reflective practitioners? Do we have an appropriate system of monitoring? Are we satisfied with the process of evaluation of curriculum? Are we considering teachers' role as central to the curriculum? Before we try to find answers to these questions, we need to 'unseat' our notion of curriculum as a cold and mysterious document which sits on the shelf of a policymaker or in the cupboard of the head teacher and gathers dust. A curriculum is much more than that. It is a living and vibrant phenomenon of which students, teachers, teaching materials, and school culture are important components.

Since textbooks are manifestations of a curriculum, education policies generally discuss the issue of textbooks along with the discussion of curricula. Writing a textbook is a highly technical job which requires teamwork and detailed planning. This process entails different steps to ensure quality. In Pakistan, however, the textbooks used in mainstream public schools do not follow a systematic writing process and thus pose a number of problems including content, language, organization, and presentation.

The content may not be sensitive in terms of gender, ethnicity, social class, and religion. The language may be complex in terms of vocabulary, syntax, and semantics and can be biased against certain social groups (Siddiqui, 2010). The organization could be in violation of pedagogical principles of moving from simple to difficult or concrete to abstract and the treatment could be insensitive to the sociopolitical fabric of marginalized groups of society. These potential textbooks problems could be aggravated in the conservative paradigm of education where the whole emphasis is on transmission rather than transformation and teachers find themselves passive followers of these books. Neither teachers nor students, in this paradigm, dare to step out of the holy circle of textbooks. In this paradigm the chances of developing independent thinking are minimal.

The central question that needs to be raised is why one fixed textbook should be used if the objectives of the curriculum could be realized better by using an alternative textbook. The idea of using alternative books is to break the hegemony of one fixed textbook written by a certain writer and offer a variety of choices to the teachers and students instead. The diversity of teaching materials on the one hand can create positive competition among writers and publishers, which is currently non-existent, and on the other hand can provide freedom of choice to schools to select a book that they think is more relevant to their environment and is more sensitive to the sociocultural identities and beliefs of their students.

The 1959 Commission on National Education recommended establishing a textbook board. The commission also emphasized that writing textbooks is a team process. The 1969 proposals for a new educational policy recommended books by several authors. To create more space for teachers and students, the 1970 Policy proposed to encourage more than one textbook. The policy also recommended permitting private publishers to publish textbooks. The 1972 Policy proposed to set up a National Book Foundation responsible for publishing books and also announced the provision of free books to schools. The policy underlined the need to reorganize the textbook board and recommended the constitution of a National Education Council. The 1992 Policy recommended allowing the production of more books in the private sector. The policy announced the designing of models of evaluation of textbooks by the Ministry of Education.

Despite recommendations by different policies (e.g. GoP, 1970; GoP, 1992) textbook writing and publishing remained a highly bureaucratic affair and private publishers were not allowed to bid for the textbooks. In 2007, during Musharraf's regime, the Ministry of Education released a document titled 'National Textbook and Learning Materials Policy and Plan of Action', which allowed private publishers to bid for the writing and publishing of books.

SUMMARY

A curriculum is considered to be one of the major components of education. Books are a direct manifestation of the curricula. Subsequent education policies of Pakistan discussed the issues related to curricula but their perception of a curriculum was limited and confined only to the topics prescribed in the curriculum. The textbooks which were used, especially in the mainstream public educational institutions were, by and large, not relevant, contemporary, and intellectually challenging in terms of contemporary information. The format, paper quality, and quality of visuals were also questionable. For a long time private publisher's books were not used as textbooks. Besides textbooks, the actual execution of the curriculum is important. No matter how many education policies come up with wonderful ideas about the curriculum, the real part is its execution and that largely depends on the quality of teachers.

Chapter 13

Teachers and Teacher Education

There has been a growing realization of the pivotal role of teachers in the teaching and learning process. Connelly and Clandinin (1988) suggest that among the four commonplace elements of a curriculum, i.e. students, teachers, teaching materials, and school milieus, teachers, because of their central position, can play a significant role in enhancing and enriching the given curriculum. Contemporary research from developing and developed countries supports the pivotal role of teachers in improving the quality of education. Pakistan, since its independence in 1947 faced some serious challenges in the domain of education, with the shortage of qualified teachers being one of them. On the one hand, schools did not have a full quota of teachers and on the other hand most of the teachers were not properly qualified. This problem was more acute in case of female education as there were not many qualified female teachers available. Another aspect of the problem was the low motivation levels of school teachers due to a lack of incentives, which impacted their performance.

Since teacher education has been considered crucial for the improvement of the educational system of a country, all the education policies and plans underscored the importance of teacher education and proposed measures for teacher empowerment. The policies seemed to grapple with the issues related to a shortage of teachers, teacher education, supply challenge in case of female teachers, low social status of teachers, low income of teachers, and lack of linkage between research and teaching. This chapter offers a critical review of the major policy documents with special reference to teachers and teacher education, identifies inter-policy tensions, and explores factors responsible for the failure in achieving the promised targets.

PAKISTAN EDUCATIONAL CONFERENCE, 1947

The Pakistan Educational Conference was held from 27 November to 1 December 1947 to deliberate on the major educational challenges faced by the nascent country. A number of committees were formed for specialized discussions on different educational issues. The committee responsible for teachers and teacher education underlined the importance of trained and well-paid teachers. The committee (1947: 24) recommended that, '... [a] sufficient number of first-rate teachers training institutes for women be established by the government at the various educational centres in Pakistan for imparting special training in the teaching of nursery and primary classes.' The committee recommended proper training of teachers and adequate scales of salary. The committee also realized the need for a large number of trained teachers and thus recommended short-term teacher training courses and underlined the need of research departments along with training institutions to have a proper blend of theory and practice. To encourage candidates to join the teaching profession, the report recommended that scholarships may be given for teacher education programmes.

This first ever policy document touched upon some important issues related to teachers in the educational system of Pakistan. These recommendations included:

- aggressive efforts to recruit teachers;
- setting up first class teacher education institutes for the training of teachers;
- offering short-term courses;
- improving the conditions of service in various types of schools;
- increasing the salary of teachers;
- giving incentives to persuade qualified people to join the teaching profession;

- stepping up efforts to arrange qualified female teachers for schools;
- provision of properly trained female teachers to nursery and pre-primary schools; and
- adding research departments to training institutes.

The report of the Pakistan Educational Conference (1947) diagnosed relevant issues and offered some recommendations but the new born country faced turbulent political events that impacted the implementation of the policy. The death of Quaid-i-Azam Muhammad Ali Jinnah in 1948 and the rapid changes in the governments afterwards could not maintain the implementation process of the recommendations given by the Pakistan Educational Conference report. Table 14 summarizes the progress made with respect to teachers and teacher education between 1948–49 and 1954–55.

Table 14: Teacher Training Facilities: A Comparison of 1948–49 and 1954–55

Teacher Training	1948–49	1954–55
Primary teachers' training institutions	125	106
Annual enrolment	6,145	7,500
Total number of trained primary school teachers	35,000	75,000
Institutions for training secondary school teachers	11	22
Annual enrolment	700	1,000
Total number of trained secondary school teachers	17,500	22,500

Source: First Five-Year Plan (GoP, 1955: 541).

Keeping in view the emphasis laid on the production of trained teachers in the 1947 Pakistan Educational Conference, this performance was disappointing. The conference had lamented the poor social status and low salaries of teachers and had proposed to raise salaries and improve their service condition. The First Five-Year Plan (GoP, 1955: 561) stated that the Advisory Board of Education had 'recommended a minimum starting salary of Rs. 60 for primary teachers and Rs. 120 for secondary school teachers plus cost of living allowances in both cases.' This suggests that the recommendations of the conference regarding the preparation of an enhanced number of trained teachers and better salaries were not implemented in letter and spirit.

Despite the claims of the First Five-Year Plan, the plan period was a disappointment as far as teachers and teacher education was concerned. The number of primary teacher training institutes, instead of going up, declined from ninety-seven to seventy-five. The annual output of primary teachers was 7,400 in 1954–56 and remained the same after the five-year period. In case of secondary school teachers only two colleges could be added to the existing number of colleges making the total number twenty-three.

At the end of the next Five-Year Plan period there was slight improvement in some areas, e.g. teachers' entry qualification, in general, was raised to matriculation, postgraduate classes were introduced in the Dhaka, Lahore, and Karachi, and a department of education was opened in Rajshahi. Table 15 summarizes the progress made with respect to teachers and teacher education during the plan period.

Table 15: Teacher Training Facilities: A Comparison of 1954–55 and 1959–60

Teacher Training	1954–55	1959–60
Primary teacher training institutes	97	75
Teacher training colleges	21	23
Annual output (primary teachers)	7,400	7,400
Annual output (secondary teachers)	1,300	1,800

Source: Second Five-Year Plan (GoP, 1960: 338).

COMMISSION ON NATIONAL EDUCATION, 1959

In 1958 Field Marshal Ayub Khan imposed martial law in Pakistan and as part of a reform programme set up a Commission on National Education in 1959. The problem of shortage of teachers, which was identified and focused in the Pakistan Educational Conference in 1947, was still an insurmountable challenge. The commission (GoP, 1959: 17) observed that, 'Good buildings are of little use without good teachers. Steps must be taken to increase the number of qualified teachers, of whom we have far too few.' The commission in its detailed report laid stress on teacher training, which compared with the 1947 report that outlined the need for teacher training, discussed at length the significant role of teachers and teacher education and recommended laying emphasis on certain aspects of teacher education programmes to make them more effective. The commission (GoP 1959: 274) identified some essential attributes of an effective teacher, e.g. 'a sound grasp of the subjects, knowledge of child psychology and insight into the growth and behaviour of children at various stages of their lives, the methodology of teaching and the skill to use up-to-date techniques and a high sense of professional ethics.'

The commission recommended in-service teacher education programmes and refresher courses for keeping the teachers abreast with contemporary knowledge. It laid emphasis on the role of research in teacher education and recommended postgraduate study in education at the doctorate level in some universities. It made two major recommendations in this regard, which were instituting fundamental academic research in training colleges and university departments of education and setting up a Council of Educational Research at the centre to coordinate and stimulate research work on education. Besides professional empowerment of teachers, the commission (GoP, 1959: 275) proposed steps to enhance extrinsic motivation of teachers as well, e.g. setting up a scale of salary consistent with qualification and experience, social status, and provision of benefits like a provident fund and retirement benefits.

The commission, similar to the 1947 Pakistan Educational Conference, emphasized the significant role of 'content knowledge' of teachers as pedagogical skills can only be effective if the teachers are familiar with the content of the subject (GoP, 1959: 1047). The commission also emphasized the need for research in teacher education and a strong link between teaching and research. Another important recommendation of the commission was to offer postgraduate education for teachers. In line with the Pakistan Educational Conference and the commission two Institutes of Education and Research (IERs) were set up in Lahore and Dhaka (then capital of East Pakistan, now capital of Bangladesh) with the help of Indiana University, USA. After the initial positive start, the IERs were turned into traditional teacher education institutes where 'trained teachers' were churned out without acquiring the balance between theory and practice and research and teaching. We see some initiatives as a result of the commission report but the major issues of teachers' availability, their socio-economic status, shortage of female teachers, and developing a strong link between teaching and learning remained inaccessible targets.

PROPOSALS FOR A NEW EDUCATIONAL POLICY, 1969

The Proposals for A New Educational Policy, prepared by a committee during Yahya Khan's rule (25 March 1969–20 December 1971), acknowledged the central role of teachers in the educational system of the country. The policy (GoP, 1969: 6) acknowledged the important role of teachers and observed that a teacher's, '... position in society must be such as to attract the best of its products to teaching. If this is not so, academic standards must fall.' The policy identified the problems faced by the teachers, e.g. low salaries, lack of intellectual freedom, dependence on bureaucrats for appointments, promotions, and transfers. The policy (GoP, 1969: 7) put forth recommendations to uplift the teachers' status including:

- discontinuation of the practice of placing teachers in class I, class II, class III, etc.;

- a raise in teachers' salaries comparable to those of other services and professions;
- one National Pay Scale for the teaching profession with different segments for different qualifications, experience, and ability;
- discontinuation of the practice of transferring teachers like ordinary government servants;
- delegation of financial powers within approved budgets and establishment of an effective teachers' voice in the governance of educational institutions;
- full autonomy in the establishment of universities. and
- establishment of a University Grants Commissions in the provinces.

The policy also emphasized that the Educational Research Institutes should be strengthened. Some of the recommendations, e.g. raising salaries, better working conditions, and links between research and teaching, etc. were highlighted by the Pakistan Educational Conference in 1947 and the Commission on National Education in 1959. It was thus strange to notice that the 1969 policy (GoP, 1969: 6) claimed that 'The educational policies of Pakistan have never taken account of this fact.' The fact remains that the previous policies did acknowledge the significant role of teachers and gave some useful recommendations but during the period of 1947–1969 the recommendations could not be implemented properly.

The 1969 policy, apart from reiterating some previous recommendations, focused on the teachers' intellectual freedom and emphasized reducing bureaucratic influence on them. The policy proposed a National Pay Scale for the teaching profession with different segments for different qualifications, experience, and ability. One very important recommendation put forth by the 1969 policy was that universities should be given more autonomy and a University Grants Commissions should be set up in the provinces.

THE NEW EDUCATION POLICY, 1970

The New Education Policy, 1970 (GoP, 1970: 2) acknowledged 'the paramount importance of quality in education and the crucial role of teachers in the improvement of educational quality.' It proposed that teachers should have basic education and professional training. The policy (GoP, 1970: 20) recommendations included:

- qualification for primary, middle, and high stages of schools as matriculates, intermediates, and graduates respectively with professional training;
- initiation of crash teacher training programmes on an emergency basis;
- provision of residential accommodations;
- provision of facilities in terms of library resources and research;
- appointment on higher position in consideration with qualification and research;
- creating a system of sabbatical leave;
- creating good conditions of service;
- preparation of efficiency and disciplinary rules to discourage arbitrary action;
- provision of supplementary materials and teaching guides;
- relaxation of basic academic and training requirements for women to qualify as teachers; and
- setting up a comprehensive programme of in-service training of teachers.

The policy (GoP, 1970: 20) underlined the significance of educational research and stated that 'The two most important needs in educational research are the development of an institutional structure and the coordination of research carried out by various agencies in the country.' It is interesting to note that this policy was introduced just one year after the launch of 1970 policy during the same regime of Yahya Khan. A number of recommendations, e.g. crash courses for teachers, linkage of research and teaching, and improvement of service conditions, were the same as in the previous policies.

THE EDUCATION POLICY, 1972–1980

The 1972 Education Policy flagged the need for 225,000 additional teachers to deal with the challenge of universalizing education. It is important to note that though this policy came after the separation of East Pakistan (now Bangladesh) which had a majority of Pakistan's population, the problem of shortage of teachers still persisted. The problem which was flagged in the Pakistan Educational Conference in 1947 remained a challenge for the policymakers. According to the policy (GoP, 1972: 23), 'In order to meet the massive requirement of teachers at all stages, facilities for teacher education will be increased by reorganizing teacher education programmes and by introducing innovative techniques.'

To deal with the challenge of shortage of teachers the policy proposed to offer the subject of education in secondary schools and in general colleges. The students passing this subject at the matriculation, intermediate, or degree level examinations would qualify as primary, middle, and high school teachers, respectively. In addition to the regular teacher education programmes, crash courses for teachers were proposed. The shortage of teachers was more seriously felt in case of female educational institutions. The lack of female teachers was certainly a constraint for female education as a number of parents in Pakistan, for sociocultural and religious reasons, would not allow their daughters to be taught by male teachers. To induct more female teachers, the policy proposed that basic academic and training requirements should be relaxed so as to enable a large number of women to qualify as teachers. The policy proposed the establishment of an academy for teachers and educational planners/administrators and a provision of opportunities to teachers with suitable background, experience, and aptitude to serve in various administrative, supervisory, and advisory cadres in the government.

During the period of Zulfikar Ali Bhutto's rule (1971–1977), the salaries of teachers were raised substantially together with the announcement that the teachers, like other government officials, would enjoy National Pay Scales. The 1972 policy claimed this contribution with pride. This policy (GoP, 1972), on the whole, was considered to be a pro-teacher policy that proposed concrete recommendations for the economic, social, academic, and intellectual uplift, and freedom of teachers.

NATIONAL EDUCATIONAL POLICY, 1979

The 1979 policy (GoP, 1979: 62), launched during the period of Zia ul-Haq, dumped all previous initiatives in the domain of teacher education by stating, '... unfortunately the standard of teacher education at present seems to be on the lower ebb because of multifarious reasons.' It is worth noticing that this official statement was being made after thirty-two years of the independence of the country. It is also worth recalling that teacher education was flagged as a major challenge in the Pakistan Educational Conference and certain measures were proposed in the report. The 1979 policy also observed that the emphasis in the previous policies was laid on the quantitative expansion of teacher education institutions and the qualitative aspects were ignored, thus it was time to consolidate the teacher education programmes.

Some important recommendations of the 1979 Education Policy (GoP, 1976: 63) regarding teacher education included:

- upgrading Primary Teacher Training Institutions and normal schools to colleges of elementary teachers;
- pre-service and in-service training by the Academy of Higher Education;
- strengthening of Education Extension Centres and in-service training centres in the provinces to provide at least one in-service training facility to each teacher every five years;
- responsibility of training of teachers of class X to XII from the provincial Education Extension Centres;
- Strengthening of the in-service training facilities of the Allama Iqbal Open University to offer teacher education programmes through correspondence, radio, television, periodic workshops, and seminars;
- provision of similar support to the provincial Institutes of Education and Research;

- establishment of an Academy of Higher Education for the pre-service and in-service training of university teachers;
- establishment of an Academy of Educational Planning and Management to provide in service training to administrators and supervisors;
- emphasis on the training of teachers in science, mathematics, industrial arts, agriculture, commerce, and home economics;
- modifications of curricula of P.T.C., C.T., BEd and MEd;
- development of a code of ethics for teachers;
- introduction of a comprehensive system of accountability and evaluation of teachers and administrators;
- introduction of a reward system for teachers; and
- the construction of flats for teachers.

The hallmark of the 1979 policy, however, was its aim to Islamize the educational system of Pakistan. The policy (GoP, 1979: 65) acknowledged the central role of teachers and made explicit the attributes of an effective teacher:, '[The] Teacher is the pivot of the entire educational system. Effective teaching demands that besides possessing adequate knowledge of the subject matter and techniques of teaching, our teacher must also exhibit full commitment to the Ideology of Pakistan.' The policy, thus, proposed that commitment to the ideology of Pakistan should be a prerequisite for the appointment of teachers. To re-orientate the massive number of existing teachers in the ideology of Pakistan and their respective fields of specialization, the policy proposed in-service training courses throughout the country. This policy had far reaching repercussions as it influenced curriculum and teachers with concrete measures to Islamize every bit of education.

EDUCATION POLICY, 1992

The 1992 Education Policy deliberated on teacher education in detail. The policy (GoP, 1992: 1) acknowledged the major role of teachers in implementing the education policies and alluded to the recurring problems of indiscipline and decline in professional standards of teachers. The 1992 policy (GoP, 1992: 14) followed the spirit of 1979 policy and proposed, '... a major change in the training programmes of teachers, diverting part of their training to study the basis on which the Islamic worldview stands.' The policy, in this regard, recommended the inclusion of religious education in the teacher education curricula in order to enhance their understanding of the worldview of Islam. The 1992 policy, like all previous policies, faced the similar challenge of shortage of teachers and to address this, the policy promised the training and recruiting of 265,000 new primary school teachers and proposed a relaxation in the upper age for the appointment of teachers. It was also recommended that retired and unemployed educated persons could be approached for teaching. It was suggested that female teachers should be appointed in primary schools.

The policy (GoP, 1992: 26) proposed measures for the improvement of teacher and teacher education including:

- separate units for organizing teacher training in each provincial education department and at the federal level;
- mobile training units for on job training of teachers, strengthening of teacher training institutions and updating the faculty in terms of knowledge and skills;
- updating of teacher training curricula;
- making teaching practice compulsory in teacher education programmes;
- regular in-service training programmes for teachers at all levels including use of distance education;
- compulsory computer education component;
- special scholarship scheme for those holding secondary or higher secondary qualifications in order to attract them to the teaching profession;
- a system of incentives to encourage teachers to undergo in-service training;
- special awards for inventions and creative work;
- encouragement of private sectors to set up Teachers Resource Centres (TRCs) to which government school teachers may be nominated for training;
- updating of teacher training curricula and assessment;

- the need for increasing the duration of teacher training;
- teaching practice as a compulsory and necessary part of pre-service training programmes; and
- setting up a national commission for teachers for examining the problems of teachers and for suggesting ways and means for their solutions.

The policy (GoP, 1992) also stated that the 'Primary Kit' would be updated and workbook and guides would be translated into local languages. Teachers would be trained to use this kit and funds for the purchase of consumables would be provided to each school. The policy proposed an increase in the salary structure and service conditions of PTC teachers, raised salaries of the *moallima* of *mohalla* schools and the imam of mosque schools, performance-based incentives for teachers, announcing equal allowances for urban and rural teachers, introducing education cadre for teachers at par with other services and setting up a national commission for teachers.

NATIONAL EDUCATION POLICY, 1998–2010

The 1998 Policy (GoP, 1998: 2) acknowledged the significant role of teachers by considering them 'the backbone of an educational system'. The policy was a comprehensive document that discussed teachers and the challenges faced by them. The policy proposed a detailed list of initiatives to be taken to uplift teachers and teacher education. Some of these initiatives (GoP, 1998: 29–30) included:

- revision of service structure and transparent personnel management mechanism to promote merit-based hiring of teachers;
- assigning schools to teachers on the basis of empirical need and reduction in transfer rate by recruiting local teachers for schools;
- revision of attendance and leave regulations and the enforcement of strict action to check teachers absenteeism

- revamping of in-service training for existing teachers over a period of five years;
- reformation and strengthening in-service teacher training;
- raising the entry qualification for primary teacher certificate from secondary school certificate to higher secondary school certificate gradually;
- Simultaneous launch of a new stream of (10+3) diploma course for elementary education;
- reformation of pre-service teacher training by revision of curricula;
- revamping textbooks and instructional materials;
- institution of a career structure for teachers at the elementary level including promotion possibilities and the revision and enforcement of better standards of professional behaviour;
- efficient distribution and optimum utilization of teachers;
- redeployment of teachers from schools where there is a surplus to the schools where there is a shortage;
- revision of Annual Confidential Reports (ACRs) to record performance and link performance to promotion possibilities;
- institutionalization of incentives and an accountability system for teachers to improve their performance;
- relaxation of qualification requirements for the appointment of female teachers where none are available; and
- relaxation of age limit for female teachers to facilitate entry into the profession.

NATIONAL EDUCATION POLICY, 2009

The 2009 Education Policy expressed dissatisfaction about the quality of teachers which was negatively affected for a number of reasons. According to the policy (GoP, 2009a: 42) 'Poor quality of teachers in the system in large numbers is owed to the mutations in governance, an obsolete pre-service training structure and a less than adequate in-service training regime.' The policy (GoP, 2009a: 42–3) offered a list of recommendations to improve teacher education. Some major recommendations included:

- requirement of a bachelor's degree with a BEd for teaching at elementary level and a masters with a BEd for teaching at secondary and higher secondary levels by 2018;
- standardization and institutionalization of accreditation and certification procedures;
- development of a separate cadre of specialized teacher trainers;
- merit-based teacher recruitment, promotions, postings, and professional development;
- a three-year cyclic teacher education programme;
- career progress to be linked to professional development;
- use of science kits and provision of science kits to all primary and middle schools;
- development of effective accountability mechanism;
- assessment of training on the basis of research and training programmes;
- steps to improve social status and morale of teachers;
- incentives for teachers in rural or other hard areas;
- teacher training institutions to develop the capacity of teachers and school managers for school development plans;
- short-terms courses for improvement of language skills for teachers of rural areas;
- giving due consideration to the voice of teacher associations in decisions;
- tapping the private sector through public-private partnerships;
- harnessing international development partners' resources within a broad national programme of teacher improvement; and
- waiving of maximum age limit for recruitment of female teachers.

The 2009 policy reiterated some of the old resolutions, e.g. steps to improve social status, effective accountability system, use of scientific kits, and waiving of maximum age limit for recruitment of female teachers. The most important proposition of the policy, however, was the required qualification of teachers—to teach at elementary level, a teacher has to have a bachelor degree and a professional degree of BEd. Another point of emphasis was the enhanced role of the private sector in education.

ANALYSIS AND DISCUSSION

Subsequent education policies grappled with some major challenges faced by the education system in Pakistan with regards to teachers and teacher education including the shortage of teachers, non-availability of female teachers, inadequate teacher education, low social status, merit-based hiring, promotions and transfers, obsolete curricula of teacher education programmes, poor salary scales of teachers, disconnect between teaching and research, the dearth of teaching resources especially in science subjects, minimum qualification for joining the teaching profession, the lack of intellectual freedom, and the inadequate accountability of teachers.

Almost all education policy documents in Pakistan underlined the central role of teachers in the process of learning and teaching. One major problem that has figured in every policy document is the shortage of teachers. A number of measures were suggested for the quantitative expansion of teachers. It was proposed in policies (GoP, 1970; GoP, 1972) that relaxation should be given in the qualifications for female teachers, allowing candidates with lower qualification to apply for teaching. This step did increase the number of female teachers but had an adverse impact on the quality of education imparted by those teachers.

In Zia ul-Haq's regime, three kinds of indigenous schools, *mohalla* schools, mosque schools, and village workshop schools were introduced to increase the literacy rate. Imams (prayer leaders) and *moallimas* were supposed to teach students in mosques schools and *mohalla* schools respectively. This step certainly increased the number of schools and teachers but the quality of teaching learning process offered by imams and *moallimas* was not satisfactory. Apart from these schools a number of other initiatives were also launched to enhance literacy. The teachers employed for these projects were deficient either in subject matter or pedagogical skills. Such initiatives increased the number of 'literates' but negatively impacted the quality of education.

To deal with the challenge of a shortage of teachers the 1972 policy proposed that any student who studied the subject of education in matric or intermediate would be qualified to teach (GoP, 1972). This was a proxy to teacher education qualification and allowed a number of people without proper teacher education qualification, to join the teaching force. These measures could be useful in the quantitative expansion of the teaching force but they were not helpful in the qualitative improvement of teaching. This tension between quantity and quality is visible in most of the education policies of Pakistan.

Over time, salaries of public sector schools did rise but their performance in the classroom is considered to be relatively poor as compared with the private schools. Andrabi, et al., (2010: 2) concludes that, 'Public school teachers are paid better, have more training, and are more experienced than their private school counterparts. It is therefore particularly surprising that public school quality, as demonstrated by the learning levels, is so low.' One explanation of this poor performance could be that rewards are not linked with performance in public sector schools, rather it is the length of service that entitles teachers to benefits. Another explanation for poor performance of school teachers in public sector schools is the lack of a monitoring and accountability system. Education policies such as 1979 and 1992 did refer to the need of accountability but the policy proposal could not be implemented in public sector schools.

Besides shortage of teachers, a related challenge was that a large number of teachers were not trained. Almost all the policies underscored the importance of teacher education. Most of the policies focused on the pedagogy of teachers, i.e. exposing them to new methods and techniques of teaching, taking for granted that they possessed strong content knowledge. However, the Pakistan Educational Conference in 1947 referred to the importance of having a strong knowledge base of the respective subject. A number of studies in the Pakistani context (Kardar, 1998; Andrabi, et al., 2007; *The Task Force on Education*, 2011) found that teachers lacked content knowledge. Thus most of our policy discussion missed the issue of content knowledge. Teacher development has three directions, i.e. knowledge, skills, and attitude. The whole emphasis of policies seemed to be only on developing skills and knowledge whereas attitudes were hardly tapped. The ultimate outcome of this skewed approach was that a holistic vision of teacher education could not be adopted. The attitudinal change remained a forgotten target in education policies (Siddiqui, 2010). Teacher education programmes need to have a strong blend of theory and practice but most of the teacher education programmes lacked meaningful teaching practices. The Education Policy, 1998, proposed that the practice of teaching needs to be treated as a separate entity and students need to pass the teaching practice module as well.

To deal with the challenges of the lack of trained teachers, the education policies proposed crash courses and short-term courses (GoP, 1947; GoP, 1970). Such short courses could be useful in exposing teachers to a few techniques but could not bring a sustainable change at a conceptual level. This is another typical example of tension between quantity and quality. Subsequent education policies, time and again, determined minimum educational and professional qualifications for teachers but interestingly for all practical purposes, these requirements were for public sector schools and the private schools never followed these instructions.

The Pakistan Educational Conference (GoP, 1947) referred to the scale of salaries for teachers. The proposal to raise teachers' salaries was reiterated in the report of the Commission on National Education, 1959, thus we see a reasonable rise in the salaries of teachers in public schools. Another related proposal was the provision of a provident fund and retirement benefits. Teachers in the public sector generally enjoy these facilities. However, the salaries of *educators,* a term used in Pakistan for teachers hired on contract basis in schools, are very low. Generally teachers in the private sector do not enjoy retirement benefits and provident funds facilities, thus the proposals of education policies have the least impact for the teachers of private schools.

As a number of measures stated in the education policies were based on imported ideas, they were not compatible with indigenous sociocultural practices and constraints. One such idea (GoP, 1992: 8) was 'introducing science kits for creative laboratory experiments.' It was decided to provide science kits to public schools to enhance the quality of teaching. A number of schools never received these kits. A large number of teachers who received these kits did not use them. According to the BRIDGES study, cited by Warwick, et al., (1992: 298):

> ... only about half of the 1000 teachers interviewed had kits available for use in their schools. Among them about half (53 per cent) stated that they had used it. Teachers were also asked if they had ever received training in how to use a teaching kit. Only one quarter of those with access to a kit said that they had received such training.

Similarly the idea of mobile vans, proposed in the Fourth Five-Year Plan, to share modern pedagogical skills with teachers, was a failure. Despite the failure of this initiative the same proposal was offered again in the 2009 Education Policy (GoP, 2009a).

The recommendation for revision of curricula of teacher education programmes invariably figured in all education policies. Different governments tried to revise curricula according to their wishes. For instance there was an emphasis on the technical and vocational aspect of education in the 1959 Commission report and we see a reflection of that during Ayub Khan's era (1958–1969). In Zia ul-Haq's period (GoP, 1979), Islamization was the order of the day and the teacher education curriculum was modified and Islamized with a stress on creating an ideological awareness in the country. In Musharraf's era (1999–2008), the theme of 'enlightened moderation' was highlighted. The revision of the curricula remained a theoretical exercise as the teachers were not professionally prepared to implement the changes in curricula.

The 1979 policy (GoP, 1979), in order to encourage female teachers to teach in schools located in distant places, proposed to provide them accommodation. According to this proposal, flats were to be constructed on a large scale. The focus was to provide accommodation to single teachers. The initiative failed as female teachers, because of cultural and social reasons, did not occupy the flats. Warwick et al. (1991: 11) observed that the main reason for the failure of this program was cultural as 'Single women in Pakistan usually do not live alone. They stay with their families and if they must travel to outlying areas they do so in the company of male relatives or other women.' Thus an expensive initiative was aborted midway.

Another aspect of teacher empowerment was their social status. Most of the education policies stated the need to enhance the social status of teachers but they ignored the fact that social status is a complex and multi-layered construct and a number of constituents are involved in its construction. Thus a rise in salary cannot ensure a rise in social status. In the 1979 Education Policy, a code of ethics was proposed for teachers. It is interesting to note that the 1959 Commission had mentioned the need for a sense of professional ethics for teachers as well but like many other policies this also remained an unrealized promise.

The 2009 Education policy proposed merit-based hiring, promotions, and postings. This proposal was given by previous policies as well but because of political intervention, merit was compromised and a number of teachers were hired, promoted, and transferred on a political basis. The culture of political intervention in Pakistan is so deep-rooted in our educational system that just rhetoric at policy level cannot remedy it. The state needs to have a comprehensive work plan to implement such policies. A critical review of teacher education policies reveals numerous gaps between promises and actual practices. A number of announced measures could not be implemented, e.g. incentives for rural teachers, special scholarships for teacher education, raising the social status of teachers, residential flats for teachers, opportunities for teachers to serve in various administrative governmental jobs, and research based assessment of curricula.

SUMMARY

Teacher education policies reflect the professed intentions of the state to reform teaching in Pakistan. There are areas of success, as a result of these policies, in terms of quantitative expansion, e.g. there are more teacher education institutions and more trained teachers as compared to the number of teachers in 1947. As proposed in the Education Policy 2009, an accreditation committee has also been set up to accredit teacher education programmes but there are a number of targets which could not be achieved. The major unrealized promise relates to the qualitative improvement of teachers and teacher education. The major factor that hampered the implementation process was the lack of political will on part of the ruling parties. Education did not seem to be a priority with the state. A number of education policies were not products of the consultative process of stakeholders but were largely personality driven. Most of the policies were not even shared with the stakeholders. One can see more ambitious political rhetoric and less practical achievable plans. The implementation phase of policies lacked an effective monitoring system and an appropriate accountability mechanism; as a result a number of promised targets could not be achieved in the stipulated period of time.

Chapter 14

Implementation: Challenges and Recommendations

Despite a number of detailed policies and plans educational outcomes have remained unsatisfactory. According to the Global Competitive Index (GCI), cited by the National Education Policy, 2009 (GoP, 2009a: 12) Pakistan's score on health and primary education is 108, which is dismal when compared with Bangladesh (90) China (55), India (93), Malaysia (42) and Sri Lanka (36) (the higher the number, the lower the performance). Pakistan lags behind the rest of the countries mentioned in the list.

There has been a growing realization of the significant role of the implementation process in the success of policies and plans. Researchers such as Huber and Miles (1984), Fullan (1986), McLaughlin (1987), and Schorr & Schorr (1989) explored processes, steps, and factors involved in the process of implementation. Most of these researches were situated in the North American experience and attempted to discuss the implementation of reforms related to school development. In the Pakistani context the implementation is studied by Bengali (1991), Ahsan (2003), Warwick et al., (1991 & 1992), Ali (2006), and Siddiqui (2011).

THE DISCOURSE PATTERN OF EDUCATION POLICIES

While reading policy documents one can observe the politics of discourse employed by the policies. Most of these policies have been used by various governments as a tool to glorify their image and denigrate their opponents (usually the previous government). A critical analysis of education policy documents reveals a common discourse pattern in the policy documents. This discourse pattern has five distinct themes which are stated below:

- Stating the significance of education and related educational aspects
- Use of rhetoric, hyperbole, and politically correct expression
- Lamenting about issues, problems, and gaps
- Responsibility of problems assigned to 'others'
- Setting new targets

Apparently most of these policy documents look promising in terms of identifying major educational challenges and professed plans to take on these challenges. What could, then, fail the implementation process of these policies? What were the factors responsible for hampering the process of change? According to the 1992 policy (GoP, 1992: 1), 'the limitation of financial resources, poor appreciation of educational priorities, inadequate delivery systems, and population pressure has never allowed a full expression of the desired change.' Some reasons are also highlighted by the Fourth Five-Year Plan, (1970: 143):

> The priority accorded to education in the drafting of plans, however, has not always been reflected in the implementation of plans. Required funds have been denied to the Education and Training Sector because of pressure for resources in other economic sectors.

This chapter discusses the factors that were instrumental in slowing down the process of implementation especially in achieving the goals of Universal Primary Education (UPE), literacy, and female education.

POLITICAL WILL

Policies and plans succeed or fail mainly because of the presence or absence of strong political will. McLaughlin (1987: 172), underlining the importance of political will, suggested that:

> Dollars can be provided. Consultant can be engaged to furnish missing expertise. But will, or the attitudes, motivation, and beliefs that underlie an implementer's response to a policy's goals or strategies, is less amenable to policy intervention.

Unfortunately in Pakistan the required political will to facilitate the success of policies is missing. The Task Force on Education (2011) observed that none of these policies attracted the sustained political will. Policies are made for the sake of policies and every new government finds it fashionable to offer an education policy. Mostly policies are used as a platform for political rhetoric, thus most of the educational reforms announced in Pakistan are without the backing of strong political will of the decision-makers at a state level. This lack of political will impacts each step of the policy implementation process.

UNRELIABLE STATISTICS

Educational policies and plans are designed largely using the statistics of different aspects of education. The numbers in some cases are inflated, e.g. the percentage of literacy is usually inflated in order to attain a socially desirable effect. As a result, statistics issued even through official channels become unreliable. For instance in 1992–93 four different literacy rates, 41.3, 34.0, 31.0, 35.0, (Ahsan, 2003: 274) were published in official documents.

LACK OF OWNERSHIP

Policies in any sector need consultations with different stakeholders to lead the way to ownership which is an important condition for successful implementation (McLaughlin 1987, Warwick, et al., 1991, 1992). In Pakistan, however, the policies, plans, and ideas usually come from the ruling elite headed by the chief executive. For instance a Martial Law order was issued on 12 March 1972 (GoP, 1972: 43) by the Civil Martial Law Administrator at the time, Zulfikar Ali Bhutto, ordering the following:

> As from the first day of September 1972, all privately-managed colleges, together with all property attached to them, shall vest
>
> (a) in the Central Government, if they are situated in the Islamabad Capital Territory; and
> (b) in the Provincial Government, if they are situated in a Province.

Zia ul-Haq offered a new educational policy, (GoP, 1979: 2) focusing on Islamization of education. The very first objective of the policy was:

> To foster in the hearts and minds of the people of Pakistan in general and the students in particular a deep and abiding loyalty to Islam and Pakistan and a living consciousness of their spiritual and ideological identity thereby strengthening unity of the outlook of the people of Pakistan on the basis of justice and fair play.

The policymakers, taking a cue from this statement, tried to incorporate the vision in the proposed policies. A one-man vision cannot be a replacement of participatory decision taken as a result of the democratic process. Most of such policies ceased to exist as the architect of that policy is no more in power. Similarly the 2001 devolution plan, initiated by Pervez Musharraf was a sudden breakaway from the established governance system and most of the implementers themselves were not clear about their roles and responsibilities.

CHALLENGE OF CAPACITY

One major factor that plays an important part in the process of implementation is the challenge of capacity. Lack of funds could be one impediment to the implementation process, but lack of capacity to absorb funds, spend them appropriately and actually deliver services is the real challenge. The question of capacity was obvious during the implementation process of devolution. Most of the *nazims* and councillors had no prior working experience. A number of them were not properly educated, were unclear of their roles, and were unable to deliver.

THE DROPOUT RATE CHALLENGE

The dropout rate issue played a negative role in the efforts to promote literacy. A large percentage of students drop out before they reach grade 5. This large dropout rate constantly pulls down the literary figures. Subsequent policies did not focus on the dropout issue which keeps on compounding the problem of low literacy. Fragmentation and non-coordination between organizations also proved counterproductive. The 2009 policy (GoP, 2009a) stated that splitting up education happens both at the federal and national levels and thus there was no mechanism for developing a whole-of-sector view at the national level. The language factor also played an important role in the failure of the policies. The non-formal basic education schools did not have any material to teach in the indigenous regional languages of Pakistan. The result was an extra effort required by illiterates to learn in a language which was quite alien to them.

IMPORTED PACKAGES OF REFORMS

Some reforms of policy initiatives were funded by foreign donor agencies. These funded projects usually have inbuilt consultancies, thus reforms designed by the foreign consultants do not realize the subtleties of local culture. A pertinent example is the construction of 320 residences in all four provinces of Pakistan for single female teachers, a project which was funded by the World Bank. The apparent purpose of the project was to facilitate female teachers to cope with the problem of accommodation while working away from their homes. The experiment, however, did not succeed as most of these residences were either not occupied or were vacated soon after occupation. Explaining the failure of this project Warwick et al. (1991: 11) noted, 'The main reason for the failure of this program was cultural. Single women in Pakistan usually do not live alone. They stay with their families and if they must travel to outlying areas they do so in the company of male relatives or other women.' Similarly the initiative of teaching kits, distributed in public sector schools, was never utilized to its true potential because of indigenous ground realities—in some public schools, class sizes are very large and the only effective way for teachers to teach is through one-sided lectures.

RESOURCES

The role of resources (financial, physical, and human) is crucial in the implementation of policies. It is important to understand that just the availability of resources is not enough, the actual activation and proper utilization of these resources is necessary to facilitate the process of implementation.

FINANCIAL RESOURCES

The budgetary allocation for education has been very low, suggesting the low priority given to the sector of education. Glancing over the percentage of GDP we have been allocating in the national budget of Pakistan, we can realize the 'priority' we have been giving to education. For a comparative study let us look at the allocations being made for education in the countries in the region.

Table 16: Comparison of Public Sector Spending on Education

Country	Public Sector Spending (as % of GDP)	Literacy Rate in (%)
Bangladesh	2.6	59.8
Bhutan	4.8	52.0
India	3.4	73.8
Iran	3.36	85.0
Maldives	12.7	99.0
Nepal	5.0	66.0
Pakistan	2.1	60.0
Sri Lanka	2.6	91.2

Source: UNESCO (2016).

As is clear from Table 16, the percentage of allocation for education of the total GDP in Pakistan was 2 per cent. This allocation is less than the amount allocated by other countries in the region like Bangladesh, Bhutan, India, Iran, Maldives, Nepal, and Sri Lanka. This trend suggests that as we are moving forward with greater education needs, instead of enhancing the spending, we are reducing it substantially. According to the Fourth Five-Year plan (GoP, 1970: 144):

> At the initial stage, however, because of the war with India, the priority of education had to be put at a lower level than stipulated in the Plan. The result was that in the first four years only about 50 per cent of the total Plan allocation for education could be earmarked in the Annual Development Programmes. Actual utilization of funds was even lower.

The Musharraf regime got a huge amount of funding for education reform in the wake of 9/11. In the Economic Survey of Pakistan (2006–7: 161) it is stated that:

> Government realizes the importance and generational impact of education on the lives of people and on the overall economy and has therefore committed to improve the quality of education as well as enhance the educational facilities.

This would naturally mean an increase in the allocation of money for education in the national budget. In the Federal Budget 2007–08 Rs. 24,147 million had been allocated for education whereas Rs. 275,000 million were set aside for defence. These figures clearly show the government's priorities.

The Education Policy 2009 (GoP, 2009a: 14) quoted the Planning Commission, 'We cannot spend only 2.7 per cent of our GDP on education and expect to become a vibrant knowledge economy.' This shows that just having a vision is not sufficient and that financial resources are equally important to realize the vision. If we look at the trend in the allocation for education in the last three years we realize the reason for reluctance to believe in the promise made by the National Education Plan (2010). In 2006–7 the allocation was 2.50 per cent of the GDP. In 2007–8, this amount was reduced to 2.47 per cent of the GDP. In the year 2008–9, the amount further came down to 2.1 per cent of GDP. These declining figures allude to the ground realities where one can see a gaping chasm between professed ideas and actual deeds (Siddiqui, 2010).

The Task Force (2011: 20) report suggested:

> The best available estimates suggest that around Rs. 80–100 billion is needed per year to reach the education MDG, a 50 per cent increment on today's expenditure. A much greater increase will be needed to provide education for all 5–16 year olds, fulfilling Clause 25a of the Constitution.

ACTUAL UTILIZATION

A usual criticism heard in the educational domain is that the allocated money for education is paltry and there cannot be two opinions about this fact. The allocated money is insignificant as compared to the amount of budget we allocate for defence, for example. So far we have seen a formidably low allocation of funds for primary education. This situation takes a far more serious turn when we come to the actual spending of allocated money. Here I will focus the five-year plans to elaborate my point that actual spending has always been far less than the allocated amount. This is quite evident from the following tables which have been cited in the Education Policy 1998–2010 (1998: 138).

In the 2nd Plan (1960–65) the allocated money for primary education was 78 million rupees whereas the actual expenditure for the purpose was 18.80 million rupees which is less than one third of the allocated money. Similarly in the 8th Plan (1993–98) the allocated money was 32,669 million rupees whereas the actual expenditure was 23,340.37 million rupees. This trend of spending far less than the allocated money can be seen in all eight plans. One possible reason for this could be the long bureaucratic channel necessary to draw money. There are, it is said, multiple steps before you could draw the allocated money. The Education Policy (GoP, 2009a: 18) states:

> The governments shall commit to allocating 7 per cent of GDP to education by 2015 and necessary enactment shall be made for this purpose. Formula for proportional allocation (out of available funds) to different sub-sectors of education shall be evolved by the provincial/area governments.

Despite all such claims only 1.5 per cent of the GDP is going to public schools (Task Force report, 2011).

APPROPRIATENESS OF UTILIZATION

Having looked at the low allocation and the actual expenditure we now turn to the utilization of funds. It is a common feeling that funds are utilized inefficiently without getting the desirable results. Lack of financial resources is just one aspect of the problem; the other aspect is the poor governance of financial resources. We are familiar with *ghost schools* which boast beautiful buildings and able teachers with a sizeable number of students. The only problem with these schools, however, was that they existed on paper and not in reality. The interesting part of the story was the regular drawing of salaries by the ghost staff. This is just one example of misappropriation of funds. Many such examples of wastage of funds can be quoted.

A glaring example of such mismanagement is that of the Iqra surcharge which was introduced in the national budget of 1985. This 5 per cent surcharge on all imports yielded substantial revenue. This innovative initiative fell prey to the political motives of the government of the time. The money accumulated in the name of Iqra surcharge disappeared in a 'mysterious manner'.

It is important to note that countries that made tremendous economic progress made their base stronger by spending more than 70 per cent on primary education. A related point is that, contrary to many countries in the world, our fees for higher education are very low. For instance countries like Indonesia, South Korea, Nepal, and India have higher fee rates for higher education as compared to Pakistan.

PHYSICAL RESOURCES

The presence of facilities required for reform enhances the possibilities of success (Warwick, 1991: 4). The target of UPE is linked with the availability of schools and the facilities present in the schools. Currently 30,000 schools need major repairs or are in a dangerous condition, while 21,045 schools have no buildings at all (Task Force Report: 2011). According to this report many schools lack basic facilities, e.g. 65 per cent have drinking water, 62 per cent have a latrine, 61 per cent have a boundary wall, and 39 per cent have electricity. Schools located at a distance from homes and schools without boundary walls discourage parents from sending their daughters to schools. Thus a lack of appropriate physical resources played an important part in jeopardizing the efforts to attain the targets stated in the policy documents.

HUMAN RESOURCES

Pakistan has about 1.5 million teachers. In a number of public sector schools, there is a shortage of teachers. Besides the problem of shortage, teachers remain absent and the classes remain unattended. According to the Task Force on Education (2011), 'On a given day 15–20 per cent public school teachers won't be in classrooms.'

The quality of teaching is usually linked with the content knowledge of students. Kardar (1998: 9) reported that a test of grade 3 level was administered to female teachers of public and private schools. On the basis of 50 per cent pass marks, 4 female teachers failed in both tests in the five districts of the Punjab, when the pass mark was raised to 90 per cent, 45 males (66 per cent) and 147 female teachers (78 per cent) failed to pass both tests. School distance, poor facilities at school, and classrooms without teachers are a few factors that deter parents from sending their children, especially their daughters, to schools.

Table 17: Allocation and Expenditure of Funds from First to Eighth Five-Year Plans

Sub-Sector	1st Plan		2nd Plan		3rd Plan	Non plan period		5th Plan		6th Plan		7th Plan		8th Plan		9th Plan	
	1955–60		1960–65		1965–70	(1970–78)		1978–83		1983–88		1988–93		1993–98		(1998–03)	
	Allocation	Expenditure	Alloc.	Expr.	Alloc.	Alloc.	Expr.	Alloc.	Expr.	Alloc.	Expr.	Alloc.	Expr.	Alloc.	Expr.	Alloc.	Expr.
Primary Education	51.40	21.20	78.00	18.80	67.51	473.93	443.76	3049.70	1413.10	7000.00	3172.40	10128.00	6399.17	32669.00	23340.37	69860.00	
Secondary Education	68.10	44.00	96.40	95.30	294.18	502.52	541.55	3257.00	1090.10	4125.00	3231.02	6404.00	5507.31	16521.20	4930.36	33140.00	
Teacher Education	23.30	4.90	17.40	17.50	36.01	109.90	114.01	380.00	290.30	305.00	156.75	287.00	260.26	3360.00	616.93	2000.00	
Technical Education	–	–	–	–	–	–	–	–	–	1315.00	857.95	2000.00	943.17	2447.00	2373.32	5000.00	
College Education	31.80	29.50	17.00	68.30	64.04	314.81	374.02	767.00	536.60	1300.00	991.95	61500.00	1730.54	2507.50	2350.80	2000.00	
University Education	48.50	36.50	47.50	58.90	91.95	334.05	398.78	725.00	687.00	2100.00	1629.70	1800.00	1890.86	4100.00	1727.75	4000.00	
Scholarships	2.60	1.00	18.70	49.10	91.00	257.74	289.87	430.00	349.60	660.00	663.67	760.00	867.12	1400.00	1215.74	15000.00	
Literacy and Mass Education	–	–	–	–	–	–	–	–	–	750.00	724.09	300.00	510.31	1750.00	409.16	1000.00	
Libraries & Textbooks	–	–	–	–	–	–	–	–	–	455.00	128.32	86.00	26.85	200.00	19.20	300.00	
Miscellaneous	29.80	39.10	137.80	55.24	83.55	519.54	397.50	287.00	526.10	570.00	3663.97	150.00	1216.44	3877.00	1217.85	1000.00	
Sub-Total	255.50	176.20	412.80	363.14	728.24	2512.49	2559.49	8895.70	4892.80	18580.00	15219.81	22530.00	19345.98	68831.70	38201.50	119800.00	
Other Divisions	49.43	21.76	77.20	85.65	358.36	485.65	843.16	1802.3	750.70	250.00	1368.20	154.78	880.95	200.00	165.99	200.00	
Total Education	3043.93	197.96	490.00	448.79	1086.60	2998.14	3402.65	10698.00	5643.50	18830.00	16606.01	22684.78	20226.94	69031.70	38367.47	120000.00	

TENSION BETWEEN QUALITY AND QUANTITY

There has been a constant tension between quantity and quality in all the policies and plans. In this tension, the ultimate winner has been quantity. Thus we see a number of initiatives proposed by the policies like mosque schools, *mohalla* schools, Nai Roshni schools, Literacy Corps, and lowering the required qualifications for female teachers. All these initiatives were geared towards crunching numbers. Another tension was between functional literacy and critical literacy. Most of the policies, however, focused on functional literacy.

POLITICAL INTERFERENCE

The negative political factor played an important role in obstructing the implementation of educational initiatives. In donor funded projects, the top slot appointments were usually made on the basis of political affiliations and a number of initiatives could not achieve their set targets because of political interference. Politicians interfered in appointments, promotions, and transfers and a large chunk of the project funding was used on the publicity of the rulers.

Similarly, discontinuation of policies leads to abortive endings of some useful initiatives. Merit is compromised as incompetent personnel are supported by politicians in organizations and important positions on projects are usually given on the basis of acquaintance. A glaring example of the political interference was the huge literacy project of the *Nai Roshni* schools that was initiated in 1986. The project, potentially an effective project to enhance literacy in the country, was marred by political interference. The project was for children of 11–14 years who would receive an education in the evening in the buildings of pre-existing public schools. As the project was set to take off, a political decision was made that 30 per cent of the teachers would be appointed by the elected members of the national assembly (MNAs) and senators and 30 per cent by members of the provincial assemblies (MPAs), 10 per cent by the Prime Minister's quota for the disabled and 30 per cent by LAMEC (Warwick, 1991). Consequently a potentially positive project suffered a serious setback because of incompetent teaching staff hired largely on the basis of political affiliations.

UNREALISTIC TARGETS

One of the factors responsible for the failure of plans and policies regarding UPE, literacy, and female education is the ambitious and unrealistic targets set by the policies. There seems to be a visible disconnect between the enormity of targets and the available resources and commitment. For instance, in the 1947 Educational Conference, the targets of UPE were set to be achieved in twenty years, i.e. by 1967. This target was quite ambitious for two reasons. Firstly as a result of the 1947 migration, a large number of the school-going population came to Pakistan and secondly the resources (financial, physical, and human) were not sufficient to cope with the challenge of achieving the mammoth target. Similarly target dates to achieve literacy and female education kept on moving partly because the targets were set without keeping in view the local realities.

Besides the ambitious targets the measures to ensure these targets were equally unrealistic. An interesting example of this was quoted by Bengali (1999: 15) who referred to a Literacy Ordinance promulgated in 1985 prohibiting an illiterate person from obtaining a passport or a driving license. The ordinance, however, was never enacted and lapsed after 120 days.

The targets set for implementing Urdu as a medium of instruction in all schools were also not realized in the given period of time. In 1959, the Commission on National Education (GoP, 1959: 295) stated that '... a period of approximately fifteen years will be needed to replace English as the medium of instruction in a large number of subjects taught at the university level.' Similarly, the 1973 Constitution (GoP, 1973: 148) promised that 'The National language of Pakistan is Urdu and arrangements should be made for its being used for official and other purposes within 15 years from the commencing day.'

LACK OF CONSISTENCY

A crucial factor responsible for the failure of policies is their inconsistency. There are a number of examples of such inconsistencies. In the 1969 policy, the proposal of a National Literacy Corps was floated. In 1970 its name was changed to the National Education Corps. After two years, the name was changed back to the National Literacy Corps. In 1979, a reference was made to a Student Volunteer Corps. In the 1992 policy, the title of Student Literacy Corps was used. In the 1998 policy, this title was reduced to Literacy Corps. In the 2009 policy there was no mention of any literacy corps at all. Similar was the case of The Literacy and Mass Education Commission (LAMEC) which was established in 1981. In 1989, this Commission was reconstituted with a different name as the National Education and Training Commission. In 1995 the name of this commission was changed to the Prime Minister's Literacy Commission. Usually a new government, for political reasons, tends to discard the names given by the previous governments and come up with new titles to dissociate the projects with the previous governments. One such example is the establishment of the People's Open University by Zulfikar Ali Bhutto. The name of this university was changed by Zia ul-Haq when he came to power in 1977. The new name given to the university was Allama Iqbal Open University.

Besides tinkering with the names we see some serious inconsistencies. We see a recurring proposal (GoP, 1959; GoP 1955; GoP, 1960; GoP 1965) of using non-formal methods to complement the formal method in order to raise literacy. The Seventh Plan (1988–93) completely rejects the non-formal approach for being more expensive and less effective. Referring to the non-formal initiatives of the Sixth-Year Plan, the Seventh-Year Plan (GoP, 1988: 252) stated, 'The Sixth Plan experience has shown that a shortcut to literacy is not only expensive but is hard to monitor. There is no substitute for formal education.' In the 1992 policy, however, use of a non-formal approach to complement the formal approach was proposed again.

Every new government in Pakistan finds it imperative to formulate a new education policy instead of continuing the implementation of the previous one. A number of policies could not survive their announced tenure as new policies were announced. For instance, before the completion time of the 1972–1980 policy, a new Education Policy was announced in 1979 with emphases different from those stated in the previous policy. Similarly before the completion of 1998–2010 policy, the work for a new policy was started in 2005 and the policy was announced in 2009.

In 1970 Education Policy (GoP, 1970: 2) one of the stated objectives focused on decentralization:

> Decentralization of educational administration to ensure academic freedom and administrative and financial autonomy required for healthy and efficient growth of educational institutions particularly in the higher stage.

Quite contrary to this, in the 1972 Education Policy a decision was made to nationalize all colleges, universities, and schools. As a result 3,334 educational institutions were nationalized. This included 1,828 schools, 146 *madrasahs*, 155 colleges, and 5 technical institutions (GoP, 1979: 23). This was a decision with long-term repercussions for the future of these educational institutions in terms of their management, faculty members, campus environment, teaching/learning process, and overall quality of education. The 1979 Education Policy (GoP, 1979: 23) notes major repercussions of the nationalization of schools:

> The nationalization did not result either in the expansion or qualitative improvement of education. However, the national exchequer had to bear an additional burden of more than Rs. 15 crore recurring expenditure per annum. Further investment by private sector in education was blocked.

The decision of nationalization discouraged educational initiatives in the private sector and negatively impacted the efforts to achieve targets in UPE and literacy. Similarly the devolution initiative that brought major structural changes could not be continued with the same spirit in the post-Musharraf era.

FRAGMENTED INITIATIVES

A trend that emerged in the recent past is the patchwork of reforms funded by donor agencies in the areas of UPE, literacy, and female education. Such patchwork strategy may prove good for neatly written end-of-the-project reports bragging their success but they are of little use for sustainable outcomes. A number of initiatives in the areas of UPE, literacy, and female education were started that died shortly and now not many people know about them. For instance LAMEC initiated nine projects, e.g. the Afternoon School projects, the Iqra projects, *Razakar Muallim* projects, mosque projects, NGOs Volunteer Literacy Corps projects, *Sipah-e-Idrees* projects, Social Welfare Agencies Literacy projects, Literacy Village projects, and *Azafi* Literacy Centres projects (Bengali, 1999: 13). These projects started and ended without achieving any significant success.

THE GOVERNANCE ISSUE

Another important factor responsible for the failure of policies was poor governance. An initiative was launched and without giving it time to deliver, it would be replaced by another initiative. This happened more conspicuously in 1980's when with quick succession more than a dozen initiatives were tried to enhance literacy. The ultimate result was that none of those initiatives could get the desired results.

Governance plays a major role in the process of implementation. Availability of resources is important but their appropriate activation and management is crucial. The governance includes the management from the top to the low level tiers as their roles influence the implementation of target reforms. According to Task Force on Education (2011) '... Leadership is the most important "secret ingredient" for translating good education policies into results.'

In Pakistan there are competing governance units with little internal coordination. This fragmented approach to different initiatives in achieving UPE, literacy, and female education impeded the process of implementation (Siddiqui, 2010). McLaughlin (1987: 173) acknowledges the influence of competing centres of authority in implementation willingness. The governance of education is being looked after by a number of ministries. Aly (2007: 6) commenting on the scattered governance observes:

> Higher Education is exclusively and autonomously dealt with by the Higher Education Commission. Inclusive Education (Special Education) is dealt by a separate Ministry. Science and Technology is being dealt by the Ministry of Science and Technology and Technical Education and Vocational training is being pursued in NAVTEC which resides in the Prime Minister's Secretariat. Ministry of Labour and Manpower is also concerned with skill training. These Ministries are acting in a disconnect and divorce from one another and not in harmony to make the effort wholesome and convergent.

The fragmented and uncoordinated governance, instead of benefitting from each other's experience, usually replicates pre-existing initiatives.

ENVIRONMENTAL STABILITY

Environmental stability is considered as an important condition for implementation (McLaughlin, 1987). In Pakistan, since its independence we have had at least four military regimes with the civil governments hardly given a chance to complete their tenure. Pakistan has also engaged in two major wars with India in 1965 and 1971, which halted the journey of progress and consumed resources which could have been used for educational development. This political instability was further aggravated with the Afghan War and post 9/11 situation. There was also massive scale destruction of schools in floods. A number of educational initiatives fell prey to sociopolitical events.

MONITORING AND ACCOUNTABILITY

Most of the projects in literacy, UPE, and female education lacked effective monitoring systems. So after their initiation the projects came to an end without bringing any significant sustainable change in the target areas. The lack of monitoring systems was coupled with the absence of accountability measures. Thus a number of initiatives consumed substantial financial and technical resources with little outcomes but the people responsible for financial corruption and the poor educational outcomes got away without any accountability.

RECOMMENDATIONS

Some achievable recommendations can be suggested to enhance the chances of success in the process of implementation. Some major ones are given below:

PARLIAMENTARY COVER

All education policies should be presented, discussed, and passed in parliament to achive a broad ownership by elected members of the assemblies. This will not only make it more acceptable to the different segments of the society but it will also give constitutional backing to the policy as well.

SUPPORT BY THE RULING ELITE

The major reason of not achieving the stated targets of any policy is the lack of political will, which emanates from the low priority set for education. For successful implementation of a policy it must be supported by the ruling government and the masses and this support should be visible to the different tiers of implementers.

CONSULTATIVE PROCESS

All policies and plans need to be designed through a consultative approach by bringing different segments of society on board.

A broad-based consultation process leads to ownership by the stakeholders and enhances the chances of success.

COMBINATION OF PRESSURE AND SUPPORT

Fullan (1986) suggests that successful implementation generally requires a combination of pressure and support. McLaughlin (1987: 173) notes that for effective implementation, pressure is important but he qualifies his statement by suggesting that 'pressure alone cannot effect those changes in attitudes, beliefs, and routine practices typically assumed by reform policies.' Along with pressure, support is essential for successful implementation.

CONSISTENT AVAILABILITY OF RESOURCES

Sustained availability of resources (financial, physical, and human) is crucial for successful implementation. To ensure an uninterrupted flow of financial resources requires joint planning by the Ministry of Education and the Ministry of Finance.

EFFECTIVE MONITORING SYSTEM

There needs to be an effective monitoring mechanism. This could be in the form of a committee presided over by a retired judge and having government and private members on it, to monitor and issue a quarterly report on the implementation of policies. The committee should also identify problems and recommend solutions.

COORDINATING SYSTEM

Governance at all levels should have an effective coordination system and should include informing and empowering one another. Coordination would keep them on the same page and help them avoid any replication.

SUMMARY

Implementation of policies has been a serious problem, especially in developing countries. In Pakistan a number of comprehensive policy documents were produced that contained some realistic recommendations but because of poor implementation the desired results could not be achieved. This chapter discussed some of the factors that impede the process of implementation. These factors included a lack of participatory approach, unreliable data, unrealistic goals, lack of political will, ineffective monitoring and accountability systems, political interference, inconsistency, lack of political stability, lack of resources, lack of capacity, poor governance, and fragmented efforts. The chapter also proposed some feasible recommendations to strengthen the process of implementation which has been a perennial problem in developing countries.

Chapter 15

Post-2009 Education Initiatives

This chapter focuses on the state's educational initiatives in the post-2009 period. The year 2009 is important as this is when the PPP government launched the National Education Policy, details of which have been discussed and analysed in previous chapters. The important educational policies discussed and analysed here belong to the post-2009 era and were initiated by three different governments—the PPP, PML-N, and PTI.

THE EIGHTEENTH AMENDMENT AND ARTICLE 25-A

The Eighteenth Amendment to the Constitution of Pakistan had a significant impact on education in Pakistan. Passed by the National Assembly on 8 April 2010 and the Senate on 15 April, it became an Act of Parliament after being signed by the President on the same day. Under the Eighteenth Amendment, the department of education, along with some other departments, was devolved to the provinces. The Ministry of Education was renamed Ministry of Federal Education and Professional Training. One obvious outcome of the Amendment was more autonomy to the provinces, and a major outcome for education was that the curriculum, syllabus, planning, policy, centres of excellence, and standards of education came under the purview of the provinces.

An important clause, Right of Education (25-A), was added to the Constitution (GoP, 2012: 26). The clause reads as below:

> The State shall provide free and compulsory education to all children of the age of five to sixteen years in such manner as may be determined by law.

The Eighteenth Amendment had a significant impact on the education system of Pakistan and on the implementation of the Education Policy which had been announced just a year earlier. These implications will be discussed later in this chapter.

NATIONAL EDUCATION POLICY, 2017 (DRAFT)

The PML-N came to power in 2013. Though no official national education policy was formally announced, the PML-N government did make an attempt to devise a new one during its tenure (2013–17). For this, an advisory committee comprising 13 sub-committees was constituted. Each sub-committee was to work on a given theme with its objectives, strategies, and the way forward. The Committee had prepared a draft but before the policy could be finalised, the PML-N's tenure came to an end in July 2017.

The draft policy, 2017, was prepared after the Eighteenth Amendment that devolved the Department of Education to the provinces. Referring to this important development, the then Federal Minister of Education, Muhammad Baligh-ur-Rehman, claimed that the policy was developed:

> with the consent of [the] IPMC [Inter-Provincial Education Ministers Conference] which proves to be a viable, sustainable and competent forum to play [an] effective role in establishing coordination among all Federating units of the country (GoP 2017: 4).

In the introduction to the draft policy document, it is claimed that in 2015, at the education ministers' conference, it was unanimously decided to revise the 2009 education policy. The draft policy designed by the advisory committee proposed 18 policy chapters with a standardised template/format for each chapter. The format included conceptual framework, constitutional/legal provisions and their importance and significance, situation analysis, issues and challenges, goals, objectives, targets, policy provisions, and an implementation strategy.

Goals, Objectives, and Key Areas of the Education Policy

The draft policy has a detailed list of goals which included character-building, meeting learning needs (knowledge, skills, and values), Pakistani nationhood and national integration, right to education, expanding access, quality of education and institution building, quality assurance of academic programmes, enhancing the education budget, science and technology, and harmonization of curriculum and standards.

Islamic Education

The draft policy is visibly tilted towards the Islamization of education. There is a dedicated chapter, entitled 'Islamic Education', that underlines the significance, objectives, and targets of Islamic education. It reproduces the Objectives Resolution (1949) and concludes that:

> The only justification for our existence is our commitment to Islam to be adopted in our practical life. Therefore, our Education Policy should focus on Islamic Education and to suggest how to translate the Islamic Ideology into our beliefs, worships and actions in daily life (GoP, 2017: 23).

The emphasis on Islamization of education in the draft policy was in line with the spirit of the 1979 education policy prepared by the Zia ul-Haq regime. A number of provisions (GoP, 2017: 27) were mentioned in the draft policy including the following:

- Islamiyat will be introduced as compulsory subject from class III to Intermediate classes extending up to graduation in all general and professional institutions as in the past. For Early Childhood Education (ECE) and classes I to II, it will be integrated in other subjects, including Urdu text book.
- Non-Muslim students will be offered Ethics (Moral Education) in lieu of Islamiyat compulsory from classes III

to XII and they will not be required to read lessons on Islam in ECE and classes I to II.

- Islamiyat (compulsory) from classes III to XII will comprise Al-Quran (Nazirah of 30 *paras*, *hifz* of some selected *ayaat* and short *surahs*, translation of about 300 *ayaat* and *masnoon dua*, hadith, *imaniyat*, *ibadat*, *seerat*, good (*mumlat*) behaviours, *huqooqullah*, *huqooqul-ibad*, day-to-day problems and their solution in Islam, prominent personalities of Islam, etc.
- Arabic as compulsory part will be integrated in Islamiyat from Middle to Higher Secondary level to enable the students to understand the Holy Quran. All possible arrangements shall be made to provide opportunities for seeking higher studies in Arabic and Islamiyat through scholarships both at home and abroad.

Early Childhood Care and Education

Another area that got due emphasis in the 2017 draft policy was early childhood care and education (ECCE). A separate chapter was allocated to it, and the target set in line with the goal of the draft education policy was:

> Free and compulsory quality pre-primary education for children of age group four to five years and equal access to early childhood education and holistic development for the children of age group three to four years by 2030 (GoP, 2017: 30).

There is a long list of wishful, overambitious provisions in the ECCE: language development and cognitive development; child-friendly, inclusive, attractive, friendly and playful school; activity-based and play-way method; teaching-learning and instructional material; teaching kits and ICT-based AV aids; ECE-trained teachers with ECE teacher assistants; governess; teacher-student ratio; policymakers, planners, managers/administrators, teachers, parents and other concerned will be mobilized and sensitized about the importance and significance of early childhood education, care, and development; improvement in coordination and linkages amongst service providers and various stakeholders; encouragement and facilitation of the local community to open and run early childhood education centres; revising, updating, and implementing ECE curricula; comprehensive ECE statistical data; child health care and nutrition; allocation of separate and adequate budget for ECE; and joint ECCE planning in collaboration and consultation with all the concerned ministries.

Literacy and Non-formal Basic Education

The chapter on literacy refers to the framework devised by the UNESCO. It reiterates the national and international commitments Pakistan has made with respect to literacy. The goal of literacy was: 'To strengthen Pakistan by making it a literate country and enhancing participation of masses in decision making at various levels' (GoP, 2017: 40).

The targets set by the policy included achieving 90 per cent literacy by 2025 in accordance with Pakistan Vision 2025, enabling Pakistan to achieve SDG 4 target of 100 per cent literacy rate by 2030, and contribute for provision of non-formal learning opportunities to 22.5 million out of school and dropped out children aged 5–16 years. Policy actions to achieve the literacy targets included expanding access to literacy and non-formal basic education programmes, and a long and ambitious list of actions in areas of quality improvement, organization, management and governance, resource mobilization, and monitoring and evaluation, including building a database.

Primary Education

The chapter on primary education starts by stating the significance of primary education and then makes a reference to the newly inserted Article 25-A. Some major objectives (GoP, 2017: 47) stated were:

a) Universalize access/enrolment by bringing all the primary age group children in school.
b) Universalize retention/completion by ensuring 100 per cent completion of primary education.
c) Universalize achievement on the basis of minimum standards of learning outcomes.

The policy document refers to a long list of promised provisions together with an ambitious list of actions required to achieve the goals.

Secondary Education

The draft education policy underlines the significance of secondary education and sets the goal for secondary education as, 'to prepare students to be responsible citizens to contribute productively in the job market and pursue higher education of their interest' (GoP, 2017: 57). The following targets were set to achieve the goal:

- Up-gradation of 50 per cent existing public sector primary schools to middle level by 2025.
- Up-gradation of 40 per cent existing public sector middle schools to secondary/high schools level by 2025.
- Up-gradation of 20 per cent existing high schools to higher secondary school level by 2025.
- Increase the gross participation rate at middle level from 62 per cent to 85 per cent and net participation rate from 27 to 50 per cent by 2025.
- Increase the gross participation rate at secondary level from existing 58 per cent to 70 per cent and net participation rate from 27 per cent to 40 per cent by 2025.
- 50 per cent increase in gross and net enrolment rates at higher secondary education level.

The draft policy also states a long list of provisions for secondary education.

Teacher Education

At the outset, the draft policy highlights the significance of teacher education and provides a situation analysis. It sets the following objectives (2017: 63):

- Setting standards and monitoring mechanisms to nationalize and internationalize the types and quality of teacher education programmes.
- Reorienting the teacher education system from supply-driven to demand-driven, ensuring need-based supply of teachers at various levels of teaching and subjects/streams of study in line with the Pakistan Vision-2025.
- Reorienting offering of concurrent teacher education programmes by encouraging out-of-subject compartmentalized approach/infusion of subject based structure of academic departments at universities.
- Developing linkages between the pre-service/initial induction and in-service teacher education programmes and institutions.
- Make continuous professional development a regular feature linked to the up-gradation and promotion of teachers and other teaching personnel.
- Set common minimum requirements of academic and pre-service teacher education qualifications for employment of teachers in the public, private and private-public-partnership schools.
- Set minimum salary/BPS for teachers at various levels both in the public, private and public-private-partnership schools.
- Establish mechanism for the certification of teachers at various stages and strengthen accreditation of teacher education programmes.
- Make teaching an attractive profession for the talented youth.

Technical and Vocational Education and Training (TVET)

The draft policy alludes to the high percentage of youth in the population of Pakistan with little opportunities for appropriate education. Only a small percentage of children opt for technical and vocational education and training (TVET). The draft policy sets the following objectives (GoP, 2017: 71) to improve the relevance of TVET in industrial and economic development needs:

- To enhance access and equity
- To assure quality of TVET
- To improve social image of TVET

The draft policy offers a long and ambitious list of provisions as well.

Higher Education

The draft policy highlights the role of higher education in national development and refers to some of the challenges, e.g., access, quality, relevance, post-Eighteenth Amendment situation, low GER (gross enrolment ratio), low number of PhD faculty, poor governance, and low ranking of universities.

The draft education policy gives a long list of policy actions for the uplift of higher education including expanding equitable access and participation rate, improving quality and ranking of universities, faculty development, promoting innovative research, strengthening linkages with industry, governance and management of universities, and financing of higher education.

NATIONAL CURRICULUM FRAMEWORK PAKISTAN

In the post-Eighteenth Amendment scenario, when education was devolved to the provinces, a major concern was to keep some uniformity in terms of themes and standards. To cope with this challenge, the National Curriculum Council (NCC) was constituted by the PML-N government. A major task assigned to the NCC was to develop a national curriculum framework (NCF). The NCC, in consultation with different stakeholders, including the federating units, prepared a comprehensive document that provided guidelines for the following areas of the curriculum (GoP, 2018):

- Rationale and Format for National Curriculum Framework
- Process of Curriculum Development
- Textbooks and Supplementary Learning Materials
- Teacher Education and Continuous Professional Development
- Learning Environment in Schools
- Medium of Instruction and Teaching of Languages
- Assessment and Examination
- Feedback Mechanism
- Mechanism for Informal Sharing and Harmonization

MINIMUM STANDARD FOR QUALITY EDUCATION (2017)

This detailed document prepared during the PML-N government focuses on minimum standards for quality education in Pakistan. The document aims to provide guidelines for attaining standards for improved learning outcomes and school effectiveness. The document discusses the components of standards of quality education (GoP, 2017) including elements of quality education, significance of quality, implementation of the quality cycle of education, standards for learners, standards for curriculum, standards for textbooks and other learning materials, standards for teachers, standards for assessment, early learning and development standards, and standards for school environment.

CURRICULUM SUPPLEMENT ON VALUE EDUCATION

This document, prepared during the PML-N government, deals with the significance of values in quality education. The document identifies and focuses on values such as truthfulness, honesty, tolerance, respect, peaceful coexistence, environmental awareness and care, democracy, human rights, sustainable development, global citizenship, personal care, and safety and integrates the themes across the curriculum. The document is claimed to be a product of mutual consultation of different organizations including the National Accountability Bureau (NAB), National Accreditation Council of Teacher Education (NECTE), Ministry of Climate Change, and Ministry of Human Rights. Values were incorporated from primary grade to Class 12 on the basis of the feedback/demand of the above organizations.

CURRICULUM 2017 FOR ICT SCHOOLS

The PML-N government undertook the curriculum review for the Islamabad Capital Territory (ICT) schools. An internal presentation was developed in the Ministry of Federal Education and Technical Training, focusing on the guidelines for preparing the curriculum including national policies; aspirations and standards; emerging international trends; focus on holistic development of students; integration of core values across the subjects; promoting intellectual, spiritual, aesthetic, emotional, social, and physical development of learners; move away from rote memorization; focus on application of knowledge; development of analytical, critical, and creative thinking; integration of modern teaching methodologies promoting student centeredness; and maximum opportunities for problem solving, logical reasoning, inquiry, project work, process skills, and life skills.

THE COMPULSORY TEACHING OF THE HOLY QURAN ACT

Another important development during the PML-N regime was an Act for making the teaching of the Holy Quran compulsory for the Muslim students in all educational institutions. The Act (Act XXX of 2017) states:

> Whereas it is expedient to provide for making compulsory teaching of the Holy Quran to Muslim students in all educational institutions in the Islamabad Capital Territory and in all the public sector educational institutions owned and controlled by the Federal Government wherever they may be and for matters connected therewith and ancillary thereto.

TVET POLICY FOR PAKISTAN

This document, prepared by the taskforce set up in September 2014 by the PML-N government, is claimed to be the first national technical and vocational education and training policy. The TVET policy document states the objectives and the rationale of the policy at the outset. It emphasizes the need for an integrated national TVET system; a national qualification, assessment and certification system; an invitation to the private sector to enter a partnership to build the country's skills; continuing and accelerating reform; collaboration across all government departments; TVET and gender education; governance and institutional structure of TVET; and funding and finance. A detailed description of the roles of the federal and provincial governments regarding policy, regulation, funding, and delivery is also given.

EDUCATIONAL INITIATIVES SINCE 2018

Following elections, the PTI assumed power in 2018. The PTI government was initially interested in issuing the NEP 2017 prepared by the PML-N government after making certain modifications in the draft. Some work was also done in the Ministry of Education to that effect but finally, the idea of tweaking the NEP 2017 (draft) was dropped and instead another document, the National Education Policy Framework 2018 (GoP, 2018a), was issued. Besides the National Education Policy Framework, some other policy papers were produced, including the SNC, guidelines for textbooks, medium of instructions, HEC undergraduate policy (GoP, 2020), and a new PhD policy (GoP, 2021).

National Education Policy Framework 2018

The National Education Policy Framework 2018 (GoP, 2018a) is a twelve-page document which was prepared during the PTI government's tenure. The first three pages are the usual recap of educational challenges, e.g., net enrolment at the primary level, public expenditure on education as a percentage of the GDP, out of school children, the multi-educational system in Pakistan, medium of instructions in private and public schools, the quality of education, and tertiary and skills training. It sums up the major educational challenges faced in the following table:

Table 18: Summary of Educational Challenges

Out of School Children	Uniform Education System	Quality	Skills and Higher Education
Low and inequitable access and participation	Lack of coordination in policy formulation and implementation across the country	Low student learning outcomes	Low and inequitable access and participation
High levels of poverty in certain disadvantaged areas resulting in high OOSC	Lack of coherence and coordination in curriculum frameworks, textbooks, and exam systems	Poor teacher quality and accountability	Poor quality and relevance of teaching and research conditions
Limited investments in early childhood education resulting in high dropout rate in early grades	Discrepancies in systems of schooling, i.e. across public, private, and madrasah education system	Lack of school leadership—School principals/head teachers	Weak linkages with industry
Low quality of non-formal and accelerated learning programmes	Variation in management of school systems	Poor school environment multi-grade teaching, limited facilities in schools, and poor infrastructure	Inadequate sector governance and management
		Inadequate use of student learning outcome data to inform policymaking	

Source: GoP, (2018a)

The framework defines the following four-point agenda:

1: Decrease Out of School Children (OOSC) and Increase School Completion
2: Achieve Uniformity in Education Standards
3: Improve the Quality of Education
4: Enhance Access to and Relevance of Skills Training

Single National Curriculum 2020

The SNC document prepared during the PTI government's tenure claims to lead to one system of education in terms of curriculum, medium of instruction, and a common platform for assessment. The following objectives are stated in the document:

- All children have a fair and equal opportunity to receive high quality education
- Social cohesion and national integration
- Alleviation of disparities in education content across the multiple streams
- Equal opportunities for upward social mobility
- Equity in education
- Holistic development of children in light of emerging international trends and local aspirations
- Smooth inter-provincial mobility of teachers and students

The SNC, according to the Government, will be implemented phase-wise at different levels of education, starting from the primary level.

Medium of Instruction

Certain guidelines for the medium of instruction are given in the SNC with reference to the status of English, Urdu, and the mother tongue. It is claimed that English will be taught as a language rather than a subject. It is also resolved that greater focus than before will be on the communicative competence of the language for which interactive and collaborative pedagogical strategies are proposed. Guidelines for assessment along with scoring rubrics/ marking schemes have been included for four language skills, including listening and speaking, which were not included in the 2006 curriculum. The initial thought was to use books written in Urdu except for the subject of English but later it was decided that English, Mathematics, and Science will be in English and General Knowledge, Social Studies, Islamiyat, and Urdu will be in Urdu. There is still resistance in some provinces against the shift from English to Urdu. Thus, the future of the medium of instruction regarding different subjects is still vague and uncertain.

Undergraduate Education Policy 2020

The Higher Education Commission proposed an undergraduate education policy that deals with Educational Programs leading to BS, professional degrees, and the associate degree (AD). The stated objective of the policy is to 'enhance the likelihood of student success' (GoP, 2020: 1). The specific objectives of the policy include competency-based learning (knowledge, skills, and professional and interpersonal attributes), balance between breadth and depth, specialization, application of knowledge, emphasis on creativity, and converting BS into terminal degrees.

The following is a systematic representation of the undergraduate policy:

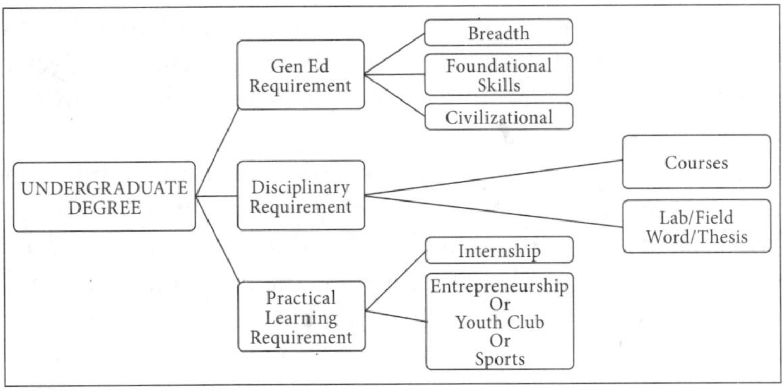

Source: GoP (2020)

The proposed framework of the policy is 'designed to balance disciplinary or concentration requirements with two other types of requirements namely, General Education requirement and practical learning requirement' (GoP, 2020: 2).

The general requirement of a programme in the proposed policy is supposed to have a broad variety of fields of inquiry and aligns with the educational framework of the twenty-first century. The policy has three major components, i.e. General Education, Major/Concentration/Discipline, and Practical Learning requirement. General Education comprises three areas of courses denoting breadth, foundation skills, and civilizational knowledge. The second component of the policy deals with concentration/major discipline.

The third component is the practical learning requirement, which aims to equip students with skills they will need to succeed in such roles. This component has been divided into two categories, internship and practical learning lab. The minimum hours to qualify for a BS degree is 120 credits.

PhD Policy 2021

The Higher Education Commission of Pakistan announced a new PhD policy (GoP, 2021) which was supposed to be implemented on 1 January 2021. The HEC's new PhD policy has some structural changes. One major change is in the minimum requirement of study years for admission to a PhD programme. According to the new policy, this minimum criterion has been reduced from 18 to 16 years of study. This allows a four-year BS degree holder to directly apply to a PhD programme, making it clear that an MS/MPhil degree is not a pre-requisite anymore.

The BS degree holders who succeed in obtaining admission to a PhD programme, however, are supposed to put in 48 credit hours, compared to 24 credit hours for MS/MPhil degree holders. Contrary to the previous PhD policy, the new policy does not require students to take GRE Subject but just GRE General for admission to a PhD programme. Another important change in the new policy is that students may apply to a PhD programme which is from their BS discipline. In this case, however, they require extra courses.

Another important change is that it is not mandatory to send the PhD thesis to foreign experts for evaluation and in case the researcher publishes a research paper in an X category journal, only one external expert is required for thesis evaluation. The duration of a PhD programme proposed in the new policy is three to eight years.

ANALYSIS AND DISCUSSION

The Education Policy 2009 (GoP, 2009a) made tall claims regarding the education targets that, like the previous education policies, could not be realized. The first setback to the policy was the announcement of the Eighteenth Amendment, which devolved a number of departments, including the education department, to the provinces. This change in the roles of the federal and provincial governments did have a major impact on the implementation phase of the Education Policy 2009. A number of targets could not be achieved because of the ongoing tussle between the federal and provincial stakeholders.

The 2009 Policy proposed construction of residential schools under the banner of *Apna Ghar* for the underprivileged in all districts but were constructed only in Punjab under a different name, i.e. Danish Schools, in 14 districts.

The 2009 Education Policy proposed a separate cadre for management, but this recommendation was implemented only in two provinces, KP and Sindh. Despite recommendations of the NEP 2009, free textbooks up to Class 10 are not being provided in all the Gilgit Baltistan and Azad Jammu and Kashmir regions. Contrary to the NEP 2009, no systematic student counselling arrangements have been made available for students at the elementary level.

Post-Eighteenth Amendment, it was considered important to have at least some common themes in curriculum and uniform standards. A ministerial committee was constituted and tasked with preparing a national framework for designing the curriculum.

The National Curriculum Framework was a well thought-out and comprehensive document that deals with some important aspects of a curriculum including rationale, format, development process, textbooks, teacher education, learning environment, assessment, and feedback.

A similar document focusing on the minimum educational standards, entitled *Minimum Standards and Quality Education*, focuses on the quality of education for curriculum, textbooks, assessment, and environment. The document also sets standards for learners and teachers. It discusses standards for commonalities across the curriculum, i.e., students, teachers, teaching materials, assessment, and school environment. However, an abrupt appearance of the theme of Early Education seems to have been forced into the list.

The *Curriculum Supplement on Value Education* focuses on the significance of values in quality education. The issue with such documents, however, is that just insertion of these values is not enough—they must be practised in the school environment by the respective teachers. The Curriculum 2017 for ICT Schools (GoP, 2017) claims to be based on holistic development for children. Besides focusing on values, the curriculum includes analytical, and critical thinking skills. The issue, however, is that teaching analytical and critical skills requires creative and inquiry-based pedagogy. So, the question then is: do we have trained teachers in our schools to teach such skills?

The Compulsory Teaching of the Holy Quran Act was passed by the PML-N government for ICT and federal government schools situated in different parts of the country. This act was implemented by the PTI government, making the teaching of the Holy Quran compulsory to Muslim students in all educational institutions.

The Draft Education Policy (GoP, 2017) was planned and prepared over a period of over two years in consultation with different stakeholders. After consuming time and financial and human resources, the PML-N government decided not to announce the policy. The TVET Policy was claimed to be the first national one. Technical and vocational education has always been a theme in our educational policies. Unfortunately, technical education at the school level is considered a socially inferior option.

Different education policies offered solutions to integrate technical courses with regular courses being taught in schools. This document seemed to be another addition to the literature already piled up on the subject, which attracted criticism from one section of society. A meaningful change can only take place if some concrete, consistent, and coordinated efforts are made to implement the policies.

The Education Policy Framework 2018 (GoP, 2018a) announced by the PTI is a crisp document that contains four agenda points including access, quality, uniformity and relevance. These agenda points are not new; they have been a recurrent theme in previous educational policies with barely any concrete outcomes.

A proper critique of the four targets can only be made at the end of the tenure of the government by giving the planners ample time for implementation. Interestingly, the area of ECCE, highlighted in the draft policy of 2017, could not find place in the National Education Policy Framework issued by the PTI government.

The Single National Curriculum (GoP, 2018c) is claimed to provide equal opportunities for students to receive quality education, alleviate disparities, and provide equal opportunities for upward social mobility. The expectation of bridging the socioeconomic gaps through the SNC looks over-simplistic. The curriculum is not just a document but has other commonalities like students, teachers, teaching materials, assessment systems, and school milieu. Having the same curriculum document cannot produce the desired results in the presence of asymmetrical socioeconomic status of students, unequal knowledge and competencies of teachers, uneven school milieus, and different assessment systems.

Another important issue is the post-Eighteenth Amendment scenario, where education has come under the purview of the provinces. A single curriculum and using the same text involves willingness of the provinces. One doable option is to set the standards and give provinces the freedom to select their own content to meet the set standards. Too much control in the form of a single curriculum, uniform books, and single language will be detrimental to the spirit of pluralism and diversity, which is a constitutional right of each citizen in Pakistan.

The language issue remained a serious challenge since the inception of the county in 1947. There have been political slogans for the promotion and implementation of the national language, Urdu, but no concrete efforts were made to enrich and associate Urdu with the power domains in the country.

The 2006 Language Policy generously admits the significance of English in the social, economic, educational, and cultural domains. Keeping in view the important role of English in the modern world, Punjab, the largest province of the country, decided to implement English as a medium of instruction at the primary level. The argument for this drastic decision was that English, being the dividing force between the elite and non-elite, will empower the students in the public sector schools right from the beginning. This decision resulted in all books being written in English.

This practice lasted for almost 14 years, when the chief minister of the PTI-led provincial government of Punjab announced through a tweet that Urdu, not English, would be the medium in the future. Books for the SNC are being written in Urdu, which has triggered a lot of debate. There is genuine concern from parents and private schools on the exclusion of English across the curriculum.

The mother tongue argument used in the debate is not relevant as the examples of countries that progressed using their mother tongue enriched their own language through a robust translation mechanism on a large scale with accelerated speed. The result was that the latest books in English, which contained the maximum information, were translated to their national language. Unfortunately, in Pakistan, despite tall claims, no concrete and consistent efforts were made to enrich Urdu or the other Pakistani languages.

The Undergraduate Policy (GoP, 2020) issued by the Higher Education Commission claims to bring structural changes by making the BS and similar degrees more holistic and richer in terms of breadth and depth to empower students in the domains of knowledge, skills, and professional and interpersonal attitudes.

The policy makes it clear that the courses just constitute minimal education in the general education area. The policy clarifies that though the HEC would prepare model programmes for general requirement, the universities can plan, design, and offer their own programmes in this regard. The adoption date given to the universities for the Undergraduate Policy is end of January 2021. The implementation deadline is Fall 2021. The policy claims to employ competency-based education (CBE) but the implementation of the policy will not be a straightforward process.

There will be challenges in admission, curriculum, major/minor distribution, faculty training, and assessment systems. Another potential challenge would be the professional degrees, especially when a student leaves after two years with only a year and a half of exposure in general education.

The new PhD policy (GoP, 2021) is criticized for not adopting a proper consultation process. The universities were not consulted, and the notification came to them as a surprise. A major concern in academic circles is that lowering the years of study requirement from 18 to 16 will decrease the quality. There is a three-tier academic structure at the higher education level—MA/MSc, MS/MPhil, and PhD—in most foreign universities. Thus, the new policy is not in line with international standards. Another point of criticism of the policy is: how will our BS degree holders with 16 years of study be eligible for PhD programmes abroad?

The duration of a PhD programme proposed in the new PhD policy is three to eight years. It is difficult to understand how the scholars can finish a PhD degree in three years when they are supposed to study courses worth 48 credit hours, conduct research, and write a research thesis.

Contrary to the previous one, the new policy does not require students to take GRE Subject. Instead, they only need GRE General for admission to a PhD programme. This will affect the quality of the admissions process.

Removing the pre-requisite of the same discipline of concentration in BS to apply for a PhD programme in that discipline is another proposed change. This will result in an increase in quantity of applicants but a decrease in quality of the PhD programmes.

Another important change is about thesis evaluation. Contrary to the previous policy that required two positive evaluation reports from the experts of technically advanced foreign countries, under the new policy, it will no longer be mandatory to send the thesis to foreign experts for evaluation. According to the new education policy, a thesis may be evaluated by two Pakistan-based experts and if the scholar manages to publish their research paper in an X-category journal, the thesis can be evaluated by only one expert, who can be from Pakistan. This is likely to reduce the quality checks for PhD theses.

The proposed changes in the new PhD policy, instead of ensuring qualitative improvement, will further reduce the quality of PhD programmes in the country.

SUMMARY

This Chapter focuses on the educational initiatives of the different governments since the last official education policy was announced in 2009 by the PPP government. It includes the Eighteenth Amendment and the insertion of Article 25-A on free and compulsory education. Some educational initiatives were announced during the PML-N government's tenure, including the draft Education Policy 2017, National Curriculum Framework Pakistan, Minimum Standard for Quality Education, Curriculum 2017 for ICT Pakistan, Compulsory Teaching of the Holy Quran Act, and TVET.

The PTI government, which came into power in 2018, initially wanted to announce the draft education policy 2017 prepared by the PML-N government but then abandoned the idea and instead presented certain policy documents on education, which include the National Education Policy Framework (2018), Single National Curriculum, Undergraduate Education Policy 2020, and New PhD Policy 2021.

Chapter 16

Where Do We Stand Today?

What is the status of the education system of Pakistan after more than seven decades? This chapter analyses factors such as public expenditure, literacy at different levels, female education, early childhood care, higher education, out of school children, dropouts from schools, quality of education, curriculum initiatives, and medium of instruction issues.

PUBLIC EXPENDITURE FOR EDUCATION

The inherent paradox in the governments' policies is that the funds allocated are insufficient to realize the overambitious targets set. The governments in Pakistan, time and again, express their desire to increase funds for education but in practice, the funds always remained far below in comparison to other countries in the region. In the 2009 National Education Policy, it was proposed that allocation for education should be 7 per cent of the GDP by 2015. This figure, however, has remained an unfulfilled dream. Interestingly, when a new official document is issued, it tends to forget the old targets and their deadlines. In the 2020–21 budget, the allocation for education (Table 19) fell to 1.92 per cent of the GDP—even lower than last year's allocation of 2.04 per cent. In fact, it is the lowest allocation for education as a percentage of the GDP in the last two decades. This figure is also the lowest in South Asian countries.

THE LITERACY SCENARIO

Access to schools is one of the major challenges for education in Pakistan, because of which the literacy rate, compared to the

Table 19: Expenditure on Education Affairs and Services 2020–1 (in Rs. million)

Province	Current Expendi-ture	Development Expenditure	District Education Authorities	Total
Federal	83,363	34,235	-	117,598
Punjab	71,802.60	31,551.48	290,000.00	393,354
Sindh	236,161.37	27,516.28	-	263,678
KP	35,817.28	15,357.91		51,175
Balochistan	70,358.25	349.65		70,708
		Total		896,513
		GDP		46,629,000*
		Public expenditure on Education (% of GDP)		**1.92**

Source: Annual Budget Statement 2020–1(Calculated and shared in personal correspondence by Dr Vaqar Ahmed, Joint Executive Director, SDPI).

literacy rates of other South Asian countries, is very low. According to the Dakar Framework for Action Education for All (2000–15), Pakistan was to achieve 86 per cent literacy rate by 2015. Pakistan is one of the signatories to the 17 SDGs of the UN. SDG 4 is about Education with seven sub-goals. The second sub-goal refers to early childhood education, which the signatory countries commit to achieve by 2030. According to SDG 4.2 (UNESCO, 2018), 'By 2030, ensure that all girls and boys have access to quality early childhood development, care and pre-primary education so that they are ready for primary education.'

The literacy rate was 57 per cent in the year the Education Policy 2009 was announced (GoP, 2009: 65). The Policy claimed that the: 'Literacy rate shall be increased up to 86 per cent by 2015 through upscaling of ongoing programmes of adult literacy and non-formal basic education in the country' (GoP, 2009a: 39). This could not be achieved even by 2020. According to the PSLM Survey 2018–19

(GoP, 2019: xii), the literacy rate of 10 years and older is 60 per cent. Interestingly, the Economic Survey of Pakistan (GoP, 2018b: xii), instead of quoting government figures (GoP, 2019), quotes 62.3 per cent—the figure given in the one-year older Labour Survey 2017–18. This literacy rate is far less than the target (86 per cent) which was to be achieved by 2015.

Table 20: Literacy Rates (10 Years and Older)

Region/Province	Literacy %
Pakistan	**60**
Punjab	64
Sindh	57
Khyber Pakhtunkhwa, excluding Merged Areas	57
Khyber Pakhtunkhwa, including Merged Areas	55
Balochistan	40

Source: GoP (2019)

Youth Literacy Rate at the Provincial Level

People aged 15–24 comprise the youth bracket of the population. According to the GoP (2019), 72 per cent of the people can read and write a simple statement in any language coherently. The following table outlines youth literacy percentages at the provincial level.

Table 21: Youth Literacy Rate (15–24 Years) (in %) at Provincial Level

Region/Province	Literacy %
Pakistan	**72**
Punjab	79
Sindh	64
Khyber Pakhtunkhwa, excluding Merged Areas	72
Khyber Pakhtunkhwa, including Merged Areas	69
Balochistan	47

Source: GoP (2019)

Adult Literacy

The adult literacy rate (age 15 years and older) at the national level is 56 per cent. At the provincial level, Punjab leads with 61 per cent, and Balochistan lags far behind, with 37 per cent. This scenario invites the attention of decision makers to invest more in Balochistan.

Table 22: Adult Literacy Rates (in %) (Age 15 Years and Older)

Province/NER	Literacy %
Pakistan	**56**
Punjab	61
Sindh	55
Khyber Pakhtunkhwa excluding Merged Areas	52
Khyber Pakhtunkhwa including Merged Areas	49
Balochistan	37

Source: GoP (2019)

EARLY CHILDHOOD CARE AND EDUCATION (ECCE)

Early childhood care and education has been mentioned in several policy documents including the National Education Policy 1998; National Education Policy 2009; and, in more detail, in the draft National Policy 2017. The first national curriculum for ECE was prepared in 2002 and was further refined and improved in 2006. Unfortunately, most of these curricular, pedagogical, and administrative plans could not be realized. Strangely, ECCE, which was highlighted as one of the major areas of reforms in the 2009 Education Policy and the draft Education Policy 2017, could not find any place in the four major areas identified by the National Education Policy Framework 2018. Unfortunately, two-thirds of students aged 3–4 years do not receive education in school. According to the draft National Education Policy, 2017 (GoP, 2017: 27), '... only one third of ECE age group children are in school and remaining two third are out of school (rural 61 per cent : urban 42 per cent).'

NET ENROLLMENT RATE AT PRIMARY LEVEL

Net enrollment rate is the ratio of children of official school-going age who are enrolled in school to the population of the corresponding official school age. According to the GoP (2019), the NER at the primary level, ages 6–10 years in Pakistan, is 66 per cent. Province-wise NER at the primary age is given in Table 23.

Table 23: NER at Primary Level (Class 1–5 and Age 6–10)

Province/NER	NER%	NER% (Urban)	NER% (Rural)
Pakistan	**66**	**75**	**61**
Punjab	73	80	70
Sindh	58	71	48
Khyber Pakhtunkhwa, excluding Merged Areas	66	75	65
Khyber Pakhtunkhwa, including Merged Areas	64	-	-
Balochistan	40	54	36

Source: GoP (2019)

As can be seen in the table above, NER at the primary level differs in provinces. Moreover, there is further discrimination in terms of urban/rural and gender. NER at the primary age (6–10) in urban areas is 75 per cent, compared to 61 per cent in rural areas.

NER AT MIDDLE SCHOOL LEVEL

As we go up the ladder, the NER reduces mainly because of a large number of students dropping out from schools. The NER at middle school-level in Pakistan is 38 per cent. The province-wise NER is 45 per cent in Punjab, 30 per cent in Sindh, 39 per cent in Khyber Pakhtunkhwa excluding merged areas and 36 per cent including merged areas, and 20 per cent in Balochistan. It is important to note that Balochistan is the only province where the NER has declined instead of being higher at the middle school-level.

Table 24: NER at Middle Level (Class 6–8 and Age 11–13)

Province/NER	NER %
Pakistan	**38**
Punjab	45
Sindh	30
Khyber Pakhtunkhwa, excluding Merged Areas	39
Khyber Pakhtunkhwa, including Merged Areas	36
Balochistan	20

Source: GoP (2019)

NER at Matric Level

The NER at the Matric level, ages 14–15 in Pakistan, is 27 per cent, including 29 per cent male and 26 per cent female students. The province-wise NER is in the table below.

Table 25: NER at Matric Level (Class 9–10 and Age 14–15)

Province/NER	NER %
Pakistan	**27**
Punjab	33
Sindh	21
Khyber Pakhtunkhwa, excluding Merged Areas	25
Khyber Pakhtunkhwa, including Merged Areas	23
Balochistan	12

Source: GoP (2019)

THE DROPOUT CHALLENGE

A serious educational challenge for Pakistan has been that of children dropping out of school. According to the GoP (2009a), the dropout rate in the public sector fell from 43 per cent in 2001–2 to 28 per cent in 2005–6. It rose to 41 per cent during 2007–8 for primary education. The latest figures available in the official document, Pakistan Education Statistics 2017–18 (AEPAM, 2017b) (Table 26), show that the survival/retention rate in Pakistan at the primary level (Class 4) is 63 per cent, which suggests that 37 per cent of the students drop out before they reach Class 5. The situation gets worse at the middle and secondary levels. The survival/retention rate at the middle level (Class 5–8) is 45.5 per cent, indicating that 54.5 per cent of the students leave school. The retention rate at the secondary level falls further to 36.5 per cent, denoting that 63.5 per cent of the students drop out before they reach Class 10.

Table 26: Survival/Retention Rate

Province/ Level	Grade I-V		Grade VI-VIII		Grade IX-X	
	Survival/ Retention Rate%	Dropout Rate%	Survival/ Retention Rate%	Dropout Rate%	Survival/ Retention Rate%	Dropout Rate%
Pakistan	63	37	45.5	54.5	36.5	63.5

Source: AEPAM (2017b)

OUT OF SCHOOL CHILDREN

The number of out of school children (OOSC) is alarmingly high in Pakistan. According to Pakistan Education Statistics 2016–17 cited in the National Education Policy Framework (GoP, 2018: 3), 22.5 million children are out of school. The PSLM Survey 2018–19 reflects that 30 per cent of the children aged 5–16 are out of school.

According to the government (2019), 61 per cent of the children have never attended a school. This number can be further analysed in terms of location (urban 75 per cent, rural 53 per cent) and gender (male 73 per cent, female 50 per cent). The number of students who ever attended school can be seen in the following table, along with their location and gender distribution:

Table 27: Children Ever Attended School (Age >= 10 Years)

Pakistan	Children Ever Attended School 2018–19				
	Urban	Rural	Male	Female	Total
	75	53	73	50	61

Source: GoP (2019)

A common problem in all the provinces is that more female students are out of school. Similarly, there are more out of school children in disadvantaged districts compared to the advantaged ones. There is a large gender, economic, and geographic disparity in education enrolment across the country. The out of school children disaggregated by levels of education shows an alarmingly high number at the middle (Classes 6–8) and higher level (Classes 9–10). This is not surprising because the number of middle and high schools across the country is much less compared to primary schools (GoP, 2018: 3). As displayed in Table 28, about 30.13 per cent of children (aged 5–16 years) are out of school. Maximum out of school children in this age bracket are in Balochistan (58.98 per cent), followed by Sindh (41.56 per cent), Khyber Pakhtunkhwa (31.15 per cent and 28.32 per cent), and Punjab (28.32 per cent).

Out of School Children in Urban and Rural Areas

There is a significant disparity in terms of out of school children in urban and rural areas (Table 28). The percentage of out of school children in urban areas is 20.40 per cent, whereas in rural areas, it is 34.99 per cent. The province-wise out of school children percentages can be seen in the following table. The situation is not very encouraging in all provinces but in Balochistan, on average, more than 50 per cent of the children are out of school. This is certainly an alarming situation which needs urgent attention.

Table 28: Percentage of Out of School Children (Age 5–16 Years) in Urban and Rural Areas

Region/Province	Urban Areas %	Rural Areas %	Total %
Pakistan	**20.40**	**34.99**	**30.13**
Punjab	13.55	24.75	20.89
Sindh	26.54	55.42	41.56
Khyber Pakhtunkhwa, excluding Merged Areas	20.69	29.71	28.32
Khyber Pakhtunkhwa, including Merged Areas	21.70	32.79	31.15
Balochistan	48.53	62.77	58.98

Source: GoP (2019)

CHILDREN WHO HAVE NEVER BEEN TO SCHOOL

The most serious challenge Pakistan is facing is that the number of children (23.56 per cent) who have never been to school (age 5–16 years) is very high. Province-wise statistics suggest that the number of children who have never been to school is highest in Balochistan, followed by Sindh, KP, and Punjab.

Table 29: Children Never Been to School (in %) (Age 5–16 Years) in Urban and Rural Areas

Region/Province	Urban Area %	Rural Area %	Total %
Pakistan	**13.98**	**28.34**	**23.56**
Punjab	7.02	17.24	13.71
Sindh	20.37	49.33	35.44
Khyber Pakhtunkhwa, excluding Merged Areas	14.24	23.42	22.01
Khyber Pakhtunkhwa, including Merged Areas	15.61	26.67	25.03
Balochistan	41.30	58.95	54.25

Source: GoP (2019)

FEMALE EDUCATION

One of the cornerstones of educational inequalities is gender. This disparity is visible in different categories and levels of education (Table 30) in the Gender parity index (GPI). The GPI in literacy is 0.69, 0.81 in youth literacy, 0.92 in primary education and 0.89 in secondary education.

Table 30: Gender Parity Index (GPI)

Literacy Level	Percentage
Literacy	0.69
Youth Literacy	0.81
Primary	0.92
Secondary	0.89

Source: GoP (2019)

Gender-wise Literacy Rates

The literacy disparity (10 years and older) on the basis of gender is evident at the national and provincial levels. At the national level, the literacy rate is 60 per cent (GoP, 2019) with 71 per cent male and 49 per cent female. Gender-wise literacy rates at the provincial level are outlined in Table 31.

Table 31: Gender-wise Literacy Rates (10 Years and Older)

Province	Male	Female	Total
Pakistan	**71**	**49**	**60**
Punjab	73	57	64
Sindh	68	44	57
Khyber Pakhtunkhwa, excluding Merged Areas	76	40	57

Khyber Pakhtunkhwa, including Merged Areas	75	36	55
Balochistan	54	24	40

Source: GoP (2019)

Gender-wise Youth Literacy Rate at the Provincial Level

Let us look at the category of youth literacy rate (aged 15–24 years) on the basis of gender. At the national level, the literacy rate is 72 per cent, which increases disparity between male (79 per cent) and female (64 per cent). This disparity between male and female literacy rate at the provincial level is outlined in Table 32.

Table 32: Gender-wise Youth Literacy Rates (15–24 Years) (in %) at Provincial Level

Province	Male	Female	Total
Pakistan	**79**	**64**	**72**
Punjab	82	75	79
Sindh	73	55	64
Khyber Pakhtunkhwa, excluding Merged Areas	88	56	72
Khyber Pakhtunkhwa, including Merged Areas	88	50	69
Balochistan	60	32	47

Source: GoP (2019)

Gender-wise Adult Literacy Rates

The adult literacy category also shows a disparity in terms of gender. The adult national literacy rate (aged 15 year and older) is 56 per cent, with males at 69 per cent and females at 45 per cent. Gender-based disparity in adult literacy persists in all the provinces (Table 33).

Table 33: Gender-wise Adult Literacy Rates (in %) (Age 15 Years and Older)

Province	Male%	Female%	Total%
Pakistan	**69**	**45**	**56**
Punjab	70	53	61
Sindh	68	42	55
Khyber Pakhtunkhwa, excluding Merged Areas	72	34	52
Khyber Pakhtunkhwa, including Merged Areas	71	30	49
Balochistan	52	21	37

Source: GoP (2019)

Gender-wise NER at Primary Level

The net enrollment ratio in Pakistan at the primary level in 2018–19 was 66 per cent (male: 68 per cent and female: 63 per cent). We can see here that the difference between male and female NER is reducing, which is a good sign. In the case of provinces (Table 34), there is no difference between male and female NER in Punjab, but the disparity is highest in Balochistan.

Table 34: Gender-wise NER at Primary Level (Class 1–5 and Age 6–10)

Province	Male NER %	Female NER %	Total NER %
Pakistan	**68**	**63**	**66**
Punjab	73	73	73
Sindh	64	52	58
Khyber Pakhtunkhwa, excluding Merged Areas	72	61	66

Khyber Pakhtunkhwa, including Merged Areas	70	57	64
Balochistan	45	35	40

Source: GoP (2019)

Gender-wise NER at Middle Level

The NER in 2018–19 at the middle level was 38 percent, with 40 per cent male and 36 per cent female. Provincial data is given in Table 35.

Table 35: Gender-wise NER at Middle Level (Class 6–8 and Age 11–13)

Province	Male NER %	Female NER %	Total NER %
Pakistan	**40**	**36**	**38**
Punjab	44	45	45
Sindh	33	26	30
Khyber Pakhtunkhwa, excluding Merged Areas	45	32	39
Khyber Pakhtunkhwa, including Merged Areas	42	28	36
Balochistan	25	15	20

Source: GoP (2019)

Gender-wise NER at Matric Level

The national enrollment rate at the matric level in 2018–19 was 27 per cent, with 29 per cent for males and 26 per cent for females. The provincial-level statistics are below (Table 36).

Table 36: Gender-wise NER at Matric Level (Class 9–10 and Age 14–15)

Province	Male	Female	Total
Pakistan	**29**	**26**	**27**
Punjab	33	33	33
Sindh	23	20	21
Khyber Pakhtunkhwa, excluding Merged Areas	30	19	25
Khyber Pakhtunkhwa, including Merged Areas	30	16	23
Balochistan	15	9	12

Source: GoP (2019)

QUALITY

Another educational challenge Pakistan is facing is the lack of quality in mainstream educational institutions. This includes physical facilities as well as human resource (qualified teachers), curriculum, textbooks, pedagogy, and an effective assessment system. A number of surveys reflect that students' performance is far less than the required national standards. It is interesting to note that as far as facilities are concerned, the public sector schools have more facilities than the private schools.

The other aspect of quality is the actual teaching/learning quality in schools. According to the ASER report of 2018, students in the public schools performed lower than the required standards. In comparison, however, the students of private schools performed better than those of public schools. It is important to understand that the students' performance is directly linked with the quality of pedagogy and educational governance in schools (ASER, 2018: 82).

INTERNET FACILITY

In recent times, online education is not just an option but a necessary tool. This has proved true during the COVID-19 phase when most educational institutions were closed, and teachers and students were forced to switch to online mode. There are countless sources of information on the Internet and a large number of courses from the top universities of the world are available in the form of mass open online courses (MOOCs). However, this requires access to the Internet. In Pakistan, according to the PSLM survey 2018–19 (GoP, 2019), only 34 per cent of the population has access to the Internet. The province-wise breakup is given in the Table below.

Table 37: Status of Internet Facility

Provinces/Region	Internet Facility (2018–19) %
Pakistan	**34**
Punjab	33
Sindh	37
Khyber Pakhtunkhwa, (excluding Merged Areas)	41
Khyber Pakhtunkhwa, (including Merged Areas)	37
Balochistan	19

Source: GoP (2019)

CURRICULUM STATUS

The government plans to implement the SNC from Class 1 to Class 12. In the first phase, the SNC will be implemented at the primary level. In Phase 2, it will be implemented in middle schools (Classes 6–8), and in the third phase, for Classes 9–12, by March 2023.

LANGUAGE ISSUES

The significance and role of the English language was made evident in the National Education Policy 2009. Consequently, schools were instructed to teach subjects of science and math in English. In the SNC (2018), it was emphasised that there would be one medium of instruction. The document reads:

> The vision of Single National Curriculum (2020) stated that one system of Education for all, in terms of curriculum, medium of instruction and a common platform of assessment so that all children have a fair and equal opportunity to receive high quality education. Single National Curriculum is a step in that direction. (GoP, 2018c: 1)

DISCUSSION AND ANALYSIS

There is a significant relationship between education and national development since the former can provide a more level playing field in terms of social, economic, and educational opportunities. A highly qualified and skilled human capital plays an important part in national progress. The UNDP (2020: 345) published the Human Development Index (HDI) of 189 countries of the world. The HDI includes indicators such as life expectancy at birth, expected years of schooling, mean years of schooling, per capita gross national income (GNI), and GNI per capita rank minus HDI rank. Pakistan is ranked 154 out of 189 countries with the HDI value of 0.557 (with 1 being the maximum value) as compared with Sri Lanka at 72, Maldives at 95, India at 131, Bhutan at 129, Bangladesh at 133 and Nepal at 142. Afghanistan is the only country below Pakistan in South Asia. All other countries performed better than Pakistan in this respect. It is important to note that the HDI of Pakistan in 2009 was 75, which simply means that instead of improving in terms of human development, Pakistan slipped down to the 154th position.

The low socioeconomic ranking is linked with poor performance on education indicators. As we saw in this chapter, the literacy rate even after seven decades could not go beyond 60 per cent, which is one of the lowest literacy rates among South Asian countries. The net enrollment rate at the primary level is 66 per cent; middle level, 38 per cent; and matric level, 27 per cent. These are not enviable figures. The literacy rate is also asymmetrical in terms of gender. Similarly, the NER at the primary, middle and matric levels shows a disparity in terms of gender, tilted in favour of boys.

As far as quality is concerned, students in school are performing at lower than required standards (ASER, 2018). Around 22.5 million (GoP, 2018a: 3) children could not even cross the school threshold. This huge number rises further with the addition of children who drop out on a yearly basis, further impacting the overall literacy rate. As a result, the literacy rate of Pakistan is stuck at 60 per cent.

Quality is a core challenge for the country's system of education that needs urgent attention from primary to higher education. Yet another aspect of our educational practices is the gap between what is being taught in educational institutions and societal needs. This gap can only be reduced if the curricula are updated on a regular basis, keeping in view the external changes and learners' needs.

The SNC initiative has its own inherent problem as it is assumed that its introduction will reduce the socioeconomic gap. This assumption ignores the other important educational factors, such as students, teachers, teaching materials, assessment system, and school milieu, which play an important role in unequal education systems. Another problem hindering the implementation of the SNC is the devolution of education to the provinces. All provinces are not on the same page in terms of SNC implementation details. Another significant component of SNC is language. The terms on medium of instruction are vague; it is not clear whether it is applicable to all provinces or all kinds of educational institutions in both the public and private sector. Most of the reasons for the failure of policies and plans have been discussed in detail in Chapter 14 of the book. The conflict and tension between the federal and provinces governments aggravated after the Eighteenth Amendment as the center appears to be reluctant to delegate powers to the provinces on the same old pretext that provinces do not have capacity to run the affairs. The major reason for not achieving the goals remained lack of political will. Ironically, funds to complete existing education projects and carry out new initiatives have decreased instead of increasing.

SUMMARY

This chapter provides a detailed scenario of education in Pakistan, after more than seventy years of independence. We have seen in this chapter that Pakistan is lagging behind other countries in the region in terms of literacy, female education, dropout rate, and out of school children. The literacy rate according to the government (GoP, 2019) is 60 per cent, which is one of the lowest in the South Asian region. We have not been able to achieve our targets in net enrollment at different levels of education. The literacy rate, despite all claims and proclaimed deadlines, remained the same. The number of out of school children could not be reduced. The disparity in terms of educational opportunities between urban/rural and male/female in different domains and categories still exists. The funds allocated for education have decreased instead of increasing. A major reason for the country's unsatisfactory performance in the domain of education is failure of policies in the implementation phase.

Appendices

Appendix-A

Quaid-i-Azam's Message to the Pakistan Education Conference in 1947

'I am glad that the Pakistan Educational Conference is being held today in Karachi. I welcome you to the capital of Pakistan and wish you every success in your deliberations which I sincerely hope will bear fruitful and practical results. You know that the importance of education and the right type of education cannot be over emphasized. Under foreign rule for over a century, sufficient attention has not been paid to the education of our people and if we are to make real, speedy and substantial progress, we must earnestly tackle this question and bring our educational policy and programme on the lines suited to the genius of our people, consonant with our history and culture and having regard to the modern conditions and vast developments that have taken place all over the world.

'There is no doubt that the future of our State will and must greatly depend upon the type of education we give to our children, and the way in which we bring them up as future citizens of Pakistan. Education does not merely mean academic education. There is immediate and urgent need for giving scientific and technical education to our people in order to build up our future economic life and to see that our people take to science, commerce, trade and particularly well planned industries. We should not forget that we have to compete with the world which is moving very fast in this direction.

'At the same time we have to build up the character of our future generation. We should try, by sound education, to instil into them the highest sense of honour, integrity, responsibility and selfless service to the nation. We have to see that they are fully qualified and equipped to play their part in the various branches of national life in a manner which will do honour to Pakistan.'

Source: GoP (1947: 5).

Appendix-B

Speech of Fazal-ur-Rahman in the Pakistan Education Conference in 1947

Ladies and Gentlemen!

It is my pleasant duty to extend to you a cordial welcome to this, the Pakistan Educational Conference of Pakistan. You will, I am sure, warmly associate yourselves with me in paying sincere homage to that great architect of our state, Quaid-i-Azam Muhammad Ali Jinnah, to whose wise and courageous statesmanship we owe the birth of Pakistan. We are meeting at a time when our hearts are still heavy with grief for our kith and kin who have suffered so terribly both in life and property in the disturbances which have convulsed large portions of the two Dominions. The overriding concern of the Government of Pakistan is naturally the speedy rehabilitation and resettlement of the refugees but, overwhelming as this national calamity is, we are determined that it should not obscure from our view the long-term objectives of national development of which education is one of the most important. It is, therefore, a matter of profound satisfaction to me, as it must be to you, that we have now before us the opportunity of reorienting our entire educational policy to correspond closely with the needs of the times and to reflect the ideals for which Pakistan as an Islamic State stands. This is a great, indeed a unique, opportunity, but even greater is the magnitude of the task which it imposes upon us. For the task is no less than the building up of a modern democratic state whose citizens are equipped by the requisite training of body, mind and character to live the good live and to make their contribution to the common efforts of a tormented humanity for the establishment of global peace and security. This calls for a supreme act of dedication for which I can think of no higher sanction than that of Islam which came as a mission of mercy to the world and unfolded the vision of the universal brotherhood of man. It is to this vision which was transformed into reality by the followers of Islam in its early days that the materialistic civilization of the West is at last directing its eyes after more than thirteen centuries of human misery, strife and bloodshed. And it is for making this vision a living reality once again that Pakistan stands.

The impression that Pakistan, being an Islamic State, is a Theoretic State is being sedulously fostered in certain quarters with the sole object of discrediting it in the eyes of the world. To anyone who is conversant with the basic principles of Islam, it should be obvious that in the field of civics Islam has stood for complete social democracy and social justice, as the history of the early Caliphs will show, and has not sanctioned government by a sacerdotal class deriving its authority from God. The ruler and the ruled alike are equal before Islamic law and the ruler, far from being a vice-regent of God on earth, is but a representative of the people who have chosen him to serve them. Social relations apart, even in the realm of spiritual relations, i.e. relationship between man and God, Islam has not recognized any distinction between man and man based on sex or race or worldly position. Within the framework of such a democracy, Islam has enjoined the granting of full freedom of conscience, security for life and property and opportunity for development and progress to all non-Muslims who are members of the body-politic. I consider it of vital importance that our educational system should be animated and guided by these principles. Where but in Islam could we find the democratic virtues of tolerance, self-help, self-sacrifice, human kindliness, the protection and succour of the weak and the oppressed? And what better ideas could we postulate for our educational theory than these?

Our existing educational system, as originally conceived by Macaulay, was intended to serve a narrow, utilitarian purpose and its growth has been largely a matter of artificial improvisation. It has been rightly condemned for its lack of realism and its inability to adjust itself to the needs of a rapidly changing society, its over-literary bias and its utterly uninspiring soulless character. It has no common faith or a common body of principle to animate it and has conspicuously failed to inculcate and maintain the stern moral and intellectual discipline which is the hallmark of true education. Thus its products, with their minds crammed with an unassimilated mass of unrelated ideas and facts passing for knowledge, have gone out into the world only to discover that they are unfitted for the business of living. The growing realization of these grave deficiencies and their paralysing effect on national life inevitably bred acute dissatisfaction in the minds of all thinking people and has of late years led to a considerable concentration of energies on a complete overhaul of our entire educational structure. The Plan for the Post-War Educational Development in India is the first concerted attempt to provide an efficient system of education for the whole subcontinent. It, however, failed to embody the ideals which I have briefly stated above. The establishment of Pakistan now provides us with the opportunity to plan our education in conformity with our genius and aspirations.

Within the limited time at my disposal, I can only indicate what I consider to be fundamental problems and to offer for your mature consideration my personal views thereon in the hope that in the light of your advice I shall be able to formulate definite policies for approval by the government.

For a succinct but brief summing up of the aims of education in a democratic society, I cannot do better than quote a living authority on education. 'Education', he says, 'is a vast continent and it will make for clearer thinking if we divide it into three provinces, corresponding to the three main needs of human life. All men need to make a living—not a base one, but the best that conditions allow. All men live in a society. All men have a personality to develop and the power of living ill or well. For all these education must provide, and it must therefore include, a vocational element, a social or, as the Greeks would have called it, a political element, and a spiritual element. Men must learn to earn a living, to be good members of a society, to understand the meaning of the phrase "the good life"; and education must help them to achieve these three ends'. It must do this not for a limited class but for every citizen, though it will do it in different ways for different people.

Of these three elements of education, I attach the highest importance to the spiritual element, for its neglect, which has characterized modern education, has had disastrous consequences. The experience of two world wars, as also the vast technological inventions of recent years, fraught as they are with incalculable possibilities of destruction, have brought home to us the realization that unless the moral or spiritual growth of man keeps pace with the growth of science, he is doomed to utter extinction. It is surely a profoundly disturbing thought that every step forward in the domain of knowledge should be attended with not a diminution but an increase in barbarism and frightfulness so that the pursuit of knowledge becomes a self-defeating process. To arrest this process, to purge men's minds of barbarism and turn them to humanitarian purposes is the great task which our education must attempt if we are to help mankind to survive. The provision for instruction in the fundamentals of religion in schools is, therefore, a paramount necessity for without such knowledge we cannot hope to build character or lay the foundations for an adequate philosophy of life. What form this instruction should assume is a matter for your careful and detailed consideration but you will agree with me that it must be catholic in outlook and must eschew sectarian or narrow doctrinal lines.

Next in importance is the training for citizenship. The possession of power by a person ignorant of the privileges and responsibilities of citizenship is like the playing of a child with dynamite and is responsible for endless corruption and political instability. Our education must, therefore, instil into the young mind the fundamental maxim of democracy, that the price of liberty is eternal vigilance and it must aim at cultivating the civic virtues of discipline, integrity and unselfish public service. We have been far too prone in the past to think in terms of Bengalis, Punjabis, Sindhis, and Pathans, and it is to be deeply regretted that our education has failed to extirpate this narrow and pernicious outlook of provincial exclusiveness which, should it persist, will spell disaster for our newborn state. There cannot be a greater source of pride and a better object of undivided loyalty than the citizenship of Pakistan, no matter what political, religious or provincial label one may possess.

There is one aspect of training for citizenship which deserves special emphasis for it is only in recent years that we have slowly come to appreciate its importance. I refer to physical training. Although our secondary schools have on the whole made fair provision for it, our primary schools are gravely deficient in this respect with the result that the proper physical development of our young national stock is ignored just at the stage where it is in the greatest need of scientific care and supervision. I trust that this deficiency will soon be made good and a rational, well-coordinated programme of compulsory physical training in all stages of education will be introduced and rigorously enforced. We must also encourage to the maximum such group activities as are typified by the Boy Scout Movement and are directed towards the promotion of 'esprit de corps' and of qualities of physical endurance, self-reliance, courage, initiative, enterprise and social service. It is also time we paid more attention to the question of military training in colleges. I am strongly of the opinion that no student, unless he is physically debarred, should be allowed to pass out of a college without his undergoing a prescribed course of military training.

In mentioning the third clement of education—namely, vocational education—last, I should not be understood to minimize its importance. In as much as it must provide for the material existence of society, it must receive first consideration in any plan of educational reconstruction. In the last analysis, however, all the three elements—spiritual, social and vocational—must cohere and form an integral whole for thus alone can we achieve a complete fusion between the spirit and substance of education.

So vast is the field covered by the term education and so far-reaching are its implications that I can only briefly refer to some of the most important problems wherein it is necessary for us to have boldly-conceived and well-defined objectives.

Our first and foremost concern must inevitably be a determined and vigorous attack on the formidable problem of illiteracy and its evil consequences. It goes without saying that the existence of a large bulk of illiterate population constitutes a grave menace to the security and well-being of the state. There is now general agreement that the state in its own interests should provide to its boys and girls, universal, compulsory and free basic education which is the primary requisite of training in democracy. Whether the financial resources of Pakistan can permit the undertaking of so vast an enterprise is a matter which will need to be gone into carefully, but it is vitally important that we must devise means to overcome within the shortest period of time whatever obstacles stand in our way. No less important is the provision of facilities for adult education which should aim at banishing ignorance through literacy, improving the general standard of living and breaking the centuries-old isolation of our vast rural community. Whatever little that has been done so far in the field of adult education has been half-hearted, haphazard and ineffective. We have now available to us through the United Nations Educational, Scientific, and Cultural Organization a common pool of experience and expert advice and I trust that our participation m the activities of this Organization for whose membership we are applying will provide the requisite stimulus to our drive for the abolition of illiteracy and ignorance.

In the sphere of higher education which seeks to create a class of the elite that will determine the quality of our civilization and will direct and plan our national life, there is urgent need for drastic reform. We must do all we can to prevent the present aimless drift of all and sundry to high schools and colleges and the colossal wastage which the absence of any selective principle involves. The universities, in particular, should cease to function as mere mechanical purveyors of knowledge in the form of cheap degrees. They are essentially homes for the promotion of learning and have a vital role to play in raising the moral and intellectual tone of society and of unfolding before it endless possibilities of human development. I hope that through the establishment of an Inter-University Board or any other coordinating agency our universities will not only strive to raise their existing standards of scholarship but also through a frequent interchange of teachers, the institution of inter-university extension lectures, and discussion of common problem make a worthy contribution in all departments of human knowledge.

Living as we do in an age dominated by science with its ever-increasing tempo of technological development we cannot afford to neglect the problem of technical education. The dire consequences which have flowed from this neglect in the past—our all-round industrial backwardness, the primitive state of our agricultural economy, our helpless dependence on foreign countries for technical personnel—are all too obvious. It was especially during the last war that the weakness of India in the industrial field was painfully demonstrated and we came to realize that in the highly competitive conditions of modern life the bullock-cart is a poor rival of the jet-propelled aeroplane. Pakistan is rich in raw materials and other natural resources which to be properly exploited must be scientifically organized and planned. And in any plan of economic development the first priority must inevitably be accorded to the training of technical personnel. The partition of India has in this respect deprived us of facilities for technical training at many a first-rate technical institution. It is, therefore, a matter of supreme concern to us that we should lose no time in strengthening and enlarging the scope of the few technical institutions that remain with us and in establishing, if necessary, as many as may be required by our own needs. It is unavoidable that in the initial stages we should seek facilities for advanced technical education in foreign countries. You have in this connection before you the proposal for the continuance of the Overseas Scholarships Scheme inaugurated by the late Government of India and I shall welcome your views on the usefulness of the scheme and any suggestions for its improvement or modification. The Government of Pakistan have already set up a Scientific Manpower Committee with the object of assessing the requirements of technical and scientific personnel in Pakistan and I have no doubt that the recommendations of this Committee will provide the necessary basis for a planned programme of technical education.

Poor as Pakistan is in the existence of facilities for technical training, it is poorer as compared with the Indian Dominion in the field of scientific research which is indispensable for industrial and agricultural development. The extent of our poverty in this respect is to be measured from the fact that out of 87 research institutions which were functioning in India in 1945, only six are located in our Dominion and even these are not of a sufficiently high standard of the Indian Council of Scientific and Industrial Research and curiously enough not one of them is in Pakistan. Even our universities, of which we have only three as against eighteen in the Indian Dominion, are poorly equipped and staffed to undertake research on certain specific problems which is generally done by University laboratories in foreign countries. We cannot but feel the gravest concern at such a state of affairs and unless we immediately set about organizing and planning scientific research on a scale commensurate with the requirements of our economic development plans we should cease to aspire to that rank in the comity of progressive nations which is our due as the fifth largest state in the world. I propose to appoint in this connection a high-powered commission which will survey our existing resources as far as government institutions, universities and private industry are concerned and suggest a coordinated plan for the consolidation and development of facilities for scientific research in Pakistan.

You have also before you a proposal for the establishment of a Pakistan Academy whose membership should be regarded as a sign of distinction based on recognition of outstanding contributions in the sphere of art, science and philosophy. I am personally inclined to the view that the proposed Academy, which, if formed, will forge a strong cultural link with foreign countries, should be an independent non-official body. The scope and functions of this Academy, the terms and conditions as also the extent of its membership and the means of financing it are matters on which I would welcome your advice. I need hardly assure you that my assistance in the establishment of the proposed Academy will always be available to you.

The language problem has long baffled our educationists for, with the exception of Russia, it is more complex in India than in any other country. In seeking a practical solution we will do well to study the Russian experimentation in this as in many other fields of education. With as many as 2,000 groups of distinct nationalities ranging from the highly civilized to tribes still in the primitive stage of devil-worship and with 200 languages and dialects some of which did not even have a written alphabet, to deal with Russians, statesmen and educationists had certainly a Herculean task to perform, but it is a tribute to their political sagacity that instead of forcing different national groups into the narrow Russian cultural mould they have made all such languages the medium of instruction as have showed some evidence of culture, of capacity to grow into a creative tool and to express thought processes. Today education in Soviet Russia is carried on in no less than ninety languages. I commend the Russian example to you because it shows how diversity has been encouraged without endangering the fundamental unity of a common culture which has been ensured by the making of Russian as the first compulsory foreign language in all non-Russian schools. We may not subscribe to the Russian ideology but we can certainly benefit from their handling of the linguistic problem. We in Pakistan must provide the maximum scope for growth to our provincial languages not merely as media of instruction but also as instruments for the dissemination of the culture they embody without at the same time sacrificing the unity of our common culture. To ensure this unity, we need a language for interprovincial communication and in this connection the claims of Urdu call for special consideration. In, the brief period of its existence it has shown an extraordinary vitality and sensitivity both as an instrument of communication and as a vehicle for the expression of the subtlest shades of thought and the most ethereal flights of fancy. The facility with which it can borrow and assimilate words from foreign languages, its historic affiliations with Persian, Arabic, Sanskrit, and English and its high creative output in prose and poetry constitute to my mind unassailable grounds for its establishment as the 'lingua franca' of Pakistan.

As regards English, while the injurious effects of making an alien language the medium of instruction have been widely recognized, it must for some considerable time to come retain its pride of place both in the sphere of our university education and as a means of international communication. During the last three or four decades it has displaced French as the leading language of the world and the recent emergence of Basic Education is likely to extend its dominion still further. Besides, from purely self-regarding motives we should not easily throw away a language which gives us so easy an access to all the secrets of Western science and culture. The study of other foreign languages, especially Arabic and Persian, which are the repositories of our vast cultural heritages, will doubtless occupy a prominent place in our educational system. In fact, I would go so far as to say that at each University in Pakistan I envisage the establishment of special chairs of provincial and oriental languages including Sanskrit for the promotion of higher research and cultural contacts.

Two matters which are interrelated have been greatly exercising my mind for some time. They are the drawing up of syllabi and the preparation of textbooks. Hitherto there has been practically no coordination among the Universities and the Provincial Education Departments in an attempt to rationalize our syllabi and relate them under a coherent educational ideology to the problems of life. I trust that in the light of the fundamental principles that I have enunciated you will lay down the general lines on which our syllabi should be framed so as to bring them into vital relation with the necessities and ideals of our country.

As regards textbooks, you will agree with me that the current practice of entrusting their preparation to commercial firms is educationally unsound for, apart from the profit-motive which overrides all other considerations, commercial firms do not command sufficient talent of the requisite intellectual calibre to produce textbooks of a consistently high standard. I am, therefore, strongly of the opinion that there should be special government organizations to undertake the preparation of textbooks. This will not only ensure the observance of approved educational principles on which textbooks are to be based but will also bring together talent of sufficient width and diversity in academic attainment to give the textbooks a degree of objectivity and high scholarly merit not to be met with in the ordinary commercial textbooks.

Of the need for fostering through education a spirit of international cooperation, I have already spoken. Wars are invariably engendered in the minds of men by suspicion and mistrust which are due to ignorance of other peoples' ways of thought and living. Pakistan, being yet in its infancy, has a need to forge bonds of mutual understanding and cooperation with other nations who are on the whole ignorant of its culture and political aspirations. We are, therefore, genuinely interested in collaborating with all such agencies as have for their object the promotion of peace and human well-being.

Of these agencies the one in which we are especially interested is the United Nations Educational, Scientific, and Cultural Organization whose most important job is the dissemination of culture 'for the sake of the dignity of man' and the institution of collaboration among the nations to advance the ideal of equality of educational opportunity without regard to race or sex or economic or social distinctions. I am certain that our association with this organization will not only help us forward in the special tasks which our education is to undertake but will also establish our solidarity with other nations in the pursuit of common objectives.

UNESCO apart, there are sundry other ways in which we can establish cultural contacts with other countries, in particular with the Middle East with whose people we claim spiritual and moral kinship. We can, for instance, promote the interchange of teachers and students, send out scientific and educational missions, arrange for international exhibitions and conferences and thereby increase the free flow of ideas. As a nation we may not have the glittering achievements of modern science to display, though in fullness of time we hope to do that; but we have our distinct cultural traditions which have left their impress from Spain in the West to Indonesia and China in the East and have enriched the world's heritage in the domain of arts and philosophy. Coming nearer home, our past still speaks to us in the eloquent beauty of a thousand architectural monuments scattered over the length and breadth of India. Most of these monuments remain now with our sister Dominion, but we in Pakistan have not only some of the most remarkable of Buddhist sites but also have the remains of almost the entire prehistoric Indus Valley civilization. We are thus culturally one of the focal points in the history and prehistory of the continent of Asia and have a unique field for sustained research and exploration, in which we will cordially welcome international collaboration. The reorganization of the Pakistan Archaeological Department is now engaging my attention and I am confident that it will prove worthy of its task and make a noble contribution to our knowledge of ancient cultures.

In dwelling upon some of the important aspects of education I have been anxious to emphasize what I conceive to be the true spirit of education. Man does not live by bread alone. He needs something more if his life has to have any worth and significance. It is this 'something more' that education must provide and I cannot define it better than as a vision of excellence of the unchanging, eternal values summed up in three words: TRUTH, GOODNESS and BEAUTY. May our endeavours be constantly guided by this great vision.

Source: GoP (1947: 5–13).

Appendix-C

Speech of Quaid-i-Azam Muhammad Ali Jinnah at the Dacca University Convocation on 24th March 1948 (Recorded by Radio Pakistan, Dacca)

Mr Chancellor, Ladies and Gentlemen,

When I was approached by the vice chancellor with a request to deliver the convocation address, I made it clear to him that there were so many calls on me that I could not possibly prepare a formal convocation address on an academic level with regard to the great subjects with which university deals, such as arts, history, philosophy, science, law and so on. I did, however, promise to say a few words to the students on this occasion, and it is in fulfilment of that promise that I will address you now.

First of all, let me thank the vice chancellor for the flattering terms in which he referred to me. Mr Vice Chancellor, whatever I am, and whatever I have been able to do, I have done it merely as a measure of duty which is incumbent upon every *Mussalman* to serve his people honestly and selflessly.

In addressing you I am not here speaking to you as Head of the State, but as a friend, and as one who has always held you in affection. Many of you have today got your diplomas and degrees and I congratulate you. Just as you have won the laurels in your university and qualified yourselves, so I wish you all success in the wider and larger world that you will enter. Many of you have come to the end of your scholastic career and stand at the threshold of life. Unlike your predecessors, you fortunately leave this university to enter life under a sovereign, independent state of your own. It is necessary that you and your other fellow students fully understand the implications of the revolutionary change that took place on the birth of Pakistan. We have broken the shackles of slavery; we are now a free people. Our State is our own State. Our government is our own government, of the people, responsible to the people of the State and working for the good of the State. Freedom, however, does not mean license. It does not mean that you can now behave just as you please and do what you like, irrespective of the interests of other people or of the State. A great responsibility rests on you and, on the contrary, now more than ever, it is necessary for us to work as a united and disciplined nation. What is now required of us all is constructive spirit and not the militant spirit of the days when we were fighting for our freedom. It is far more difficult to construct than to have a militant spirit for the attainment of freedom. It is easier to go to jail or fight for freedom than to run a government.

Let me tell you something of the difficulties that we have overcome and of the dangers that still lie ahead. Thwarted in their desire to prevent the establishment of Pakistan, our enemies turned their attention to finding ways and means to weaken and destroy us. Thus, hardly had the new State come into being when came the Punjab and Delhi holocaust. Thousands of men, women and children were mercilessly butchered and millions were uprooted from their homes. Over fifty lakhs of these arrived in the Punjab within a matter of weeks. The care and rehabilitation of these unfortunate refugees, stricken in body and in soul, presented problems, which might well have destroyed many a well-established State. But those of our enemies who had hoped to kill Pakistan at its very inception by these means were disappointed. Not only has Pakistan survived the shock of that upheaval, but also it has emerged stronger, more chastened and better equipped than ever.

There followed in rapid succession other difficulties, such as withholding by India of our cash balances, of our share of military equipment and lately, the institution of an almost complete economic blockade of your province. I have no doubt that all right-thinking men in the Indian Dominion deplore these happenings and I am sure the attitude of the mind that has been responsible for them will change, but it is essential that you should take note of these developments. They stress the importance of continued vigilance on our part. Of late, the attack on your province, particularly, has taken a subtler form. Our enemies, among whom I regret to say, there are some Muslims, have set about actively encouraging provincialism in the hope of weakening Pakistan and thereby facilitating the re-absorption of this province into the Indian Dominion. Those who are playing this game are living in a fool's paradise, but this does not prevent them from trying. A flood of false propaganda is being daily put forth with the object of undermining the solidarity of the *Musslamans* of this State and inciting the people to commit acts of lawlessness. The recent language controversy, in which I am sorry to make note, some of you allowed yourselves to get involved even after your Prime Minister had clarified the position, is only one of the many subtle ways whereby the poison of provincialism is being sedulously injected into this province. Does it not strike you rather odd that certain sections of the Indian press, to whom the very name of Pakistan is anathema, should in the matter of language controversy set themselves up as the champion of what they call your just rights? Is it not significant that the very persons who in the past have betrayed the *Mussalmans* or fought against Pakistan, which is after all merely the embodiment of your fundamental right of self-determination, should now suddenly pose as the saviours of your just right and incite you to defy the government on the question of language? I must warn you to beware of these fifth columnists. Let me restate my views on the question of a State language for Pakistan. For official use in this province, the people of the province can choose any language they wish. This question will be decided solely in accordance with the wishes of the people of this province alone, as freely expressed through their accredited representatives at the appropriate time and after full and dispassionate consideration.

There can, however, be only one lingua franca, that is, the language for intercommunication between the various provinces of the State, and that language should be Urdu and cannot be any other. The State language therefore, must obviously be Urdu, a language that has been nurtured by a hundred million Muslims of this sub-continent, a language understood throughout the length and breadth of Pakistan and above all a language which, more than any other provincial language, embodies the best that is in Islamic culture and Muslim tradition and is nearest to the language used in other Islamic countries. It is not without significance that Urdu has been driven out of the Indian Union and that even the official use of the Urdu script has been disallowed. These facts are fully known to the people who are trying to exploit the language controversy in order to stir up trouble. There was no justification for agitation but it did not suit their purpose to admit this. Their sole object in exploiting this controversy is to create a split among the Muslims of this State, as indeed they have made no secret of their efforts to incite hatred against non-Bengali *Mussalmans*. Realizing, however, that the statement that your Prime Minister made on the language controversy, on return from Karachi, left no room for agitation, in so far as it conceded the right of the people of this province to choose Bengali as their official language if they so wished, these persons changed their tactics. They started demanding that Bengali should be the State language of the Pakistan centre and since they could not overlook the obvious claims of Urdu as the official language of a Muslim State, they proceeded to demand that both Bengali and Urdu should be State languages of Pakistan. Make no mistake about it. There can be only one State language, if the component parts of this State are to march forward in unison, and that language in my opinion can only be Urdu. I have spoken at some length on this subject so as to warn you of the kind of tactics adopted by the enemies of Pakistan and certain opportunist politicians to try to disrupt this State or to discredit the Government. Those of you who are about to enter life, be on your guard against these people. Those of you who have still to continue your studies for some time, do not allow yourselves to be exploited by any political party or self-seeking politician. As I said the other day, your main occupation should be in fairness to yourselves, in fairness to your parents and indeed in fairness to the State, to devote your attention solely to your studies. It is only thus that you can equip yourselves for the battle of life that lies ahead of you. Only thus will you be an asset and a source of strength and of pride to your State. Only thus, can you assist it in solving the great social and economic problems that confront it and enable it to reach its destined goal among the most progressive and strongest nations of the world.

My young friends, I would, therefore, like to tell you a few points about which you should be vigilant and beware. Firstly, beware of the fifth columnists among ourselves. Secondly, guard against and weed out selfish people who only wish to exploit you so that they may swim. Thirdly, learn to judge who are really true and really honest and unselfish servants of the State who wish to serve the people with heart and soul and support them. Fourthly, consolidate the Muslim League Party, which will serve and build up a really and truly great and glorious Pakistan. Fifthly, the Muslim League has won and established Pakistan and it is the Muslim League whose duty it is now, as custodian of the sacred trust, to construct Pakistan. Sixthly, there may be many who did not lift their fingers to help us in our struggle, nay even opposed us and put obstacles in our great struggle openly and not a few worked in our enemy's camp against us, who may now come forward and put their own attractive slogans, catch-words, ideals and programs before you. But they have yet to prove they are bonafide or that there has really been an honest change of heart in them, by supporting and joining the League and working and pressing their views within the League Party organization and not by starting mushroom parties at this juncture of a very great and grave emergency, when you know that we are facing external dangers and are called upon to deal with internal complex problems of a far-reaching character affecting the future of seventy million people. All this demands complete solidarity, unity and discipline. I assure you, 'Divided you fall. United you stand'.

There is another matter that I would like to refer to. My young friends, hitherto, you have been following the rut. You get your degrees and when you are thrown out of this university in thousands, all that you think and hanker for is government service. As your vice chancellor has rightly stated the main object of the old system of education and the system of government existing, hitherto, was really to have well-trained, well-equipped clerks. Of course, some of them went higher and found their level, but the whole idea was to get well-qualified clerks. Civil Service was mainly staffed by the Britons and the Indian element was introduced later on and it went up progressively. Well, the whole principle was to create a mentality, a psychology, and a state of mind that an average man, when he passed his B.A. or M.A. was to look for some job in government. If he had it he thought he had reached his height. I know and you all know what has been really the result of this. Our experience has shown that an M.A. earns less than a taxi driver, and most of the so-called government servants are living in a more miserable manner than many menial servants who are employed by well-to-do people. Now I want you to get out of that rut and that mentality and especially now that we are in free Pakistan. Government cannot absorb thousands, impossible. But in the competition to get government service most of you become demoralized. Government can take only a certain number and the rest cannot settle down to anything else and being disgruntled are always ready to be exploited by persons who have their own axes to grind.

Now I want that you must divert your mind, your attention, your aims and ambition to other channels and other avenues and fields that are open to you and will increasingly become so. There is no shame in doing manual work and labour. There is an immense scope in technical education for we want technically qualified people very badly. You can learn banking, commerce, trade, law, etc. which provide so many opportunities now. Already you find that new industries are being started, new banks, new insurance companies, new commercial firms are opening and they will grow as you go on. Now these are avenues and fields open to you. Think of them and divert your attention to them, and believe me, you will there benefit yourselves more than by merely going in for government service and remaining there, in what I should say, a circle of clerkship, working there from morning till evening, in most dingy and uncomfortable conditions. You will be far more happy and far more prosperous with far more opportunities to rise if you take to commerce and industry and will thus be helping not only yourselves but also your State. I can give you one instance. I know a young man who was in government service. Four years ago he went into a banking corporation on two hundred rupees, because he had studied the subject of banking and today he is Manager in one of their firms and drawing fifteen hundred rupees a month—in just four years. These are the opportunities to have and I do impress upon you now to think in these terms.

Finally, I thank you again Mr Chancellor and particularly you Mr. Vice Chancellor for the warm welcome you have given me and the very flattering personal references made by you. I hope, nay, I am confident that the East Bengal youth will not fail us.

Pakistan Zindabad.

Source: *http://jinnah.pk/2009/09/27/students-role-in-nation-building/*

Appendix-D

Aims and Objectives of Constitution (Objectives Resolution) passed by Constituent Assembly in March 1949

Whereas sovereignty over the entire universe belongs to Allah Almighty alone and the authority which He has delegated to the State of Pakistan, through its people for being exercised within the limits prescribed by Him is a sacred trust;

This Constituent Assembly representing the people of Pakistan resolves to frame a Constitution for the sovereign independent State of Pakistan;

In the name of Allah, the Beneficent, the Merciful:

Wherein the State shall exercise its powers and authority through the chosen representatives of the people; Wherein the principles of democracy, freedom, equality, tolerance and social justice as enunciated by Islam shall be fully observed; Wherein the Muslims shall be enabled to order their lives in the individual and collective spheres in accordance with the teachings and requirements of Islam as set out in the Holy Qur'an and the Sunnah; Wherein adequate provision shall be made for the minorities to freely profess and practice their religions and develop their cultures; Wherein the territories now included in or in accession with Pakistan and such other territories as may hereafter be included in or accede to Pakistan shall form a Federation wherein the units will be autonomous with such boundaries and limitations on their powers and authority as may be prescribed; Wherein shall be guaranteed fundamental rights including equality of status, of opportunity and before law, social, economic and political justice, and freedom of thought, expression, belief, faith, worship and association, subject to law and public morality; Wherein adequate provisions shall be made to safeguard the legitimate interests of minorities and backward and depressed classes; Wherein the independence of the Judiciary shall be fully secured; Wherein the integrity of the territories of the Federation, its independence and all its rights including its sovereign rights on land, sea and air shall be safeguarded;

So that the people of Pakistan may prosper and attain their rightful and honored place amongst the nations of the World and make their full contribution towards international peace and progress and happiness of humanity.

Source: Khan, H., 2001. Constitutional and Political History of Pakistan (Karachi: Oxford University Press).

Appendix-E

Excerpt from the speech of Sris Chandra Chattopadhyaya in the Constituent Assembly, 7 March 1949

Mr President, I rise to support the amendment for circulation of the Resolution for eliciting public opinion. I want to make a few observations about the amendment. First, in the course of the last 18 months that have passed after the partition, no 'Objectives Resolution' was brought forward. In fact after 14 August 1947, when Pakistan became a sovereign state, we thought no such Resolution was necessary at all. The thing that matters is the constitution itself and not a theoretical resolution on the aims and objects of the constitution. In fact, not even a committee of this House was formed to consider this Resolution. In India they had an Objectives Resolution because the Britishers were still there, and it was necessary to tell the people and the world what her constitution would be like after the British left. Even that was before August 1947, when the sovereignty was made over to the people of Pakistan and India. In some countries there have been Objectives Resolutions after a bloody revolution because everything was in a chaos. But the case is different here in Pakistan. Some 18 months ago, Britishers had left and we are now free to do as we like. And we have been going on without any Objectives Resolution for so long. As a matter of fact, I understand the Sub-Committee on Fundamental Rights have already finalized their report. There was no difficulty to recommend Fundamental Rights even without this Objectives Resolution. The fact is that it is the actual constitution that will matter and a theoretical resolution like the one before us may not be necessary at all. So long as we had an idea that the constitution would be based on the eternal principles of equality, democracy, and social justice. We thought that religion and politics would not be mixed up. That was the declaration of Quaid-i-Azam Muhammad Ali Jinnah in this House. But the Resolution before us has a religious basis. We got notice of it some four days back.

We have not been able to understand fully the implications of some of the paragraphs of the Resolution. They require study, consultation, deliberation with our friends, both Muslims and non-Muslims, and the citizens of our country who are our masters. We are their servants. But the time given to us for the purpose has been too short. Frankly speaking, for example, what the Resolution means and implies in the Preamble, viz, that: 'Sovereignty over the entire universe belongs to God Almighty alone and the authority which He has delegated to the state of Pakistan through its people for being exercised within the limits prescribed by Him is a sacred trust;' is a thing for which we require time to study it and understand before accepting or modifying it in any way. Then come to paragraph four: 'Wherein the principles of democracy, freedom, equality, tolerance, and social justice, as enunciated by Islam, shall be fully observed.' has been mentioned. This again is not clear to us—the non-Muslims. We need time to study it, in consultation with our friends in East Bengal and for the sake of clarification. In fact when we left East Bengal this time we had no idea that such a Resolution was to be brought forward. There was no indication of it in the Agenda papers circulated.

Liaquat opposed the motion which was put to vote that very day, 7 March 1949, and defeated.

Source: GoP, 1949. Official Report of the Fifth Session of the Constituent Assembly of Pakistan Debates. The Constituent Assembly of Pakistan Debates. Volume V. 9–10. (Karachi: Governor-General's Press).

Appendix-F

Language Formula Approved by the Constituent Assembly in May 1954

1. The official languages of Pakistan Republic should be Urdu and Bengali and such other languages as might be declared to such by the head of the state on the recommendations of the provincial legislatures concerned;
2. Members of Parliament should have the right to speak in Urdu and Bengali in addition to English;
3. Notwithstanding anything in the above Article, for a period of twenty years from the commencement of the Constitution, the English language should continue to be used for all official purposes of the Republic for which it was being used immediately before such commencement;
4. For the examination of the central services, all provincial languages should be placed on an equal footing;
5. Provision should be made to teach Arabic, Urdu, and Bengali in secondary schools to enable students to study one or two of these in addition to the language used as the medium of instruction;
6. The state should take all measures for the development and growth of a common national language;
7. A commission should be appointed ten years after the commencement of the constitution to make recommendations regarding the replacement of English; and
8. Notwithstanding anything in the foregoing Articles, the federal legislature might by law provide for the use, after the expiry of the period of twenty years from the commencement of the Constitution, of the English language for such purposes as might be specified in the law.

Source: Khan, H., 2001. Constitutional and Political History of Pakistan (Karachi: Oxford University Press).

Appendix-G

Single National Curriculum

Vision

One system of Education for all, in terms of curriculum, medium of instruction and a common platform of assessment so that all children have a fair and equal opportunity to receive high quality education. Single National Curriculum is a step in that direction.

Objectives

One system of Education for all, in terms of curriculum, medium of instruction and a common platform of assessment which will ensure:

- All children have a fair and equal opportunity to receive high quality education
- Social Cohesion and National Integration
- Alleviation of disparities in education content across the multiple streams
- Equal opportunities for upward social mobility
- Equity in education
- Holistic development of children in the light of emerging international trends and local aspirations
- Smooth inter-provincial mobility of teachers and students

Key Considerations

The development of SNC is driven by the following key considerations:

- Teachings of the Holy Quran and Sunnah
- Vision of Quaid and Iqbal
- Constitutional framework
- National Policies, Aspirations and National Standards
- Alignment with the goals & targets of SDG-4
- Emerging international trends in teaching, learning & assessment
- Outcomes based approach
- Focus on Values, Life Skills Based and Inclusive Education

- Respect & appreciation for different cultures & Religions in local and global context
- Promotion of intellectual, spiritual, aesthetic, emotional, social and physical development of learners
- Move away from rote memorization & Focus on Project, Inquiry and Activity Based Learning
- Development of 21st century skills including Analytical, Critical and Creative Thinking.
- Use of Information & Communication Technology (ICT)
- Alignment with Trends in International Mathematics and Science Study (TIMSS)

Phases of Single National Curriculum

Single National Curriculum is being developed in three phases:

1. Phase I: Development of SNC and textbooks Pre-I–V (March 2021)
2. Phase II: Development of SNC and textbooks VI–VIII (March 2022)
3. Phase III: Development of SNC and textbooks IX–XII (March 2023)

Development Process of SNC

- Before initiating development of SNC, multiple comparative studies were conducted to align SNC with international standards.
    - These include analysis of Pakistani Curriculum with Singapore and Cambridge Curriculum
    - Pakistan Learners' Standards comparison with Singapore, Malaysia/ Indonesia, & UK standards.
    - All the findings were incorporated in the SNC.

Consultation with Stakeholders

- All federating units
- public sector
- private sector
- Federal Government Educational Institutions (FGEIs) Cantts & Garrisons
- Deeni Madaris
- Cambridge University UK for English, Maths, and Science
- LUMS and AKU-IED

Workshops and National Conference

- National workshops on Life-Skills Based Education, Critical Thinking, and SDG-4
- Four-Day Provincial and Area workshops in all federating units

- The inputs and feedback received was incorporated in the SNC
- Four-Day National Conference on Single National Curriculum from 11–14 February 2020 and the draft was finalized and signed by all the representatives from Federating Units, FGEIs, Private Sector, and Ittehad Tanzimat ul Madaris Pakistan.

Salient Features of SNC

- The SNC is standards, benchmarks and outcomes based across all subjects as compared to the 2006 curriculum in which standards benchmarks and learning outcomes were not developed for each subject curriculum.
- In 2006, the subject of Islamiat was integrated with General Knowledge up to Grade 2 and started as a separate subject from Grade 3 onwards. In the SNC Islamiat starts from Grade 1 as a separate subject up to Grade 12.
- Previously the subject of Ethics was designated for non-Muslim students in lieu of Islamiat from Grade 3 onwards. Now a new subject Religious Education has been introduced for non-Muslim students from Grade 1 onwards for five minority groups of Pakistan.
- The content of the SNC for Maths and Science has been aligned to the TIMSS content framework.
- The content is aligned to the international commitments like SDG 4.
- The SNC focusses on equipping learners with principles and attributes such as truthfulness, honesty, tolerance, respect, peaceful coexistence, environmental awareness & care, democracy, human rights, sustainable development, global citizenship, personal care, and safety.
- SNC focusses on development of analytical, critical and creative thinking through a more activities-based approach rather than static teacher centric learning.
- Use of ICT is integrated in the curriculum for the first time.
- The 2006 curriculum was implemented only in government schools and some low-cost private schools. The SNC will be implemented across the board in all schools of Pakistan including government and private schools and Deeni Madaris.

Subject-Wise Salient Features

Early Childhood Care and Education (Pre-I)

- The ECCE curriculum has been revised keeping in view the local culture and environment alongside modern/innovative trends in ECCE and national & international commitments (SDG 4)
- Basic learning areas include:

    - personal and social development
    - language & literacy

  - basic mathematical concepts
  - world around us
  - physical development (newly added)
  - health, hygiene & safety
  - creative arts

- Holistic development of a child through emphasis on knowledge, skills, and positive attitudes
- Personality development through practice of patience, tolerance, empathy, and citizenship
- Respecting diversity of gender, religion, colour, cast, creed, and people with special needs
- Competencies on child security and safety and link to technology.
- Integration of 21st century skills
- Guidelines for teachers, materials developers and administrators
- Suggestions on ECCE materials, conducive environment and assessment

General Knowledge for Grades 1–3 (General Science and Social Studies)

- Integration of basic concepts of Science and Social Studies to serve as a bridge between Grades Pre-I to Grade 4.
- Fosters lifelong learning through development of inquiry and independent learning skills
- Life-Skills including child protection
- Includes activities for students to improve learning
- Increased emphasis on positive attitudes for holistic development of students

English Grades 1–5

- English to be taught as a language rather than subject
- Higher focus than before on the communicative competence of the language (listening and speaking)
- Addition of interactive and collaborative pedagogical strategies
- Guidelines for assessment along with scoring rubrics/marking schemes have been included for all four language skills including listening and speaking which was not included in curriculum 2006
- Many new themes added to guide the content development such as SDG-4, Gender Equality, LSBE and Inclusivity, Diversity of Cultures, Personal Safety, Health and Hygiene

Urdu Grades 1–5

- Focus on development of language skills and competencies

- Competencies of 'speech', 'creative writing' and 'aesthetic sense' have been added
- Integration of themes like patriotism, citizenship, promotion of social cohesion
- Creation of links between language learning and other subjects
- Promotion of diversity of culture and languages especially regional languages of Pakistan
- Understanding and application of critical media literacy

Islamiat Grades 1-5

- Islamiat is now a separate subject from grade 1 onwards
- Curriculum was revised by both the representatives of the Federating units as well as representatives of Ittehad Tanzimat-e-Madaris Pakistan
- There were no competencies, standards and SLOs in the previous curriculum 2006. Now, these have been added in the SNC along with their definition.
- Outcomes based and activity-based curriculum. From passive to active learning
- According to 'Compulsory Teaching of the Holy Quran Act 2017' the SLOs have been added
- In addition to Nazra Quran, a framework for reading of 200 Ahadith from I–XII has been added
- In addition to Hifz of Surahs, framework of hifz 40 Ahadith from I–VIII has been added
    - Addition of two strands: 'Husn-e-Muamlat o Muashrat' and 'Islami Taleemat aur Dour-e-Hazir ke Taqazay'
- For primary classes, SLOs have been developed keeping in view higher order thinking
- Instructions for teachers, textbook authors and assessment experts have been added

Mathematics Grades 1–5

- Gradual progression in teaching approach from grades 1–5 (concrete, pictorial, abstract)
- Focus on developing solid conceptual foundation based on logical reasoning
- Responds to SDG 4 goals such as communication, collaboration and independent learning
- Emphasis on linking Maths with real life situations through examples and number stories
- Several suggested activities for each content area to promote learning
- Integration of ICT through web links and students-based tasks

- Alignment with Trends in International Mathematics and Science Study (TIMSS) for the best teaching and assessment practices.

General Science Grades 4–5

- Realignment in view of latest global trends and practices in Science education
- Addition of Technology based content as separate chapters
- Integration of themes such as conservation, bio-ethics, scientific responsibilities & care for the environment and all living beings
- Promotion of inquiry-based learning
- Integration of ICT into the curriculum through web links and project work
- Integration of STEAM as a cross cutting strand

Social Studies Grades 4–5

- Organization of the curriculum in 6 strands including Citizenship, History, Government, Economics, Culture, and Geography
- Inclusion of national, global and digital citizenship education including rights and responsibilities
- New themes include local government, ancient civilizations, agriculture, entrepreneurship, anti-corruption
- Focus on democracy, patriotism and importance of rule of law
- Holistic development of students through integration of peaceful coexistence, acceptance, respect and appreciation of diversity

Appendix-H

The Objectives Resolution to form part of substantive provisions

2A. The Objective Resolution to form part of substantive provisions.[1]

The principles and provisions set out in the objectives Resolution reproduced in the Annex are hereby made substantive part of the Constitution and shall have effect accordingly.

3. Elimination of exploitation

The State shall ensure the elimination of all forms of exploitation and the gradual fulfilment of the fundamental principle, from each according to his ability to each according to his work.

4. Right of individuals to be dealt with in accordance with law, etc.

1) To enjoy the protection of law and to be treated in accordance with law is the inalienable right of every citizen, wherever he may be, and of every other person for the time being within Pakistan
2) In particular:
    a. no action detrimental to the life, liberty, body, reputation or property of any person shall be taken except in accordance with law;
    b. no person shall be prevented from or be hindered in doing that which is not prohibited by law; and
    c. no person shall be compelled to do that which the law does not require him to do.

5. Loyalty to State and obedience to Constitution and law.

1) Loyalty to the State is the basic duty of every citizen.
2) Obedience to the Constitution and law is the inviolable[2] obligation of every citizen wherever he may be and of every other person for the time being within Pakistan.

6. High treason.[3]

1) Any person who abrogates or attempts or conspires to abrogate, subverts or attempts or conspires to subvert the Constitution by use of force or show of force or by other unconstitutional means shall be guilty of high treason.

2) Any person aiding or abetting [or collaborating][4] the acts mentioned in clause (1) shall likewise be guilty of high treason.

2A)[5] An act of high treason mentioned in clause (1) or clause (2) shall not be validated by any court including the Supreme Court and a High Court.

3) [Majlis-e-Shoora (Parliament)][6] shall by law provide for the punishment of persons found guilty of high treason.

Notes

1. Inserted by Revival of Constitution of 1973 Order, 1985 (President's Order No. 14 of 1985), Art.2 and Sch. item 2 (with effect from 2 March 1985).
2. Substituted by Revival of Constitution of 1973 Order, 1985 (President's Order No. 14 of 1985), Sch. item 3 (with effect from 2 March 1985) for 'basic'.
3. Substituted by Constitution (Eighteenth Amendment) Act, 2010, Sect. 4(i) (with effect from 19 April 2010) for:
    1) Any person who abrogates or attempts or conspires to abrogate, subverts or attempts or conspires to subvert the Constitution by use of force or show of force or by other unconstitutional means shall be guilty of high treason.
4. Inserted by Constitution (Eighteenth Amendment) Act, 2010, Sect. 4(ii) (with effect from 19 April 2010).
5. Inserted by Constitution (Eighteenth Amendment) Act, 2010, Sect. 4(iii) (with effect from 19 April 2010).
6. Substituted by Revival of Constitution of 1973 Order, 1985 (President's Order No. 14 of 1985), Sch. item 1 (with effect from 2 March 1985) for 'Parliament'.

Appendix-I

Technical Assistance Management Organization

Section 4.8: English Medium Schools

4.8.1: Conversion of Govt. Schools into English Medium Schools 2009

NO.PS/SSE/MISC/2009/67
GOVERNMENT OF THE PUNJAB
SCHOOL EDUCATION DEPARTMENT

Dated Lahore, the 28th March, 2009

To
All the Executive District Officers (Edu), in Punjab.

Subject: **CONVERSION OF SELECTED GOVERNMENT SCHOOLS INTO ENGLISH MEDIUM FROM 1ST APRIL 2009 IN EACH DISTRICT.**

The General public has to face exploitation by a large number of private schools in the name of English medium instruction. This situation can only be checked if Govt. Schools provide a reliable alternate. Additionally, this has also adversely affected the enrolment in Govt. Schools. Parents of even lower middle class and poor segments of society are being attracted by private schools due to English medium instruction, smart uniform and computer literary. As a result, the Govt. Schools are losing talented students.

2. As compared to private schools, the Govt. staff is more talented, qualified and trained with better salary and job security. The successful experiment of one English medium section in selected schools has shown excellent results and proved the potential of Govt. Schools for effective English medium instruction.

3. With a view to provide a suitable alternate, it has been decided from 1st April 2009, the subjects of Science and Mathematics will be taught in English from class 6, in some of the selected high/higher secondary schools. The selected high schools with primary portion will introduce this system from the classes of Nursery, 1 and 2 as well. The remaining classes from 7th to 10th may be kept in Urdu medium. Gradually these schools will be changed into English medium schools in a period of 4 years. Quality books will be introduced in the subject of English. Where possible, SS/Pak Studies will also be taught in English. However, for Urdu, Islamiat, Arabic and optional subjects, Urdu medium books printed by Punjab Textbook Board will be used to ensure a strong Urdu language basis as well.

4. The following schools will start English medium instruction:

a) All the 144 High Schools identified as Centers of Excellence. The Central Model Schools, Comprehensive Schools, Pilot Schools, Technical and Junior Model Schools, which were not included in this list of Centers of Excellence.

b) In addition, 5% Govt. Boys High/Higher Secondary Schools and 10% Govt. Girls High/Higher Secondary Schools in each district will adopt this system. The criterion for this would be highest enrolment. (The list of this category for each district is attached).

c) All Community Model Girls Primary Schools established under Girls Primary Education Project (GPEP) will also start English medium classes of Science and Mathematics. They may introduce additional books for the subject of English. Initially they may start with Nursery, Class One and Class Two.

d) The schools already having English medium sections are required to enhance number of such sections. Any head of school from Primary to Higher Secondary level may start English medium classes.

5. The heads of these medium schools will introduce a smart uniform. The suggested uniform for boys is: **Summer:** Sky-blue shirt, dark grey pant, grey socks, black shoes (preferably with laces). For classes upto 3, Nicker may be used. Winter: Green coat/Green pullover may be added for winter. For female students, the present uniform of sky-blue Kameez and whit Shalwar with Dupatta will continue.

6. The Directorate of Staff Development (DSD) and GCETs will cater for training requirements of English medium instruction in their training programmes. PMIU will plan and arrange English medium books of the selected subject. However, training and provision of books shall not be used as an excuse to delay the English medium initiative.

7. The class size should be kept under 50 but it will be more appropriate if it does not exceed 40. The Education Department has provided a special scholarship @Rs.30,000/- to the trainee teachers of B.Ed presently studying in 33 GCETs working under DSD with the condition that they will teach in Govt. Schools (preferably in English medium schools) for one year. Around 33,00 such teachers will be available for next 3 years. The EDOs and Principal GCETs may co-ordinate to utilize their services accordingly. Six months internees of GCETs or University Colleges of Education may also be considered for this.

8. The heads of these schools may enhance Farogh-e-Taleem fund up to Rs.20/- to meet requirements of the school. However, no student will be expelled from school for non-payment of enhanced FT fund. The Heads of schools may remit FT fund in case of deserving students.

9. The staff of the selected schools be sensitized and necessary arrangements be made to start English medium classes from the new session from 1st April 2009. Banners and due publicity should be ensured to attract better lot of students from the vicinity.

(NADEEM ASHRAF)
SECRETARY SCHOOL EDUCATION

Appendix-J

Technical Assistance Management Organization

4.8.2: **Medium of Instruction for Mathematics & Science Subjects 2009**

NO.SO (SE-III)2-16/2017
GOVERNMENT OF THE PUNJAB
SCHOOL EDUCATION DEPARTMENT

Dated Lahore, the 6th May, 2011

To
All the Executive District Officers (Edu),
in Punjab.

Subject: **CONVERSION OF URDU MEDIUM SCHOOLS INTO ENGLISH MEDIUM SCHOOLS.**

The School Education Department has issue instructions to all the schools that the instructions in the subjects of Science and Mathematics at a levels will be impart in English as approved in the scheme of studies approved to impart instructions in Urdu in English Medium Schools besides their conversion into English Medium Schools.

2. It is hereby clarified that subjects of Science and Mathematics at all levels shall be taught a English as per decision approved by the Federal Government, however, in cases where students feel some difficulty in understanding these subjects in English, they may be given instructions during class in Urdu as well. However, the medium of instructions in these subjects shall remain in English for examination purpose.

3. The above mentioned instructions may be brought into the notice of all concerned.

UNDER SECRETARY (SE-III)

No. & Date Even

A copy is forwarded for information and necessary action to:-

1. The Direct Public Instruction (SE/EE), Punjab, Lahore.
2. All the District Coordination Officers in the Punjab.
3. The Programme Director, Directorate of Staff Development, Lahore.
4. The Programme Director, PMIU, Lahore.

UNDER SECRETARY (SE-III)

CC

1. The Additional Secretary (Schools)
2. PS to Secretary School Education.

References

Adam, W., 1868. *Adam's Reports on Vernacular Education in Bengal and Behar, Submitted to Government in 1835, 1836 and 1838. [With a Brief View of Its Past and Present Condition by J. Long]* (Calcutta: Home Secretariat Press).

Adams, N. L., and Adams, D. M., 1971. 'An Examination of Some Forces Affecting English Educational Policies in India: 1780–1850'. *History of Education Quarterly, vol. XI*, 157–73. http://www.jstor.org/stable/367592 accessed on 17 Sept. 2015.

Ahmed, H., 1993. 'Pakistan Main Deeni Madaras, Mukhtasar Jaiza', in M. Sajjad and S. Khalid (eds.) *Deeni Madaras ka Nizam-e-taleem* (Islamabad: Institute of Policy Studies).

Ahsan, M., 2003. 'An Analytical Review of Pakistan's Educational Policies and Plans'. *Research Papers in Education*, vol. XVIII, 259–80. doi: 10.1080/0267152032000107329.

Ali, S., 2006. 'Why does policy fail? Understanding the problem of policy implementation in Pakistan–a Neuro-cognitive perspective'. *ISEA*, vol. XXXIV, 2–20.

Aly. J., 2007. *Education in Pakistan: A White Paper revised–document to debate and finalize the National Education Policy.* http://planipolis.iiep.unesco.org/upload/Pakistan/Pakistan%20National%20Education%20Policy%20Review%20WhitePaper.pdf, accessed on 17 Sept. 2015.

Andrabi, T., Das, J., and Khwaja, A. I., 2010. *Education Policy in Pakistan: A Framework for Reform* (Lahore: International Growth Centre).

Andrabi, T., Das J., Khwaja, A., Vishwanath, T., and Zajonc. T., 2007. *Learning and Educational Achievements in Punjab Schools (LEAPS): Insights to Inform the Policy Debate* (New York: The World Bank). http://www.leapsproject.org/assets/publications/LEAPS_Report_FINAL.pdf

Apple, M. W., 1990. *Ideology and Curriculum* (New York and London: Routledge).

Barber, M., 2010. *Education Reform in Pakistan: This Time It's Going to be Different* (Brookings Institution). http://www.brookings.edu/~/media/events/2010/11/04%20education%20pakistan/barberpakistan_education%20paper.pdf accessed on 17 Sept. 2015.

Bengali, K., 1999. *History of Education Policy Making and Planning in Pakistan* (Islamabad: Sustainable Development Policy Institute).

Bray, M., 1983. 'Universal Education in Pakistan: A Perpetually Elusive Goal?' *International Review of Education, vol. XXIX*, 167–78. http://www.jstor.org/stable/3443888, accessed on 17 Sept. 2015.

Connelly, M., and Clandinin, D. J., 1988. *Teachers as Curriculum Planners: Narratives of Experience* (New York: Teachers College Press).

Cooley, J., 2000. *Unholy Wars: Afghanistan, America and International Terrorism* (London: Pluto Press).

Dharampal, 2000. *The Beautiful Tree: Indigenous Indian Education in the Eighteenth Century.* Collected Writings vol. III (Goa: Other India Press).

Fullan, M., 1986. *Improving the Implementation of Educational Change, School Organization*, 6(3), 321–26.

Eysenck and Wilson., 1978. *The Psychological Basis of Ideology* (College Park MD: University of Maryland Press).

Ghafoor, A., and Khan, A., 1995. *Literacy Efforts in Pakistan: From Rhetoric to Action* (Islamabad: National Education and Training Commission).

Gramsci, A., 1996. *Selections from the Prison Notebooks* (Hyderabad: Orient Longman).

Huberman, A., and Miles, M., 1984. *Innovation Up Close: How School Improvement Works* (New York and London: Plenum Press).

Kardar, S., 1998. The Economics of Education, in P. Hoodbhoy, ed., *Education and The State: Fifty Years of Pakistan* (Karachi: Oxford University Press).

Khalid, S., 2004. *Deeni Madaras main Taleem: Kaifiat, Massayil, Imkanat* (Islamabad: Institute of Policy Studies).

Khan, A. H., 1997. 'Education in Pakistan: Fifty Years of Neglect', *The Pakistan Development Review,* vol. XXXVI. http://www.pide.org.pk/pdf/PDR/1997/Volume4/647-667.pdf accessed on 17 Sept. 2015.

Khan, H., 2001. *Constitutional and Political History of Pakistan* (Karachi: Oxford University Press).

Leitner, G. W., 2002. *History of Indigenous Education in the Punjab: Since Annexation And in 1882* (Lahore: Sang-e-Meel).

Mansoor, S., Meraj, S., and Tahir, A., eds., 2004. *Language Policy, Planning, & Practice: A South Asian Perspective* (Aga Khan University).

McLaughlin, M. W., 1987. 'Learning from Experience: Lessons from Policy Implementation', *Educational Evaluation and Policy Analysis*, vol. ix, 171–8. http://www.jstor.org/stable/1163728 accessed on 17 Sept. 2015.

Nayyar, A., 2004. 'Madrasah Education: Frozen in Time', in P. Hoodbhoy, ed., *Education and the State: Fifty Years of Pakistan* (Karachi: Oxford University Press).

Rahman, T., 2004. *Denizens of Alien Worlds: A Study of Education, Inequality, and Polarization in Pakistan* (Karachi: Oxford University Press).

_______, 1996. *Language and Politics in Pakistan* (Karachi: Oxford University Press).

Riaz, A., 2011. 'Ham Apne Bacchon ko kia Parah Rahe Hain?' *A Study of the Textbooks of Punjab Text Book Board* (Lahore: Action Aid & Jaag).

Saigol, R., 2003. *Becoming a Modern Nation: Educational Discourse in the Early Years of Ayub Khan (*1958–1964) (Islamabad: Council of Social Sciences).

Schorr, L., and Schorr, D., 1989. *Within Our Reach: Breaking the Cycle of Disadvantage* (New York: Doubleday).

Siddiqui, S., 2014. *Language, Gender, and Power: Politics of Representation and Hegemony* (Karachi: Oxford University Press).

———, 2012. *Education, Inequalities, and Freedom: A Sociopolitical Critique* (Islamabad: Narratives).

———, 2011. 'Language Policies in Pakistan: A dilemma of linguistic choices'. *NUML Journal of Critical Inquiry, vol. IX (2).*

———, 2010. *Rethinking Education in Pakistan: Perceptions, Practices & Possibilities* (Karachi: Paramount).

Warwick, D. P., Reimers, F., and McGinn, N., 1992. 'The Implementation of Educational Innovations: Lessons from Pakistan'. *International Journal of Educational Development, vol. XII* (4), 297–307. doi: 10.1016/0738-0593(92)90005-7.

———, 1991. *The Implementation of Educational Innovations in Pakistan: Cases and Concepts* (Massachusetts: Harvard University).

Government of Pakistan Official Documents

GoP (2021). Policy on Ph.D. Degree Programs. https://www.hec.gov.pk/english/services/faculty/Plagiarism/Documents/HEC-PhD-Policy.pdf accessed on 1 April 2021.

——— (2020). Undergraduate Education Policy 2020. https://www.hec.gov.pk/english/services/faculty/Plagiarism/Documents/UGE-Policy.pdf accessed on 1 November 2020.

——— (2019). Report on Pakistan Social and Living Standards Measurement (2018–19). http://data.gov.pk/pslm_sdgs/Education/index 11 November 2020.

——— (2018a). National Education Policy Framework 2018. Ministry of Federal Education and Professional Training, Islamabad. http://mofept.gov.pk/SiteImage/Policy/National%20Eductaion%20Policy%20Framework%202018%20Final.pdf accessed on 8 September 2020.

——— (2018b). Pakistan Economic Survey. Finance Division. http://www.finance.gov.pk/survey/chapters_19/Economic_Survey_2018_19.pdf accessed on 1 September 2020.

——— (2018c). Single National Curriculum (SNC). Ministry of Federal Education and Professional Training. http://mofept.gov.pk/ProjectDetail/MzkyNDc2MjMtY2VjYy00ZDA4LTk5OTUtNzUyNDI3ZWMzN2Rm accessed on 8 September 2020.

——— (2018d). Pakistan Bureau of Statistics. Disabled Population by Nature of Disability. http://www.pbs.gov.pk/content/disabled-population-nature-disability accessed on 15 November 2019.

——— (2017). Draft National Education Policy 2017. Islamabad: Ministry of Education. http://mofept.gov.pk/SiteImage/Policy/Draft%20National%20Educaiton%20Policy%202017.pdf accessed on 8 September 2020.

_______, 2014. Pakistan Economic Survey (2013–2014). Islamabad: Ministry of Finance.

_______, 2014. Pakistan Social and Living Standards *Measurement (PSLM) Survey 2011–12*. Islamabad: Pakistan Bureau of Statistics.

_______ (2012). National Assembly of Pakistan. The Objectives Resolution. The Constitution of the Islamic Republic of Pakistan, pp. 3–5. http://www.na.gov.pk/uploads/documents/1333523681_951.pdf accessed on 8 September 2020.

_______, 2012. Pakistan Economic Survey (2011–12). Islamabad: Ministry of Finance.

_______, 2011. Pakistan Economic Survey (2010–11). Islamabad: Ministry of Finance.

_______, 2009a. National Education Policy. Islamabad: Ministry of Education.

_______, 2009b. Special Citizens (Right to Concessions in Movement) Act. Government of Pakistan.

_______, 2007. National Textbook and Learning Materials Policy and Plan of Action. Islamabad. Ministry of Education Curriculum Wing.

_______, 2006. National Plan of Action for the Persons with Disabilities. Islamabad: Directorate General of Special Education.

_______, 2004. Education Sector Reforms 2001–2, 2005–6. Islamabad: Ministry of Education.

_______, 2004. *Handbook on Literacy Education, and Gender in South & West Asia* (Islamabad: Ministry of Education).

_______, 2003. *National Plan of Action on Education for All (2001–2015)* (Islamabad: Ministry of Education). http://planipolis.iiep.unesco.org/upload/Pakistan/Pakistan%20EFA%20NPA%202003. Pdf accessed on 17 Sept. 2015.

_______, 1999. The National Policy for Special Education, Islamabad: Pakistan Ministry of Women Development, Social Welfare and Special Education.

_______, 1998. National Education Policy (1998–2010). Islamabad: Ministry of Education.

_______, 1993. Eighth Five Year Plan: 1993–1998. Islamabad: Planning Commission.

_______, 1992. National Education Policy (1992–2002). Islamabad: Ministry of Education.

_______, 1988. Seventh Five Year Plan: 1988–1993. Islamabad: Planning Commission.

_______, 1986. National Policy for Rehabilitation of the Disabled, Islamabad: Pakistan Ministry of Health, Special Education and Social Welfare.

_______, 1983. Sixth Five Year Plan: 1983–1988. Islamabad: Planning Commission.

_______, 1981. Disabled Persons (Employment and Rehabilitation) Ordinance. Government of Pakistan.

_______, 1979. National Education Policy. Islamabad: Ministry of Education.

_______, 1978. Fifth Five Year Plan: 1978–1983. Islamabad: Planning Commission.

———, 1973. Constitution of Islamic Republic of Pakistan. Islamabad: Ministry of Education.

———, 1972. The Education Policy 1972–1980. Islamabad: Ministry of Education.

———, 1970. Fourth Five Year Plan: 1970–1978. Islamabad: Planning Commission.

———, 1970. New Education Policy 1970. Islamabad: Ministry of Education.

———, 1969. Proposals for a New Educational Policy. Islamabad: Planning Commission.

———, 1965. Third Five-Year Plan: 1965–1970. Islamabad: Planning Commission.

———, 1960. Second Five-Year Plan: 1960–1965. Islamabad: Planning Commission.

———, 1959. Commission on National Education. Islamabad: Planning Commission.

———, 1955. First Five-Year Plan: 1955–1960. Islamabad: Planning Commission.

———, 1951. Proceedings of the educational conference.

———, 1949. *Official Report of the Fifth Session of the Constituent Assembly of Pakistan Debates. The Constituent Assembly of Pakistan Debates*, vol. V. 9–10 (Karachi: Governor-General's Press).

———, 1947. *Proceedings of first educational conference, 27 November–1 December* (Karachi: Ministry of Interior).

Reports

AEPAM (2021). Pakistan Education Statistics 2017–18. http://library.aepam.edu.pk/Books/Pakistan%20Education%20Statistics%202017-18.pdf accessed on 14 April 2021.

——— (2018). Pakistan Education Statistics 2016–17. http://library.aepam.edu.pk/Books/Pakistan%20Education%20Statistics%202016-17.pdf accessed on 15 March 2020.

ASER (2018). Annual Status Education Report, Pakistan. http://aserpakistan.org/document/aser/2018/reports/national/ASER_National_2018.pdf accessed on 11 November 2019.

———, 2010. *Annual Status of Education Report Pakistan 2010*. Islamabad: The South Asian Forum for Education Development (SAFED).

National Commission on Terrorist Attacks upon United States, 2005. *The 9/11 Commission Report*. Official Government Edition.

The Pakistan Education Task force, 2011. *Education Emergency Pakistan*. http://api.ning.com/files/M6olNYM1EBYF8rP3x6UIql0RCKiNnw8pxdqrGl13rzjsG3qyjRh4v13ZhUqoO2aPlDg8uINw5EExW1dGkwek4Pg4a-TNIxXy/PakistanEducationEmergency2011. Pdf accessed on 17 Sept. 2015.

UNDP (2020). Human Development Report, Beyond Income, Beyond Averages, Beyond Today: Inequalities in Human Development in the 21st century. http://hdr.undp.org/sites/default/files/hdr2020.pdf accessed on 29 April 2021.

UNESCO (2019). Literacy Rates. https://en.unesco.org/themes/literacy accessed on 11 May 2020.

_______ (2018). The Investment Case for SDG 4 Data. http://sdghelpdesk.unescap.org/sites/default/files/2018-11/investment-case-sdg4-data.pdf accessed on 10 March 2020.

_______ (2017). Global Education Monitoring Report 2017/18: Accountability in Education. https://en.unesco.org/gem-report/node/2314 accessed on 10 March 2020.

_______ (2016). UNESCO Institute for Statistics. http://uis.unesco.org/en/country/pk accessed on 15 January 2020.

_______, 2003. *Literacy Trends in South Asia.* UNESCO. http://www.un.org/Overview/rights.htm

_______, 1990. *World Declaration on EFA.* UNESCO.
http://www.unesco.org/education/nfsunesco/pdf/JOMTIE_E.PDF accessed on 17 Sept. 2015.

UNO, 1948. *Universal Declaration of Human Rights.* http://www.uis.unesco.org/ev_en.php?ID=6401

World Bank, 2012. *Gender Equality and Development.* The World Bank Group. https://siteresources.worldbank.org/INTWDR2012/
Resources/7778105-1299699968583/7786210-1315936222006/Complete-Report.pdf accessed on 17 Sept. 2015.

_______, 2000. *Higher Education in Developing Countries: Peril and Promise.* The World Bank Group. http://siteresources.worldbank.org/INTAFRREGTOPTEIA/Resources/Peril_and_Promise.pdf accessed on 17 Sept. 2015.

_______, 1998–99. *Knowledge for Development.* The World Bank Group. http://web.worldbank.org/WBSITE/EXTERNAL/EXTDEC/EXTRESEARCH/EXTWDRS/0,,contentMDK:22293493~pagePK:478093~piPK:477627~theSitePK:477624,00.html accessed on 17 Sept. 2015.

World Economic Forum (2019). Global Competitiveness Report 2019: How to end a lost decade of productivity growth. https://www.weforum.org/reports/how-to-end-a-decade-of-lost-productivity-growth accessed on 10 March 2020.

_______, 2000. *The Dakar Framework for Action.* UNESCO. http://unesdoc.unesco.org/images/0012/001211/121147e. PDF accessed on 17 Sept. 2015.

Index